DIGITAL MARKETING ANALYTICS

In Theory And In Practice

Third Edition

KEVIN HARTMAN

To my family who has loved me,

my friends who have supported me,

and my colleagues who have inspired me.

PRAISE FOR DIGITAL MARKETING ANALYTICS

"Kevin has made science accessible. With the immense potential digital holds, I'm confident this book will allow you to unlock new ways to deepen customer relationships and fatten your profits!"

Avinash Kaushik Chief Strategy Officer – Croud, Author
Web Analytics: An Hour A Day and *Web Analytics 2.0*

"Kevin combines the experience of a skilled analytics practitioner with the expertise of an academic. In this book, he presents a fresh look at the field through the lens of history: from its earliest beginnings to its modern incarnation."

Mike Chapple Director, M.S. in Business Analytics – Mendoza
College of Business, The University of Notre Dame

"Digital Marketing Analytics is an important resource for all marketers, whether you are early in your career and learning or a seasoned practitioner who wants to remain sharp. This book will help you understand the changing dynamics and apply that thinking to maximize your business results."

Karen Sauder Vice President – Google

"This book is an excellent examination of data analytics, providing both a solid theoretical foundation and a deep dive into practical application. Readers of all levels of digital savvy will benefit from Kevin's expertise across platforms, tools, and approaches."

W. Brooke Elliott Associate Dean and EY Professor
Gies College of Business, University of Illinois

"The power of *Digital Marketing Analytics* is that it provides an insightful approach to the art of analytics while demystifying its science. Whether you're a big brand or small company, Kevin's book is a fantastic resource for any marketer who wants to do more with data."

Mike Clarke Director of Product – Shopify

"Kevin has honed wisdom gathered over decades as a practitioner and lecturer to develop a strong foundation of analytics. As the evolution of marketing analytics continues to accelerate, this foundation will prepare you to successfully tackle any new challenge, approach, or data source you will encounter throughout your career!"

Stan Balanovskiy Director of Ads Measurement Product – TikTok

TABLE OF CONTENTS

INTRODUCTION   1

PART 1   2

The Day the Geeks Took Over   2

   PART 1 | LESSON 1   3

   The ART+SCIENCE Mind   3

      The Three Roles of the Analyst   4

      The Evolution of the Analyst in the Firm 6

      Characteristics of the Successful Analyst 9

      In Summary: The ART+SCIENCE Mind   11

   PART 1 | LESSON 2   12

The Early History of Data Analytics   12

      Epoch I: 'Early Maps and Diagrams'   13

      Epoch II: 'Measurement & Theory'   14

      Epoch III: 'New Graphical Forms'   14

      Epoch IV: 'The Beginnings of Modern Graphics' 15

      Epoch V: 'The Golden Age of Data Analytics' 15

      Epoch VI: 'The Modern Dark Ages' of Data Analytics 16

      Epoch VII: 'The Rebirth of Data Analytics' 19

      Epoch VIII: 'High-Definition Data Analytics' (1975–1994) 19

      In Summary: The Early History of Data Analytics 19

   PART 1 | LESSON 3   21

The Contemporary History of Data Analytics   21

      Epoch I: 'When Anything Was Possible'   24

      Epoch II: 'The Bubble and the Burst'   24

      Epoch III: 'The Seeds of Prosperity'   27

      Epoch IV: 'The Age of Unicorns'   27

      The Significance of 2014   28

      In Summary: The Contemporary History of Data Analytics 30

   PART 1 | LESSON 4   31

The Rise of Modern Data Analytics   31

      P&G's Three-Step Model of Marketing   32

      The Introduction of the 'Zero Moment of Truth' (ZMOT) 33

      Technological Influences   35

      Market Influences   39

      Placing Today's Data Creation in Context 40

      Rise of the Machines: Machine Learning and Analytics 42

      In Summary: The Rise of Modern Data Analytics 46

PART 2   47

Consumer/Brand Relationships   47

   PART 2 | LESSON 1   48

   Owned and Operated Properties   48

      Growing Importance of O&O   49

      Measuring What Matters   50

      Organizational Impediments   51

      Key O&O Metrics   52

      In Summary: O&O Properties   53

   PART 2 | LESSON 2   55

   Online Video   55

      Online Video (OLV) Market Share   56

      Consumer Behavior and OLV   57

      OLV and Television   58

      Key OLV Measures   61

      In Summary: Online Video   63

   PART 2 | LESSON 3   64

   Online Search   64

      Search Engine Market Share   65

      Search Engine Management Versus Search Engine Optimization   66

      The Importance of Search Rank   68

      Consumer Behavior and Search   69

      Key Search Measures   69

      In Summary: Online Search   71

   PART 2 | LESSON 4   72

   Display Media   72

      Display Media Market Share   73

      Evolution of Display Ad Formats   74

      Key Display Media Measures   75

      In Summary: Display Media   76

   PART 2 | LESSON 5   77

   Social Media   77

      Social Media Market Share   78

      Consumer Behavior and Social Media   79

      How Brands Use Social Media   80

      Key Social Media Measures   81

      In Summary: Social Media   83

PART 2 | LESSON 6 84

The Consumer Decision Journey 84

    The Introduction of McKinsey's CDJ 85

    The Steps of the CDJ 86

    Applicability of the CDJ 90

    How Ad Blockers Affect Digital Measurement 91

    In Summary: The Consumer Decision Journey 92

PART 3 94

The Science of Analytics 94

    PART 3 | LESSON 1 95

    Digital Data Infrastructure 95

        Categories of Data 96

        Digital Data Collection: Cookies, Tags and Sign-Ins 97

        Data Availability and Value 99

        Data Collection and the Effect of Privacy Concerns 99

        In Summary: Digital Data Infrastructure 101

    PART 3 | LESSON 2 102

    Digital Measurement 102

        The Four Categories of Digital Measurement 103

        Making the Intangible Tangible: Brand Impact 104

        Measuring Sales Levers: Consumer Outcomes 106

        Understanding What Is Important: Customer Value 109

        Assessing Marketing Effectiveness: Attribution 110

        Getting to True Lift: Incrementality Testing 117

        A Word on Clarity through Measurement Multiplicity 121

        A Word on Digital Measurement Challenges 122

        In Summary: Digital Measurement 123

    PART 3 | LESSON 3 125

    Analytics and Dataviz Tools 125

        Key Categories of Digital Analysis Tools 126

        Evaluation Criteria 1: Data Flexibility 131

        Evaluation Criteria 2: Ease of Use 135

        A Word on SQL 138

        A Word on R and Python 139

        A Word on Tools < The Analyst 140

        In Summary: Analytics and Dataviz Tools 140

PART 3 | LESSON 4 141

Digital Marketing Maturity 141

    BCG's View of Digital Marketing Maturity 142

    Bain's View of Digital Marketing Maturity 143

    Deloitte and MIT Sloan's View of Digital Marketing Maturity 144

    Benefits of Digital Marketing Maturity 145

    Building a Winning Analytics Team 146

    Get the model right 147

    Other Considerations 151

    What You Can Do Today to Build the Analytics Team for Your Future ... 156

    In Summary: Digital Marketing Maturity 159

PART 4 160

The Art of Analytics 160

    PART 4 | LESSON 1 161

Navigating to Your Big Idea 161

    The Four Steps of the Marketing Analytics Process (MAP) 164

    First Step: Plan 165

    Second Step: Collect 166

    Third Step: Analyze 166

    Step Four: Report 167

    'The Ask Behind the Ask' 168

    In Summary: Navigating to Your Big Idea 170

PART 4 | LESSON 2 171

Planning for Your Analytics Expedition 171

    When Objective-Setting Goes Awry 172

    The Six Marketing Objectives 174

    Determining Your Marketing Objective 182

    Prioritizing Objectives 186

    Building an Analysis Plan around Your Objective 187

    How to Build a Plan in a Pyramid Layout 190

    Countering Bias During Planning 196

    In Summary: Planning for Your Analytics Expedition 198

PART 4 | LESSON 3 199

Collecting Data, Data Everywhere 199

    Unstructured Versus Structured Data 200

    Collecting Data 202

    Ensuring Data Quality 204

    A Word on Data Tidying 206

    A Word on Managing Collected Data 206

    In Summary: Collecting Data, Data Everywhere 207

PART 4 | LESSON 4   208
Analyzing for Insights   208
    The Five Categories of Marketing Data Analysis   209
    A Word on the Importance of Context   210
    Finding Patterns in Data   210
    Countering Bias in Analysis   213
    In Summary: Analyzing for Insights   215
PART 5   216
Storytelling with Data   216
PART 5 | LESSON 1   217
Pictures You See with Your Brain   217
    Visual Perception and the Door Study   218
    Preattentive Attributes   220
    A Word on the Effect of Neuroscience   221
    In Summary: Pictures You See with Your Brain   222
PART 5 | LESSON 2   223
Evaluation Framework for the Visual Form   223
    Evaluating the Effectiveness of Dataviz   224
    Connecting Data Visual Elements to the Analysis Journey   226
    Understanding the Components of Visual Form   227
    In Summary: Evaluation Framework for the Visual Form   228
PART 5 | LESSON 3   229
Sophisticated Use of Contrast   229
    Size Contrast   230
    Color Contrast   232
    Shape Contrast   234
    Contrived Contrast   236
    Bringing Contrast to Numbers through Context   237
    A Word on the Importance of Sketching Visuals   240
    In Summary: Sophisticated Use of Contrast   241
PART 5 | LESSON 4   242
Ensuring Clear Meaning   242
    Properly Titling Your Visual   243
    Highlighting Messages Visually   246
    A Word on Leveraging Emotions   251
    In Summary: Ensuring Clear Meaning   252

PART 5 | LESSON 5   253

Refined Execution through Visual Polish   253

    Color in Charts   254

    Lines   259

    Shapes   260

    Space   261

    Testing to Improve the Visual   263

    A Word on Combining Tools to Refine Visuals   264

    In Summary: Refined Execution through Visual Polish   264

PART 5 | LESSON 6   265

On Your Feet and Getting Your Story Across   265

    'The McCandless Method' of Data Presentation   266

    The McCandless Method in Practice   268

    A Word on Presentation Style   273

    The Storyteller's Dash: Dashboarding Data Effectively   275

    A Word on Building Habits over Time   281

    In Summary: On Your Feet and Getting Your Story Across   281

CONCLUSION   282

GLOSSARY   283

ABOUT THE AUTHOR   320

INTRODUCTION

Even if you know nothing about digital marketing analytics, digital marketing analytics knows plenty about you. It's a fundamental, inescapable, and permanent cornerstone of modern business that affects the lives of analytics professionals and consumers in equal measure. This book is an attempt to provide the context, perspective, and information needed to make analytics accessible to people who understand its reach and relevance and want to learn more.

The contents of this book reflect my decades of work in the digital analytics space, with most of that time spent leading large analytics teams at a major advertising agency and a global technology company. I've also had the privilege of teaching analytics at the graduate level for nearly 10 years. This textbook represents the synthesis of those two worlds: the academic and the actionable, the history and the hands-on, and the analysis and the application.

I hope readers find this book to be a valuable, enlightening, and engaging review of the ever-evolving analytics field. I'm profoundly grateful for the opportunity to share my experience, knowledge, and insights with you.

Kevin Hartman, September 2020

PART 1
The Day the Geeks Took Over

Lesson 1   The ART+SCIENCE Mind

Lesson 2   The Early History of Data Analytics

Lesson 3   The Contemporary History of Data
            Analytics

Lesson 4   The Rise of Modern Data Analytics

The ubiquity of data analytics today isn't just a product of the past half-century's transformative and revolutionary changes in commerce and technology. Humanity has been developing, analyzing, and using data for millennia. Understanding where digital marketing analytics is now and where it will be in five, 10, or 50 years requires a holistic and historical view of our relationship and interaction with data.

Part 1 looks at modern analysts and analytics in the context of its distinct historical epochs, each one containing major inflection points and laying a foundation for future advancements in the ART + SCIENCE that is modern data analytics.

The ART+SCIENCE Mind

Five things discussed in this lesson:

- Data analytics affects every aspect of business
- Opportunities for data analysts have never been greater, and expectations of data analytics to influence business decisions have never been higher
- Analysts should focus on skill development in three important roles: the "Data Strategist," the "Techie," and the "Data Designer"
- Analysts' roles have evolved over time, moving from focused areas of expertise to broad and balanced skills
- Successful analysts develop deep skills but, just as importantly, develop a mindset that helps set them up for success

Digital marketing analytics, in my humble opinion, is the most vibrant and undiluted blend of art and science in today's business world. No other pursuit requires its practitioners to balance such a depth of scientific application with a more poignant need to communicate with audiences who neither understand nor have patience for the technical underpinnings of that science. The science of digital marketing analytics presents as verbose and academic. A purely artistic display of analytics output suggests the same lack of substance as a charlatan's medicine show. This pursuit only works through a harmony of the two: "ART+SCIENCE."

Data analytics – the broad science of applying data analysis to solve business problems – affects every aspect of business. From finance to operations to human resources to marketing (and everything in between), it's understood "the world's most valuable resource is no longer oil, but data."[1] As a result, everyone in a business today becomes an analytics consumer. Moreover, the stakes have never been higher for analysts as the opportunities for data analysis – and the expectations for their benefits – have reached unprecedented levels.

Given this predicament for the analyst (whether that word is in one's title or not) a broad, yet balanced skill set is required.

The Three Roles of the Analyst

Analysts should develop skills and expertise in three functional areas. Think of these functional areas as hats that successful analysts wear throughout any analysis project or endeavor. Each area of expertise has always been an important skill for successful data analysts, regardless of their industries or titles. These skills are interdependent: Strength in one area will be throttled by weakness in another. As a result, analysts should seek to balance their abilities across the three roles.

The 'Data Strategist'

The first role the analyst must play is that of the "Data Strategist." In this role, analysts must bridge the data and marketing worlds and understand their firms' business operations, objectives, and environment. The successful Data Strategist understands how data can support the firm and can interpret data in the context of what they mean to the firm's performance. The Data Strategist's required skills are often associated with titles such as Business Analyst and Marketing Strategist.

Data Strategist acumen is built primarily through business experience. The more time analysts work in their industries, the more they understand the concepts and nuances that drive business performance in those fields. Their experience helps them put data in the proper context as they

---

[1] "Regulating the Internet Giants: The World's Most Valuable Resource Is No Longer Oil, But Data," *Economist* (May 6, 2017).

understand their industries' metrics, competitors, and business processes. Furthermore, they become familiar with the terminology they need to communicate with others outside their analytics teams. In my experience, many analysts who excel in the Data Strategy functional role first worked in nonanalyst roles, such as sales, finance, or other business functions, before joining analytics teams. Their nonanalyst experience gave them strong industry understanding and command of key concepts that made them better strategists.

Data Strategist acumen can, of course, be learned. In this book, I'll provide the frameworks and approaches a successful Data Strategist needs.

The 'Data Technologist' (also known as the 'Techie')

The second role an analyst must play is that of the "Data Technologist," a role that I often refer to as the "Techie." Here, the analyst is the data owner and must know how to collect and manage data in ways that ensure quality and promote efficiency. The successful Techie has the technical know-how to solve difficult data challenges and understands a breadth of data tools. Techie skills are commonly associated with Data Scientist and Data Engineer roles.

Techie acumen is built through a blend of academic education and hands-on experience. Opportunities to earn Techie skills are growing rapidly (see "The Evolution of the Analyst in the Firm" coming up next). Indeed, analytics training is becoming more accessible than ever before through video tutorials, online courses, and workshops. Traditional academic institutions are increasingly bestowing degrees for Techie education. When done well, these opportunities offer analysts a deep, theoretical understanding of statistics and the ability to apply machine learning and other technological innovations. The Techie's "toolbox" is filled with tools like Structured Query Language (SQL), R, and Python.

In this book, I'll explain the Techie's role, tools, and approaches. While this book doesn't provide a deep dive into the statistics or tools that Techies use, you'll find links to valuable resources that explore these topics in a Google Doc I maintain here: http://tinyurl.com/dmabook-resources.

The 'Data Designer'

The last role is what we'll call "Data Designer." The successful Data Designer has strong creative skills and can turn insights into innovative visuals that people remember. This role requires the analyst to know how to express data stories and use tools to visualize those stories. Like the Techie's data analysis tools, we will discuss a variety of dataviz tools throughout this book.

The blend of these three functional areas is what I like to call the "ART+SCIENCE Mind." When the three skills are in balance, analysts are perfectly positioned to complete any analytics task and communicate their findings in interesting, compelling ways.

We'll discuss these skills in-depth in this book. First, let's look at how these three roles have been staffed over time. The analyst's role has undergone a significant and interesting evolution.

The Evolution of the Analyst in the Firm

In an earlier time, advertisers – particularly, large advertisers – would build teams of data analysts centered around each of these functions. The ability of the three distinct functional teams to work closely with one another was a key determinant of a company's success. As a result, advertisers would invest significant time and energy in ensuring cross-collaboration through specially designed information-sharing sessions that would invite analysts from various functions to experience the rough-and-tumble exchange of ideas and the unavoidable pain of collaboration. In other cases, companies created cross-functional "scrum" teams that would meet frequently to discuss progress against closely watched project plans and develop ways to mitigate the risks of handing work from one group to the next.

Progressive advertisers increasingly expect data analysts to have demonstrable skills in all of the functional areas. This expectation undoubtedly had something to do with the inefficiencies that advertisers with distinct functional teams likely experienced. Required handoffs between teams in the old model slowed progress and introduced risk. But another important reason for the growth in expectations of data analysts is the natural evolution of a role that has become increasingly critical for advertisers to compete in today's digital economy.

The proliferation of analytics initiatives across industries has led to more options for good analytical talent than ever before. Analysts' opportunities have grown in terms of geography, expanding beyond the expected hot spots of major metropolitan areas, to include nearly every area where businesses operate today. Opportunities for the analyst have also become more technically diverse. As industries mature and explore new applications for data, the need for analysts is emerging in traditional businesses as well as in so-called "mission-driven roles" that have a societal or environmental benefit, such as those that focus on the application of data to advance health outcomes, energy efficiency, or nonprofit work.

Several trends have expanded analysts' opportunities.

Data analytics tools are becoming more accessible

The advancement of open-source and vendor-developed tools has improved accessibility for challenges that were previously reserved for complex and rigorous computer science solutions. While the market's most sophisticated tools are far from being "point and click," they're evolving quickly and becoming easier for a wider audience of analysts (and even nonanalysts) to use.

Analytics know-how is increasingly becoming a requirement for all roles

With many analytics teams expanding in size and scope, businesses increasingly face the challenge of connecting technical teams to other business unit stakeholders. As a result, companies expect nonanalyst business leaders to have a greater understanding of data analytics.

The expectation for nonanalysts is an understanding of concepts and ideas related to analytics – not the development of analyst skills. In this way, nonanalysts use their expertise to be representatives for the quantitative team and free up analysts to do what they do best: advanced technical analysis.

Educational backgrounds are shifting

In addition to the evolution of analytics tools, a fast-growing number of educational choices are making analytics training more accessible. These choices include video tutorials, online courses, "master class" workshops led by subject matter experts, as well as the expansion of traditional educational programs to include analytics-focused curriculums and degrees. Degrees, certificates, and work portfolios resulting from such educational alternatives are supplementing or even replacing the bachelor's and master's degrees analysts hold today.

A perusal of job postings for "analyst" reveals a wide variety of titles, including "Market Research Analyst," "Marketing Analytics Analyst," "Marketing Strategy Analyst," "Analytics Analyst," "Social Media Analyst," and many more. While the name by which the analyst is called has grown more distinct, responsibilities remain centered around gathering, analyzing, reporting, and advancing data.

Still, segmenting "Data Scientist" roles from other analytics professionals makes sense today because of skill set differences that affect salaries. While there's no universal definition of a "Data Analyst" or Data Scientist, the generally accepted distinction of the two roles is that the Data Analyst focuses on the "current state" through the analysis of structured data while the Data Scientist works primarily with unstructured or streaming data to better understand the future. While the market values the roles differently today, both are lucrative professions.

The divide between traditional analysts and more statistics-forward Data Scientists is blurring by the day. This is primarily because requirements for Techie skills have become more common. Such skills may have once distinguished subsets of analytics professionals but are less differentiating today. While Data Scientists have long been regarded as a specialized subset of the analytics profession, I would expect fewer companies to employ distinctly scoped teams.

In its 2022 annual survey on salary ranges for the analytics market, Burtch Works Executive Recruiting's treatment of job categories illustrates the evolution of roles and their earning potential. Burtch Works collected compensation and demographic data on professionals who work primarily with structured data. The company had referred to these individuals as "Data Analysts" in the past, but categorized them as "Data Scientists" in its 2022 report. Furthermore, the report referred to those who work primarily with unstructured data as "AI Professionals." For those professionals who work with structured data, Burtch Works reported the median base salary of individual contributors ranged from $90,000 to $145,000. Those who work with unstructured data as individual contributors earned more, with median base salaries ranging from $105,000 to $175,000. Managers in both roles earned up to $275,000.[2] These figures represented increases for Data Analysts and Data Scientists when compared to previous years.

Over the course of this book, we'll explore many other industry trends that are driving the evolution of the analyst in the firm. Before we do, however, let's look at the characteristics of successful analysts.

Characteristics of the Successful Analyst

Being a successful analyst requires more than mastering the three roles discussed above. It demands a mindset. Indeed, the successful analyst demonstrates a mindset characterized by three important traits: curiosity, optimism, and a healthy dose of boldness.

---

[2] Burtch Works, "The Burtch Works Study, Salaries of Data Science & AI Professionals" (October 2022).

Curiosity

Data analytics operates on the leading edge of marketing, advertising, and technology, and that's exactly what the analyst will love about it. A new search is always on the horizon: a new framework to develop, a new challenge to quantify, a new learning to discover. The analyst should embrace these challenges with the vigor, zeal, and inquisitive nature of a "Data Frontiersperson." Curiosity compels the successful analyst forward.

Optimism

The challenges data analytics pose aren't for the weak of mind or spirit. Analysts should expect to run into more brick walls than open doors. The arduous process of analyzing data means that failure is routine. I've seen analysts who abandoned their work when it became too challenging. More often than not, this was because they were limited in imagination, resilience, and zeal. Those who succeed do so because their tenacity and passion outweigh their frustrations. Perhaps, most importantly, analysts are successful because their optimism lets them believe solutions are there to be found.

Boldness

No one is more immersed in the use of marketing numbers than data analytics practitioners. Those who succeed push the boundaries of what was thought to be data's limit. They're audaciously daring in the questions they ask and the answers they seek. They earn the right to be bold. In my experience, this boldness has driven analysts to focus on the details while they strive to provide the highest-quality work. That attention to detail is what separates outstanding analysis from merely good analysis.

Data analytics affects every aspect of business – from operations to investment planning to marketing. While opportunities for data analysts have never been greater, they come with expectations that have never been higher. To be successful in today's data analytics environment, analysts should focus on skill development in three important roles: the Data Strategist, the Techie, and the Data Designer. These roles have evolved, moving from focused areas of expertise to broad and balanced skills. Successful analysts go beyond developing deep skills in these areas to develop a mindset of curiosity, optimism, and boldness that helps set them up for success.

In the next lesson, we'll place the role of the analyst and the emergence of today's contemporary practice in the context of the long and robust history of data analytics.

The Early History of Data Analytics

Five things discussed in this lesson:

- Mankind's experience with data analytics is long and robust, evolving from rudimentary mapmaking to the flourishing ART+SCIENCE practice of today
- Data analytics has played a major role in statistics, medicine, politics, and many other fields
- Data analytics' early history can be described through eight distinct epochs, each boasting significant events that trace the growth of data analytics as a practice
- Each epoch features a distinct inflection point that moved the practice forward and ushered in the beginning of the next epoch
- Data analytics' early history ended when the creation of digital data introduced the rise of contemporary data analytics

In the beginning, there was data.

One can look back through 7,000 years of human history and see examples of mankind expressing ideas through data. The practice began in the humblest of forms – simple maps used to document and describe the world around those early humans – and has evolved to become the flourishing modern practice of data analytics that we know today, fanning into statistics, medicine, politics, and other fields. The discipline evolved over time, adding capabilities, confronting critical issues and, in the end, emerging as a balanced blend of art and science.

This long, rich history of humans using data to communicate can be traced back to nearly the beginning of time and can best be categorized around eight distinct epochs. Each period had an inflection point that moved us from one point in this history to another period.

Figure 1.1: The early history of data analytics in visual form

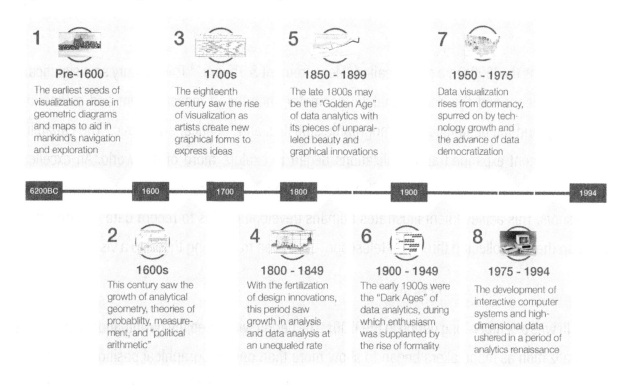

Epoch I: 'Early Maps and Diagrams'

Epoch I, the "Early Maps and Diagrams" phase, is the period before 1600.[3] The earliest seeds of visualization arose in geometric diagrams, tables of the positions of stars and other celestial bodies, and maps to aid in navigation and exploration. People used data in a functional way: creating visual objects to make sense of the world around them. Displaying information visually

---

[3] Michael Friendly and Daniel Denis, "Milestones in the History of Thematic Cartography, Statistical Graphics, and Data Visualization" (2001).

allowed people to share their knowledge, record their environment, and measure critical matters in their everyday lives.

During this period, the ability to communicate visually was critical to human development, social interaction, and humans' understanding of the world.

Epoch II: 'Measurement & Theory'

Epoch II spans the 1600s in a period called "Measurement & Theory."[4] This century saw significant growth in theory and the rise of analytic geometry, theories of measurement and estimation, probability, and the beginning of demographic statistics and "political arithmetic." The capability of measurement expanded as visualizations began to explore more of the world. An excellent example of this evolved use of data is Christoph Scheiner's visual from 1626 that charted changes in sunspots. This achievement illustrates humans developing tools to record data – in this case, spots on the sun collected through a telescope – and then translating that into a visual form.

Epoch III: 'New Graphical Forms'

Epoch III was a century-long period in the 1700s. The period witnessed the germination of the seeds of visualization as mapmakers began to show more than only geographical position. As a result, people introduced many graphic forms. In the period of "New Graphical Forms,"[5] artists began to explore new ways of visualizing information, expanding the boundaries of creative forms of communication. This period is characterized by the development of preattentive attributes – early examples of shading, size, contrast, and color – that expressed developing insights and demonstrated a growing aptitude in the science of data analysis.

---

[4] Friendly and Denis, "Milestones in History."

[5] Friendly and Denis, "Milestones in History."

Epoch IV: 'The Beginnings of Modern Graphics'

Epoch IV, 1800–1849, has been called "The Beginnings of Modern Graphics."[6] With the fertilization of design and technique innovations, the first half of the nineteenth century saw growth in statistical graphics and thematic mapping at a rate not matched until modern times. Real data visualization took root in this period. William Playfair introduced the pie chart, bar chart and line chart – all still important to data visualization.

Epoch V: 'The Golden Age of Data Analytics'

In the following epoch, Epoch V, we move into the "Golden Age" of data analytics.[7] The late 1800s saw dataviz of unparalleled beauty and many graphical innovations. Data artists used visualization to communicate their stories. Great examples from this period include John Snow's epidemiological study of cholera in London occurring around the Broad Street well. This visualization is credited for revolutionizing human understanding of cholera and its treatment methods. Florence Nightingale proved the need for improved sanitary conditions in the British army using visualization, and Charles Booth visualized poverty in London using color on a map to demonstrate how the poor were isolated.

In this epoch, we're also blessed with possibly the greatest data visualization of all time: Charles Joseph Minard's representation of Napoleon's march on Moscow. So much information is packed into this visual, including Napoleon's "triumphant" return to Paris. It includes distance and temperature, and the number of soldiers lost. This visual communicates a complex story while being simple and beautiful.

---

[6] Friendly and Denis," Milestones in History."

[7] Friendly and Denis, "Milestones in History."

Figure 1.2: Minard's masterful visual presentation of Napoleon's march

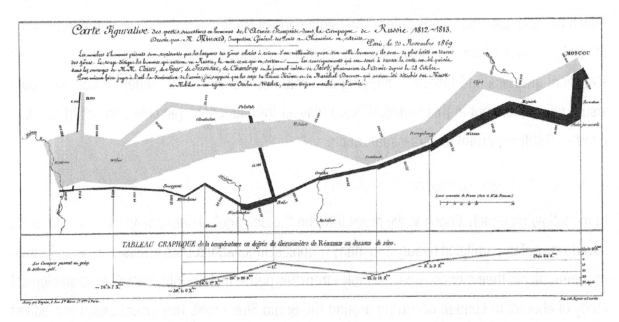

During this period, data artists begin to get a little "over their skis." New emerging graphical forms inspired people who made visualizations to create images for visual sake alone. Several examples from the time are complicated and overwrought. Graphics printed on top of graphics obscure the artists' intended meaning.

Epoch VI: 'The Modern Dark Ages' of Data Analytics

After the careless approach to data visualization triggered an inevitable backlash, we move into Epoch VI (1900–1949). If the late 1800s were the "Golden Age" of visualization, the early 1900s were the "Modern Dark Ages,"[8] as the previous period's enthusiasm was supplanted by the rise of quantification and formality. Scholars, who suspiciously watched the emergence of data analytics from their academic quarters, rose in revolt. Their primary concerns were the need for more

---

[8] Friendly and Denis, "Milestones in History."

accuracy, more controls, and a standardized language. This movement limited creativity for the sake of accuracy and introduced what we know today as the scourge that is "clip art." Individual icons represented certain data that were standardized, and frankly, threatened to knock the path of data visualization off its creative tracks.

We see redeeming introductions during this period, however. One is the famous Henry Beck map of the London Underground, which describes a complex system simply and beautifully. More importantly, Beck's map doesn't show the positions of the Underground stations perfectly. It stood as a testament to the idea that images can serve a purpose without exacting accuracy. The popularity of this graphical representation offered a counterargument to the strict and rigid practices of data visualization from the societies that promoted exactness and standardization.

Figure 1.3: Beck's perfectly imperfect map of the London Underground

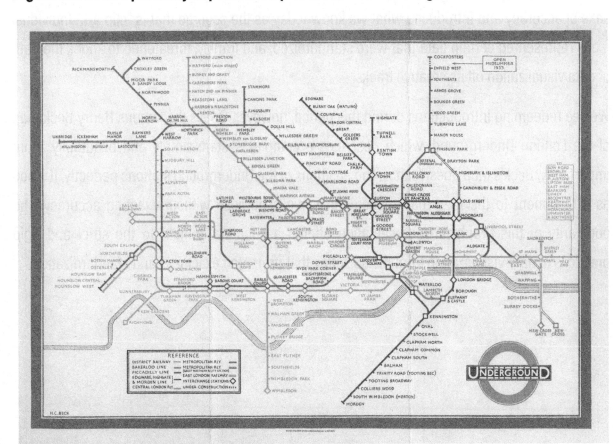

This period also introduced the Mark I, a computer developed at Harvard University. As the first computer, the Mark I was the size of a living room, but less capable than today's average smartphone. Still, this technological advancement made it possible to process information in ways that weren't possible before. Analysts could visualize larger volumes of data, generate graphics with greater efficiency, and discover patterns in data no one could find before the introduction of the computer.

The introduction of Beck's map and the Mark I are chief among the factors that moved the discipline of data visualization from the Modern Dark Ages into a period of rebirth.

Epoch VII: 'The Rebirth of Data Analytics'

Data analysts began to embrace new graphical forms and capabilities in Epoch VII, "The Rebirth of Data Analytics" (1950–1974).[9] Still under the influence of the formal and numerical zeitgeist from the mid-1930s on, data visualization began to rise from dormancy in the mid-1960s, spurred largely by technology and data democratization. Computers played an enormous role in this transformation. Analysts could bring in more data with greater sophistication and add elements that weren't previously available.

Epoch VIII: 'High-Definition Data Analytics' (1975–1994)

We move into the final epoch in the early history of data analytics, Epoch VIII (1975–1994). The development of highly interactive computer systems and new methods for visualizing high-dimensional data ushered in a dataviz renaissance period that was limited only by human imagination. We call this period "High-Definition Data Analytics,"[10] in which computers or applications created most visuals. They processed vast amounts of information and leveraged previous data visualization knowledge to create effective, efficient, and tremendously powerful visuals. The rapid advancement of data design signaled the end of the early history of data analytics and a shift to a contemporary time.

In Summary: The Early History of Data Analytics

Understanding the evolution of analytics through the eight epochs described in this lesson is important because they trace a rich and long history of humans communicating with data. The journey also shows how we've evolved from simple hand-painted maps to where we are today – using computer applications that have tremendous power to generate visuals. Throughout this fascinating history, we've confronted topics such as data scarcity, politics, data misuse, and other

---

[9] Friendly and Denis, "Milestones in History."

[10] Friendly and Denis, "Milestones in History."

issues to arrive at what is today – in my estimation – the purest, and most beautiful blend of art and science that we'll find. This early history of data analytics ended when the creation of digital data introduced the rise of contemporary data analytics, which we'll discuss in the next lesson.

The Contemporary History of Data Analytics

Five things discussed in this lesson:

- Contemporary history of data analytics saw the fully formed ideal of the role data and analysis could play in marketing and advertising
- Contemporary history of data analytics is a 20-year period that began with the introduction of the banner ad in 1994
- Contemporary history of data analytics can be described as four epochs, each boasting significant events that trace the growth of data analytics as a practice
- As with the early history of data analytics, the epochs of its contemporary history feature inflection points that advance the practice and signal the beginning of a new epoch
- Several events demonstrate the maturation of digital platforms in 2014, bringing the contemporary history of data analytics to a close

As we turn our attention to the contemporary history of data analytics, I'm reminded of a quote from Michael Fassnacht, a pioneer in the introduction of data analysis in marketing and my first boss when I entered the world of advertising. In 2006, Fassnacht said, "Over the next few years, geeks in marketing will become one of the most disruptive forces in a discipline that traditionally was driven by big creative personalities."

Fassnacht was talking about data's effect on creative and marketing processes. He was correct in this assessment, but perhaps a bit too prescient. Indeed, few advertisers had fully integrated data analytics in their marketing efforts in the years immediately following 2006. Furthermore, many advertisers still rely on traditional, comfortable methods to guide their creative and marketing endeavors.

But Fassnacht knew the opportunity to better understand consumers in a way that reduced risk for advertisers and increased accountability for their agency partners had been gaining steam for a while. Twelve years before he issued his challenge to the marketing and advertising world, a seminal event redefined the consumer/brand dynamic forever. That event was the introduction of the digital banner ad on October 27, 1994.

Figure 1.4: The world's first banner ad

AT&T purchased the first banner ad and placed it on hotwire.com. It earned a click-through rate of 44 percent,[11] an unheard-of result, especially given that today's display ads entice 0.05 percent of consumers to click them.[12] It's almost certain the novelty of the experience sparked curiosity in consumers who wondered what would happen if they followed the ad's instructions to "click your mouse right HERE."

---

[11] Adrienne LaFrance, "The First-Ever Banner Ad on the Web," *Atlantic,* (April 21, 2017).

[12] Doubleclick's Display Benchmarking Tool as cited by SmartInsights, US, Europe and Worldwide Display Ad Clickthrough Rates Statistics Summary (September 10, 2019).

This humble ad, presented in a haphazard-looking array of psychedelic colors against a plain black background, changed the way brands use the web. The ability to influence behavior and, more importantly, collect information about behavior, disrupted the economic and financial models of nearly every company from then on.

The moment also brought a new trajectory for data analytics, ushering in the next phase of this science – something I call the "contemporary history of data analytics."

Figure 1.5: The contemporary history of data analytics

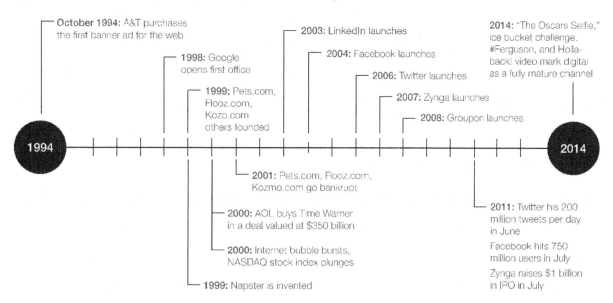

Similar to the early history of analytics, this period can be seen as a collection of distinct periods, each with its own unique characteristics and circumstances. Inflection points of technological and cultural significance transition us from one period to the next. In this way, the contemporary history of analytics is comprised of four epochs.

Epoch I: 'When Anything Was Possible'

The first epoch is something I will call "When Anything Was Possible," and encompassed the time of that first AT&T banner ad in 1994 to 1999. Some great things happened in this period. Google opened its first offices. Napster was invented, which would change the face of music forever. Other companies founded in this time are less heralded today, including Flooz.com, Kozmo.com, and Pets.com, but were just as important to the growth of digital commerce.

At this point, nearly anyone who entered an investor's office with a dot-com plan would be taken seriously. No idea was a bad idea that involved the use of digital platforms to transform (or create) businesses. The web and how it would sort itself out wasn't readily understood, but it was clear that it had the power to connect people and make information more accessible than any previous invention. As a result, investors placed bets on a wide variety of early internet ventures. Any company left standing on the sidelines of the "Internet Revolution" felt palpable anxiety emanating from its board of directors to its junior employees.

It was the inchoate period of digital "FOMO" (Fear of Missing Out), without mobile devices and apps. As a young management consultant who worked in a well-respected and established firm that had similarly well-respected and established clients, it seemed as if every day, I watched a bright, ambitious colleague announce they were leaving the consultancy to join a startup poised to revolutionize the [insert industry name here]. In private conversations, my friends would talk excitedly about being part of the dot-com experience and, should the stock options pan out as they hoped, how they would probably be able to retire in a few years.

Epoch II: 'The Bubble and the Burst'

That exuberance ended with the advent of the second epoch, "The Bubble and the Burst" (2000–2002). The NASDAQ stock index, where the vast majority of public dot-com companies were traded, rose fivefold between 1995 and 2000. But the index tumbled from a peak of $5,048.62 on March 10, 2000, to $1,139.90 on October 4, 2002.[13] That crash destroyed $2.7 trillion in market value.

More than half of all dot-com businesses founded after 1996 failed to see 2004.[14] Many signs of the unsustainability that led to the NASDAQ crash were apparent, yet apparently ignored. Kozmo, one victim of the internet bubble and burst, demonstrates the limitations of investors' strategy to forego profitability in favor of innovation.

A supply chain management company that invested heavily in innovative technology, Kozmo delivered small consumer goods its bicycle couriers could accommodate. Kozmo focused on densely populated urban areas and had a unique promise: It would deliver any item from its offered product categories in less than an hour with no recipient delivery fee. While traditional companies required consumers to invest their own time and money by shopping at retail locations or waiting days for their items from costly delivery, Kozmo promised to "extend (the supply chain) all the way to the customer's front door."[15] The company warehoused nonperishable items in its delivery areas (with a central distribution center located in Memphis, Tennessee) and collected perishable items, including Starbucks coffee and Gerald Stevens flowers, directly from retailers.

Kozmo's customer-centric focus meant it sacrificed efficiency. It carried an awkwardly broad set of 24 product categories (in line with its mantra of "delivering what the consumer wants"), including DVDs, books, food, beer, electronics, and other items that introduced tremendous complexity to its inventory management and distribution systems. Kozmo's need to attract consumers to its new shopping concept kept a tight lid on prices for consumers, yet its lack of scale prevented Kozmo from earning discounts or advantageous pricing arrangements from suppliers. The mix of low prices and high fulfillment costs meant Kozmo, like other internet-based

---

[13] Adam Hayes, *Dotcom Bubble* (June 25, 2019).

[14] Leslie Berline, "Lessons of Survival, from the Dot-Com Attic," *New York Times* (November 21, 2008).

[15] John C. Wu, "Anatomy of a Dot-Com," *Supply Chain Management Review* (November/December 2001).

delivery services operating at the time (a list that includes now-defunct Urbanfetch, Streamline, Webvan, and ShopLink), lost money on almost every delivery.

Kozmo's early performance took firm hold of investors' imagination. At the end of its first year of operations, the company grew from six markets to 11. Despite posting an operating loss of $26.3 million on revenues of just $3.5 million, Kozmo continued to attract investment to fuel its growth. After 18 months in business, the number of Kozmo customers jumped from 75,000 to 300,000. A $60 million cash infusion from Amazon in March 2000 provided further capital and by July 2000, Kozmo had more than 400,000 customers, 2,600 employees, revenues that were doubling month-over-month, and plans for an initial public offering (IPO) on the NASDAQ. Just three years after opening a single delivery shop in New York City, Kozmo featured all the top-line trajectory the internet age promised.

But for all of its tremendous growth, Kozmo's underlying financial viability remained suspect. Its ardent focus on meeting customer needs led to poor business decisions, such as its Valentine's Day offer of jewelry delivery in less than one hour. Without a clear sense of demand (outside of anecdotal consumer interest), Kozmo secured inventory and paid significantly to augment security controls yet managed to sell only 2 percent of the products it purchased. Operating mistakes like this led Kozmo to be unprofitable in all but four of its markets, despite a broadening distribution network, a homegrown inventory management system that provided innovative solutions to the company's unique delivery challenges, and on-time order fulfillment rates that hovered around 99 percent. While still attracting investment, Kozmo calculated an average order size of $5 and an average delivery cost of $7.50.[16]

The NASDAQ crash forced Kozmo to postpone its planned IPO and re-examine its operating model. As investors' money dried up, Kozmo made moves to point itself toward profitability – such as

---

[16] Wu, "Anatomy of Dot-Com."

enacting order minimums – but these moves were too little, too late. The company continued to burn through cash and layoffs began in mid-2000. Even with an (unbelievable) $30 million new round of funding raised in January 2001, Kozmo ceased operations just a few months later in April 2001.

The Kozmo experience provided a cautionary tale for investors about the importance of any company's underlying business fundamentals. Perhaps more importantly, it spurred new ventures to re-examine the use of data and analytics in assessing consumer needs and the value of collecting consumer data.

Epoch III: 'The Seeds of Prosperity'

From these ruins emerged new internet-based ventures, stronger and better-positioned than the companies that fell victim to the dot-com crash. This brings us to the third epoch, something I call "The Seeds of Prosperity" (2003–2010). In this period, a number of new ventures took root, harnessing the internet's massive reach. They didn't sell products in the traditional sense. Instead, they met consumer needs that can't be bought or sold.

These companies include LinkedIn (professional connections), Twitter (the ability to be heard), Groupon (collective savings), and, of course, Facebook (community). They were founded as the web began to recover from the NASDAQ crash, and each one fulfilled important consumer needs through the internet.

Epoch IV: 'The Age of Unicorns'

This brings us to the fourth epoch, "The Age of Unicorns" (2011–2014). The label, "unicorn," has been widely attributed to Cowboy Ventures founder Aileen Lee, who coined the term to describe pre-IPO tech startups with a market valuation of $1 billion or more. When she introduced the concept of the unicorn in 2013, 39 U.S. startups had topped the $1 billion valuation mark in the previous decade.[17]

From there, things moved quickly to the point where the existence of these once-unique startups became the norm. One year later in 2014, 20 years after the invention of the banner ad and the year that marks the close of this fourth epoch, the number of unicorns had doubled to 80, according to *Fortune*.[18] The implication of this tremendous growth is that the tech startup came of age. I would argue that an underlying explanation lies in the sophisticated use of data exhibited by each company on the *Fortune* list.

The Significance of 2014

Between 1994 and 2014, internet use grew dramatically. When the first banner ad appeared in 1994, fewer than 5 percent of North Americans used the internet. By 2014, that percentage had begun to level off around 75 percent.[19] According to Nielsen Online, ITU, PEW Research, and internet World Stats, the internet's usage in North America was a few points below 90 percent in 2019.

Expanded internet access gave rise to new, powerful uses of digital platforms, representing an unprecedented and marked shift in the way consumers interacted online. Several examples signaled that the internet had become fully mature in 2014.

Ellen's 'Oscars Selfie' Tweet

In March 2014, Ellen DeGeneres' star-studded "Oscars Selfie," snapped at the *Academy Awards* show, was shared on Twitter while the show was still filming.

---

[17] Erin Griffith and Dan Primack, "The Age of Unicorns," *Fortune*, (January 22, 2015).

[18] Griffith and Primack, "The Age of Unicorns."

[19] Hannah Ritchie, Edouard Mathieu, Max Roser, and Esteban Ortiz-Ospina, "Internet," Our World in Data (2019).

That tweet set a record with 3.4 million retweets.[20] It's been estimated that Ellen's selfie was worth as much as $1 billion in earned media for Samsung, an Oscar sponsor that year.[21] Such powerful social sharing had not been seen before.

ALS Ice Bucket Challenge Viral Sensation

Four months later, the amyotrophic lateral sclerosis (ALS) ice bucket challenge raised more than $100 million as a viral sensation arose over people videoing themselves dumping buckets of cold water on their heads after challenging others to do the same (and contributing donations to ALS research).[22] Primarily shared on Facebook, Twitter, and YouTube, these videos raced through social circles of all sizes.

One of the more popular ALS challenge videos involved Microsoft founder Bill Gates successfully completing a challenge from Mark Zuckerberg. That video racked up nearly 21 million views, demonstrating the connective power of the internet as a means for raising awareness (and funding) for social causes.[23]

#Ferguson Digital Activism

In August 2014, amid the unrest that erupted around the police shooting of unarmed teen Michael Brown in Ferguson, Missouri, social media became an engine of social activism. The hashtag, "#ferguson," was tweeted 21.6 million times during five days of protests and demonstrations.[24]

[20] Caspar Llewellyn Smith, "Ellen DeGeneres' Oscars Selfie Beats Obama Retweet Record on Twitter," *Guardian* (March 2, 2014).

[21] Rhonda Richford, "MIPTV: Ellen DeGeneres' Oscar Selfie Worth As Much As $1 Billion," *Hollywood Reporter* (April 8, 2014), quoting Publicis CEO Maurice Levy.

[22] ALS Association, The ALS Association Expresses Sincere Gratitude to Over Three Million Donors (August 29, 2014).

[23] Kimberlee Morrison, "The Top 5 Viral Events of 2014," *Adweek* (December 24, 2014).

[24] Gene Demby, "Combing through 41 Million Tweets to Show How #BlackLivesMatter Exploded," *NPR* (March 2, 2016).

In November 2014, the anti-harassment organization, Hollaback!, posted a video on YouTube, *10 Hours of Walking in NYC as a Woman*. In clear sound and images, the video demonstrated the harassment a woman faces walking the streets of New York and earned more than 6 million views in 24 hours.[25]

In Summary: The Contemporary History of Data Analytics

The contemporary history of data analytics witnessed the fully formed ideal of the role data and analysis could play in marketing and advertising. This 20-year period that began with the introduction of the banner ad in 1994, created a novel and significant change in the way analysts could gain insight into consumer behavior and measure the effects of their marketing efforts. The contemporary history of data analytics can be described as four epochs, each boasting significant events that trace the growth of data analytics as a practice. Like the early history of data analytics, each epoch of its contemporary history features inflection points that advance the practice and signal the beginning of a new epoch. Finally, we learned that several events demonstrate the maturation of digital platforms in 2014, bringing the contemporary history of data analytics to a close.

In the next lesson, we'll discuss important frameworks analysts developed to help them make sense of their consumer relationships and the role data analytics played in that understanding.

---

[25] Hermione Hoby, "The Woman in 10 Hours Walking in NYC: 'I Got People Wanting to Slit My Throat,'" *Guardian* (December 17, 2014).

The Rise of Modern Data Analytics

Five things discussed in this lesson:

- Data has become the most valuable asset for those who make decisions or attempt to influence them
- In 2005, Procter & Gamble (P&G) introduced the concept of a three-step model that detailed the role of the brand in a consumer's decision journey
- Since P&G introduced its three-step model, the amount of data consumers and brands have generated has grown significantly
- To adapt P&G's framework to the changing data landscape, Google introduced the concept of the "Zero Moment of Truth"
- Several influences drove the explosive growth of data and new customer touch points, creating new marketing opportunities that led to the growing demand for analytics in today's marketing and advertising environment

Humankind's experience with data analytics has been long and rich. Through periods of cultural, political, and technological changes, the importance of collecting, analyzing, and telling stories from data has never wavered. On the contrary, the critical role of data in nearly every aspect of marketing has grown exponentially. Data has become the most valuable asset for anyone who makes – or attempts to influence – a decision.

From the use of personal computers in the '80s, to the web's arrival in the '90s, to the advent of smartphones in the 2000s, brands' interactions with consumers have changed radically. To make sense of the changing dynamic in their relationships with consumers, brands frequently turn to frameworks, including the three-step marketing model that P&G pioneered.

P&G's Three-Step Model of Marketing

In 2005, after the internet bubble burst but before Facebook had fully taken root, P&G introduced a three-step model of marketing. Although simple in its design, the P&G framework was powerful in its relevance and insight into consumer behavior. The model sought to simplify the way consumers make purchase decisions and explain critical points along that journey.

'Trigger'

The model begins with the idea that every consumer's purchase path begins with a stimulus. For example, an ad could spark interest in learning more about a product the individual decides to purchase. Perhaps the consumer runs out of a required household staple, learns how wonderful a product is from a friend, and decides to try it. These stimuli are examples of what P&G calls a "trigger," or the first step toward the purchase of a product.

'First Moment of Truth' (FMOT)

The next major step in P&G's model is called the "First Moment of Truth" (FMOT). FMOT occurs when consumers are at the shelf, ready to purchase, and have a number of options for the products they want. Various brands boast promises through attention-grabbing packaging and compelling price discounts. Consumers may even receive samples that entice them to "try before they buy." With FMOT, consumers must choose brands based on their knowledge of the various offerings. Importantly, this was the point P&G identified as the first battleground for brands because they have to fight for attention.

The final step in the P&G model is called the "Second Moment Of Truth" (SMOT) and is realized after consumers buy products and bring them home. They appraise products against the expectations they developed during their evaluation process. When products live up to SMOT expectations, brands can win customers for life. If products falter, however, the results can be catastrophic for brands. According to P&G, fulfilling consumers' expectations was the second critical moment that brands must win.

P&G's purchase path moments are as important to brands today as they were in 2005. Brands must stand out from their competitors and persuade consumers to choose them instead of rival products.

The need to set and fulfill consumers' expectations hasn't diminished and is arguably more important today than ever before. The world, however, isn't quite the same as it was then.

The Introduction of the 'Zero Moment of Truth' (ZMOT)

As access to information grew with the increasing availability of mobile devices and brands' maturing use of the internet, the way consumers shopped underwent a dramatic change. Online information quickly became a vital source of intelligence for consumers as they evaluated products.

For that reason, in 2011, Google introduced the "Zero Moment of Truth" (ZMOT). ZMOT is the time between a stimulus, still obviously relevant, and the First Moment of Truth. Still true to the P&G framework, a brand doesn't win unless a consumer chooses it. Typically, consumers have many brands from which to choose. With ZMOT, Google captured the concept that the shopping dynamic had changed considerably. Now, consumers were going to the shelf while armed with significantly more information about the products and the brands they could purchase.

Such information could be earned from product reviews found on any number of internet sites. It could be collected from a friend's experience with the product and posted to Facebook. It could be found in a tweet from a celebrity extolling love for products and brands. The information could also come from some variety of the estimated 4,000 to 10,000 ads most Americans are exposed to each day.[26] These sources often work collectively to inform and educate consumers during ZMOT, and are joined by many others, including television, friends and family, online destinations, print media, and brick-and-mortar stores.

ZMOT isn't a neat picture. It's messy, with many things going on and is, in no way, linear. Consumers can hop between sources of information and back again as quickly as their browsers are able to load internet pages. Furthermore, consumers move between online and offline worlds fluidly – much like how they live. All of these channels are part of the pre-shopping experience in-home and in-store, ultimately leading to P&G's First Moment of Truth.

For brands, ZMOT represents a critical opportunity to influence purchase behavior. Each ZMOT touch point represents an opportunity to interact with consumers and learn their reactions to specific brands and products. These new touch points provide opportunities for brands to influence consumers which requires brands to understand consumer needs – insights that could be gleaned through the collection of profile data, and online consumer behaviors. As a result, ZMOT offers advertisers many opportunities to influence consideration, and learn whether their products satisfy consumers' needs. For marketing analysts, ZMOT represents the most important opportunity to understand consumers. It's where consumers reveal significant information about themselves.

Delivering influence required brands to understand consumer needs – insights that could be gleaned through the collection of profile data, and online consumer behaviors. As a result, ZMOT

---

[26] Ron Marshall, "How Many Ads Do You See in One Day?" Red Crow Marketing Inc. (September 10, 2015).

offers advertisers many opportunities to influence consideration, and learn whether their products satisfy consumers' needs. For marketing analysts, ZMOT represents the most important opportunity to understand consumers. It's where consumers reveal significant information about themselves.

Optimizing the effect brands had on consumer choice required brands to test messages and track results. In this way, the growth in advertiser opportunities was among many factors that drove increased demand for analytics.

Technological Influences

One driving force behind the growth of data analytics has been the ceaseless advance of technology. As technology has evolved to meet the needs of consumers and businesses, new opportunities to create and collect data have arisen. Two of the more important technological influences are consumers' swift adoption of mobile devices and the growth of marketing technology to help businesses create value from the data they collect.

Swift Adoption of Mobile Devices

The swift adoption of mobile devices has dramatically increased the volume of consumer data available to analysts. Devices facilitate the creation of consumer data in two ways. First, mobile devices provide access to online sites and apps that create data (e.g., mobile Facebook and mobile search), making it easier for consumers to generate data. Second, mobile devices produce passive data (e.g., location data) in great volumes.

Mobile device growth was rapid, as illustrated in photographs comparing the installations of Pope Benedict in 2005 and Pope Francis in 2013, seen in Figure 1.6. The ability of device users to instantly share thoughts, feelings, and experiences (as well as their locations) improved analysts' ability to understand consumers and contributed directly to the rise of analytics.

Figure 1.6: Comparison of Pope Benedict (2005) and Pope Francis (2013) installations[27]

Growth of Marketing Technology Space

The rapid growth in companies in the marketing technology (martech) space increased the value of analytics while driving the demand for analysts. This phenomenon was illustrated through snapshots of the martech industry from ChiefMartec's Scott Brinker.

In August 2011, Brinker charted the logos of providers operating in the nascent business of "marketing technology" as a way to sort out the market. There were 150.

---

[27] Luca Bruna/Associated Press (2005), Michael Sohn/Associated Press (2013).

Figure 1.7: Brinker's martech landscape in 2011[28]

The infographic was so well-received, Brinker decided to visit the martech space a year later and produce a second, updated industry snapshot. When Brinker recorded his second analysis in September 2012, the number of marketing technology firms had grown to 350. When he updated

[28] Scott Brinker, "Marketing Technology Landscape" Infographic (August 3, 2011).

his analysis in 2014, the number of firms had climbed to 1,000. A year later, in 2015, the number increased to 2,000.

Brinker's March 2016 analysis revealed an astonishing 3,500 firms in the space – almost twice the number from 14 months prior. In 2017, the number of companies in the marketing technology space reached 5,000, increasing more than 40 percent from 2016's total. 2018's graphic charts 6,829 marketing technology solutions. While that represents "only" 27 percent growth over the previous year's landscape, the increase belies the absolute scale of this space.

At the writing of this book's third edition in 2023, the number of companies in Brinker's marketing technology analysis exceeds 11,000. The extraordinary growth in the number of firms that offer services to analysts has opened their minds to the (nearly) unlimited power of data, while introducing extensive confusion as they attempt to navigate these new, roiling opportunities.

Figure 1.8: Brinker's martech landscape in 2023[29]

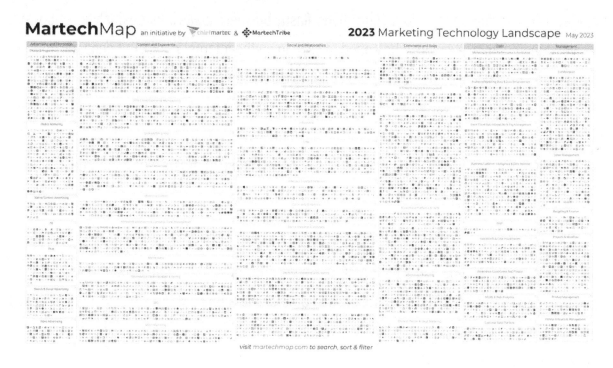

The number of firms in the space has led to innovation and technological advancement, thereby increasing the value analytics offers the business world.

Market Influences

In addition to the force of technology growth, market influences also had a profound effect on the demand for data analytics. By reducing uncertainty and creating accountability, today's digital-based business models and data analytics have played an important role in industry.

---

[29] Scott Brinker, "Marketing Technology Landscape Supergraphic (2019): Martech 5000 (Actually 7,040)" (April 4, 2019).

In the early go-go days of the mid- to late-1990s, flashy business ideas light on analytical rigor still received funding from investors who hoped to cash in on the internet boom. But once the internet bubble burst in 2000, businesses that didn't demonstrate sound financial structure surrendered their value. Companies that emerged from the wreckage of the NASDAQ crash and attracted investment in the post-bubble environment could demonstrate sound business models backed by thorough financial analysis. This heightened examination of the numbers side of internet business increased the demand for analytics.

Rise of FAMGA

Following the NASDAQ crash in 2000, FAMGA – Facebook, Apple, Microsoft, Google, and Amazon – understood the value of digital data better than others. The data FAMGA collected, analyzed, and aggregated have dramatically affected the way consumers shop for products and how businesses interact with consumers.

Since 2015, these companies have been one of the most important driving market forces behind the U.S. economy. How investors evaluate FAMGA is tied to the value of their data (e.g., Facebook's key performance indicator [Daily Average Users]/[Monthly Average Users]). Maximizing the value of FAMGA's data has fueled the rise of analytics.

Placing Today's Data Creation in Context

An extraordinary amount of digital data is generated every day. It can be easy, however, to lose context for how much data is produced. A simple infographic like the one displayed below can help us regain that context.

Figure 1.9: Comparison of daily data-creating human activity (all figures in billions)[30]

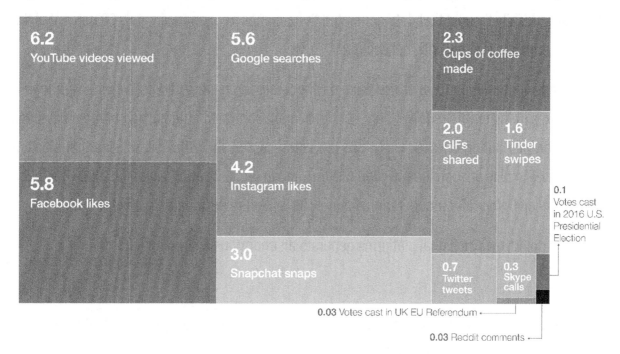

Represented in this graphic are the volumes of several consumer activities that generate important data. Each box represents a single activity, such as liking images on Instagram or tweeting on Twitter, and is scaled to its relative size. The infographic makes it possible to introduce other data-producing behaviors that add context to the digital activities represented in the visual.

Large, popular activities, including watching YouTube videos (6.2 billion each day), liking things on Facebook (5.8 billion), and searching Google (5.6 billion), stand out as vast amounts of data are created daily.[31] Those numbers appear even larger in the context of the brown box in the upper right, which represents the cups of coffee made each day. Although one can find coffee anywhere

[30] Domo (2019), BrandWatch (2019), Social Pilot (2019), Tinder (2019), Word Development (2019), U.S. Election Atlas (2019), UK Election Atlas (2019).

[31] Domo (2019).

on Earth, the number of cups made pales in comparison to the activity on YouTube, Facebook, and elsewhere, despite the fact that data generated there comes from approximately 60 percent of the world's population that has internet access.[32]

The volume of internet data generated each day becomes even more impressive when compared to two boxes in the graphic's lower right corner. In stark contrast to the hulking number of videos viewed and like buttons clicked daily, are the votes cast in the 2016 U.S. presidential election (represented in blue at approximately 100 million), and in red, the votes cast earlier that year in the UK's European Union referendum (approximately 30 million to decide the issue of Brexit).

Without a doubt, today's digital platforms generate an enormous amount of data.

Rise of the Machines: Machine Learning and Analytics

The explosion of digital data has been a catalyst for innovation. The growth of technologies to manage this volume of data and analytics tools to make sense of it have been critical developments for the analyst. The next big force for change – machine learning – is quickening the pace of innovation in several fields. Machine learning has a long and varied history, however.

IBM's Arthur Samuel introduced machine learning in 1959 to describe a computer that could be programmed to learn.[33] In the simplest sense, machine learning is the use of computer-powered algorithms to analyze data for patterns. What makes machine learning such a transformative approach to analysis is that the volume of data that can run through the algorithms is limitless. Should the computers behind the algorithms reach their data volume capacity, an infinite amount of computing power can be added to increase that capacity.

---

[32] Miniwatts Marketing Group, Internet World Stats (November 19, 2019).

[33] Arthur Samuel, "Some Studies in Machine Learning Using the Game of Checkers," *IBM Journal of Research and Development* (1959).

A subset of artificial intelligence (AI), machine learning separates itself from AI because AI algorithms depend on human-created rules. In contrast, computers that use machine learning programs can effectively create rules for themselves as they "learn." Learning in this sense refers to computers' attempts to optimize outputs from their algorithms. In other words, a machine learning algorithm designed to maximize the percent of consumers who click on a display ad (the algorithm's target "output") will churn through thousands, millions, or perhaps billions of instances when consumers saw the ad. It will then correlate what's known about those consumers and the various elements of the ad (the algorithm's data "inputs") to determine the "right" conditions for consumer engagement. While human programmers code some of the initial parameters in the machine learning algorithms, the computers take it from there to constantly test and reveal insights. The evolving field of "Deep Learning," a further subset of machine learning, provides the computer with even more latitude to adapt through the use of deep artificial neural networks.

Machine learning's modern applications are greatest in the fields of data analysis and pattern recognition, and machine learning is playing an increasingly important role in marketing. A machine learning program can find patterns in a dataset using regression models and clustering techniques to map inputs to outputs based on example input:output pairings (referred to as supervised learning). The program can also find patterns in a dataset, drawing inferences without reference to a labeled outcome (unsupervised learning). The program can do this quickly, efficiently, and without bias.

Machine learning is used in spam filters in your email inbox and recommended videos on YouTube. Computer-aided medical diagnoses that can improve disease recognition, patient care, and outcomes depend on machine learning. Self-driving cars, which can reduce the risk of automobile accidents, are powered by sophisticated machine learning programs. Anheuser-Busch has used machine learning to optimize delivery routes, improving efficiency and driver satisfaction.[34] Indeed, machine learning can improve many aspects of everyday life.

The modern applications of machine learning are felt more profoundly in digital marketing than anywhere else, given the vast amounts of accessible data in the field. Its primary function is determining consumer segments based on observed behaviors to improve and customize the consumer's journey. For example, machine learning algorithms working on consumer data can match this data with products or services that consumers who have similar interests selected. Retailers like Walmart, Alibaba, The North Face, Amazon, and eBay have all used machine learning to cater messages to individuals more precisely than ever before. Perhaps most famously, Target employed a machine learning algorithm developed by statistician and leading AI expert Andrew Pole to analyze women's purchases in an attempt to identify which shoppers were likely to be pregnant. The algorithm revealed key indicators like the purchase of certain supplements, unscented lotion, and other products that were highly correlated with subsequent baby registry enrollments. Target used these insights to send coupons to consumers the model identified, including a 16-year-old, revealing her unintended pregnancy to her father. Target adapted its strategy to mix other offers in with the pregnancy-focused promotions after finding that customers were uncomfortable with this degree of personalization. While expanding ethical concerns and growing limitations in data collection have affected the robustness of machine learning algorithms, programs built on publicly available information can still effectively tailor advertisements a person receives.

Personalized ads have long been viewed as a key to marketing effectiveness and the health of the relationships brands maintain with consumers. In a 2016 study Demand Metric conducted in partnership with Seismic, "Content Marketing's Evolution: The Age Of Hyper Personalization And

---

[34] Prannoiy Chandran, "Disruption in Retail — AI, Machine Learning & Big Data," Medium (July 23, 2018).

Automation," 80 percent of respondents said personalized content was more effective or much more effective than generic content.[35] More recently, McKinsey & Company's *Next in Personalization 2021 Report* revealed that 76 percent of consumers get frustrated when brands don't deliver personalized ads.[36] But machine learning has been shown to dramatically increase the relevance and personalization of ads by analyzing consumer behavior to build highly customized audiences around brand-specific awareness measures. Through a combination of survey and response data, machine learning algorithms can categorize consumers successfully based on their positions in the consumer journey: those requiring greater awareness, those who are working through the stage of consideration, and those who exhibit purchase intent. Audiences built in this way provide brands with the opportunity to move consumers seamlessly through the consumer journey by matching messages to their personalized needs.

The future of machine learning in marketing is exciting. In addition to better consumer understanding, other applications of machine learning are evolving quickly. Chatbots, for example, can function on the same level as human customer service representatives. Some of the most exciting advancements are in content curation and creation. A sophisticated algorithm could eventually be instrumental in the creation of digital media, whether making suggestions on end-to-end strategies for content marketing, providing content topics, or even creating content.

That said, adopting machine learning techniques in the marketer's repertoire makes the analyst's role even more important. While algorithms powering machine learning programs can identify unseen patterns, it's the analyst who interprets those patterns. These tools should be seen as enablers – not replacements – for analysts. As a result, it's imperative that analysts build their Techie skills, so they can lead the use of machine learning in their organizations. It's even more

---

[35] Demand Metric, Seismic, *Content Marketing's Evolution: The Age of Hyper-Personalization and Automation* (March 2016).

[36] McKinsey & Company, *Next in Personalization 2021 Report* (September 2021).

important that analysts hone their Business Strategist skills, so they can place machine learning insights in the context of the advertiser's broader business and make smarter, more informed decisions.

In Summary: The Rise of Modern Data Analytics

Data has become the most valuable asset for anyone who makes or attempts to influence decisions. To help make sense of the consumer journey and the role data could play, P&G introduced the concept of a three-step model that detailed the role of the brand in a consumer's decisions in 2005. The amount of data consumers and brands generate has grown significantly since then. As a result, Google adapted P&G's framework to the changing data landscape by introducing the concept of the Zero Moment of Truth. Google's ZMOT remains durable through the explosive growth of data in today's marketing and advertising environment. Several influences drove the explosive growth of data and new customer touch points, creating new marketing opportunities that led to the growing demand for analytics in today's marketing and advertising environment.

PART 2
Consumer/Brand Relationships

Lesson 1   Owned and Operated Properties

Lesson 2   Online Video

Lesson 3   Online Search

Lesson 4   Display Media

Lesson 5   Social Media

Lesson 6   The Consumer Decision Journey

The methods that brands use to build relationships with consumers – online video, search, display ads, and social media – give analysts a wealth of data about behaviors on these platforms. Knowing how to assess successful consumer/brand relationships and understanding a consumer's purchase journey requires a useable framework for parsing this data.

In Part 2, we explore each digital channel in-depth, including a discussion of key metrics and measurements, how consumers interact with brands on each platform, and ways of organizing consumer data that enable actionable insights.

Owned and Operated Properties

Five things discussed in this lesson:

- Owned and operated (O&O) digital properties include websites, campaign microsites, and landing pages for search ads that a brand produces and maintains
- O&O digital properties are an important means through which brands establish and deepen consumer relationships
- O&O digital properties offer brands the exclusive ability to own how they appear to consumers and collect first-party (1P) consumer data
- Measuring the consumer behaviors that matter through an O&O digital property requires solid organizational leadership, strategic thinking, and digital enablement (i.e., digital maturity)
- Website analytics tools that track important metrics related to consumer behaviors, acquisition, and value typically collect data used to measure O&O digital properties

Owned and operated (O&O) digital properties are the digital experiences brands create for consumers that are, as the name suggests, brand-owned and operated. Specifically, O&O digital properties are those that a brand produces and maintains, including its website, microsites, and landing pages for search ads. For most brands, these are the primary touch points that make consumer connections.

A brand's O&O properties are an extremely important component of its digital strategy. These properties are highly measurable and the only platform in which a brand can own the consumer experience and narrative. When a brand maintains a Facebook page, for example, it can be sure that its competitors are on Facebook, too. On a company's website, however, a brand can control 100 percent of the voice consumers hear and collect 100 percent of site-generated data.

Growing Importance of O&O

O&O digital properties are increasingly important e-commerce hubs and sources of consumer data, particularly first-party, or 1P, data that a brand collects directly from consumers, rather than obtaining data from another source (what we call second-party, or 2P, and third-party, or 3P, data).

Brands that sell products and services online have faced increasing pressure from online marketplaces (primarily Amazon) and traffic aggregators (such as Booking.com in the travel industry). The immense and growing presence of these marketplaces and aggregators has significantly cut into brands' profit margins by increasing consumer access to competitors and the cost of acquiring customers. In addition, as marketplaces and aggregators strive to create consumer value by reducing price, they typically take a brand-agnostic approach. Consequently, they make featured brands indistinguishable from one another (aside from their respective prices). Such a reality offers little opportunity for brands to build consumer relationships.

A brand, however, can create and cultivate such relationships through O&O digital properties. An O&O property allows a brand to establish unique, direct connections with consumers by offering online accounts. Based on the information consumers provide – names, ages, email addresses, mobile phone numbers, physical locations, transaction histories, and redemption data typical of most online accounts – a brand can better understand consumers and what they like. Linking consumer behaviors on an O&O digital platform – website pages viewed, e-newsletter sign-ups, online service requests, etc. – gives the brand unique data through which to better understand its customers. Brands can take this understanding a step further by linking each customer's Lifetime

Value (LTV) to the customer's account, helping the brand to differentiate consumers and offer corresponding levels of investment (e.g., status levels, special offers, and specific relevant marketing messages).

The data brands can collect on their O&O digital properties has become increasingly valuable, as marketplaces and aggregators rarely (if at all) share their consumer-level data. Marketplaces and aggregators recognize the importance of consumer data to their customer relationships and the threat sharing such data poses. Another reason that brands collect 1P data through their O&O digital properties is because privacy and regulatory influences have systematically limited brands' ability to acquire 3P data. The growing need for consumer consent has prevented companies from collecting consumer data. In addition, the deprecation of digital cookies has eliminated much of the consumer data these companies were collecting in the first place. As a result, much of the 3P data brands have collected is no longer viable, making 1P data critical to their marketing operations.

Measuring What Matters

The majority of interactions most brands have with consumers today happens through digital advertising engagements or company-owned properties. Website analytics platforms, such as Google Analytics and Adobe Analytics, are the tools brands use to measure consumer behavior on O&O digital properties. Tracking consumer behavior on O&O digital properties requires only a thorough set of digital tags on a brand's website. Brand goals differ with each business type. Website analytics tools that allow tracking for a variety of customer interactions meet those goals.

In addition, brands can collect additional 1P data from systems that can also help them act on insights. Online bidding systems, such as Google Ads, can supply conversion data (e.g., conversion tracking). Brands can import offline conversions, such as sales or survey data collected in a retail location, into online systems. They can then match the data to consumers through unique identifiers, such as customer IDs and loyalty card numbers, or other means. Similarly, they can import online consumer actions that other systems track.

Organizational Impediments

While it seems obvious that O&O digital properties and the 1P data they collect are valuable, many brands struggle to realize this value.

A surprising number of brands don't align on what they should measure. This is typically because executive leaders aren't clear about how their companies measure success or they've delegated measurement to lower levels of their organizations. This is where organizational silos, which promote data ownership but prevent sharing, thwart progress toward consistent, effective measurement. How finance teams define key performance indicators (KPIs) rarely aligns with that of performance marketing teams, unless a strong executive leader forces consistency and focus.

A lack of big-picture thinking can often pose challenges. For example, many advertisers define conversions as purchases. When brands focus exclusively on the results of their marketing efforts, they don't collect the information necessary to identify the root cause of consumer behaviors that inhibit or assist those results. Brands can't improve their results when they don't know which consumer behaviors to invest in and promote. To earn a more holistic, accurate understanding of the effects of digital marketing, brands must track every consumer interaction on their O&O digital properties.

Digital maturity is another obstacle. Many brands lack the people, processes, and technology to operate O&O digital properties effectively. Operating an O&O digital property effectively doesn't mean "having a website." It means knowing how to use that website to build and deepen customer relationships through connected data and actionable measurement. Doing so requires investments in skills, partnerships, teams, and cultures, as well as integrated and automated technologies.

Key O&O Metrics

Measuring consumer interactions on owned and operated properties gives brands an evaluative view into the quality and quantity of consumer experiences, as well as metrics related to customer acquisition and value.

Bounce Rate

A website analytics metric that measures the percentage of visitors who enter a website and leave without viewing other pages.

Cart Abandonment Rate

The rate at which consumers don't complete the checkout process after placing an item in an online shopping cart.

Goal Conversion Rate

Goals are specific website interactions that define a target objective. Typical goals could include a purchase or a registration, but a goal also may be defined as a consumer who visits a certain number of pages or downloads a piece of content. By tracking conversion rates, brands can determine how well marketing efforts lead to goal conversions, and use other consumer metrics to understand the factors that affect their successes or failures.

Macroconversion

A brand's ultimate goal for a consumer's journey – most frequently a sale of goods or services – and the culmination of microconversions.

Microconversion

An important, measurable step a consumer completes on the way to a macroconversion, such as viewing a webpage, downloading a coupon, etc.

Organic search traffic is traffic from users who came from a nonpaid search engine results page (SERP). Paid search is traffic from users who clicked on an advertisement on a SERP.

Revenue

Sales generated from consumers on an owned and operated property. Data provided will typically include the number of transactions, the total transaction value, and the average sales per transaction. Additional measures, such as number of items purchased and average price per item, may be included, depending on the business type.

Session Duration (Time On Site / Time On Page)

The average length of site or page visits. Along with the bounce rate, average session duration measures user engagement by tracking how long users stay on a website. It's a helpful metric for indicating engagement, which is the true value of website content.

Unique Page Views

An analytics metric that measures the number of unique pages a visitor views on a website.

In Summary: O&O Properties

A brand's O&O digital properties, websites, and other digital properties are an important component of digital strategy. These include websites, campaign microsites, and landing pages for search ads that a brand produces and maintains over its lifetime.

O&O digital properties are an important means through which brands establish and deepen consumer relationships. Importantly, O&O digital properties allow brands to collect 1P consumer data.

Measuring the consumer behaviors that matter through an O&O digital property requires solid organizational leadership, strategic thinking, and digital enablement (i.e., digital maturity). Website analytics tools that track important metrics related to consumer behaviors, acquisition, and value typically collect data used to measure O&O digital properties.

In the next lesson, we'll look at Online Video (OLV), an important way for brands to engage consumers through multisensory experiences.

Online Video

Five things discussed in this lesson:

- Online video is an important way for brands to engage with consumers
- Online video's blend of sight, sound, and motion provides brands with unique opportunities to craft consumer experiences
- YouTube is the world's largest online video platform, but the market is quickly evolving to include streaming services from traditional video creators and new entrants
- Consumer behavior has seen a significant shift in the way video content is enjoyed, its role in entertainment choices, and the influence it has on purchase decisions
- Measuring successful online video campaigns requires the use of new metrics, as well as traditional video measures adapted for online video delivery

Online video (OLV) is an important way for brands to engage consumers through multisensory experiences: sight, sound, and motion. Its emergence has revolutionized the entertainment industry, as well as the way people around the world use the internet. The 2016 announcement that OLV stars are eligible for Emmy nominations demonstrates this shift and is a testament to the fact that short-form digital content can be high-quality entertainment, regardless of where people view it.

By developing content that resonates with the interests and passions of viewers today, OLV creators have created authentic connections with their fans and amassed large followings. Stars such as PewDiePie, Smosh, and Jenna Marbles are frequently considered more popular and influential than many mainstream celebrities. In fact, a recent Variety study found that YouTube sensation PewDiePie was more popular than basketball great LeBron James among Generation Z males.[37]

Online Video (OLV) Market Share

OLV is comprised of "user-generated content" models such as YouTube and Facebook, but also includes full episode players (FEP) and over-the-top (OTT) streaming services, including Hulu, Netflix, and Disney+. Google, powered by YouTube, remains the largest online video player, reaching nearly 250 million people in the U.S., according to Comscore.[38]

Figure 2.1: Leading U.S. video properties 2022, by reach[39]

Platform	U.S. Reach (Millions)	Notes
Google Sites	248.99	Includes the world's largest video-sharing site, YouTube
Comcast NBCU	153.66	Portfolio of news and entertainment video properties
Paramount	146.93	Mass media and entertainment conglomerate
Global	140.09	Digital video services led by its flagship streaming service,
Disney	133.51	Disney+
Hulu		Subscription streaming video service majority-owned by Disney

---

[37] Todd Spangler, "YouTuber PewDiePie Is More Liked Than LeBron James Among Gen Z Males, Study Finds," *Variety* (November 5, 2019).

[38] Comscore. *Most Popular Online Video Properties in the United States in July 2022, By Reach (in Millions)* (August 1, 2022).

[39] Comscore (August 1, 2022).

Comscore reports that 85 to 90 percent of internet users in the U.S. view online video. Brands are a critical component of the OLV experience, as marketing strategist Mehmood Hanif estimates the average internet user is served 11,250 ads per month.[40]

Consumer Behavior and OLV

As OLV increasingly becomes more important, the way people watch it is changing. Google documented several recent and interesting trends. These trends are affecting consumer behavior in ways beyond how people access entertainment. In fact, OLV plays a significant role in shopping behaviors:

→ Watch time for shopping-related videos on YouTube grew in the U.S. by more than five times over the past two years.[41]

→ Over the past three years, the number of YouTube channels with more than 1 billion views has grown by five times.[42]

→ More than half of shoppers say online video has helped them decide which brand or product to buy.[43]

→ More than 90 percent of people say they discover new brands or products on YouTube.[44]

---

[40] Christopher Elliott, "Yes, There Are Too Many Ads Online. Yes, You Can Stop Them. Here's How." *HuffPost* (February 9, 2017).

[41] Google, 2019 Research Review: New Media Channels Are Emerging (December 2019).

[42] Google, 2019 Research Review: New Media Channels.

[43] Google/Ipsos, Global (U.S., CA, BR, U.K., DE, FR, JP, IN, KR, AU), "How People Shop with YouTube" Study, 18–64-year-olds who go online at least monthly and have purchased something in the last year, n=24,017 (July 2018).

[44] Google/Magid Advisors, Global (U.S., CA, BR, U.K., DE, FR, JP, IN, KR, AU), "The Role of Digital Video in People's Lives," n=20,000, A18–64 general online population (August 2018).

→ More than 40 percent of global shoppers say they've purchased products they discovered on YouTube.[45]

Such shifts in consumer behavior have been a poignant illustration of the power of digital platforms. Moreover, changes in consumer behavior have left traditional linear television companies scrambling to reimagine the way they deliver entertainment. The culmination of these influences has led marketers to rethink their approaches to advertising. The implications for analysts are far-reaching.

OLV and Television

Television has been one of the most influential creations since its inception in 1925. But its influence is waning today. According to Insider Intelligence (formerly eMarketer), the average amount of time U.S. adults watch TV has been on a steady decline. Time spent watching live, DVR, and other prerecorded television (such as video downloaded from the internet but saved locally) reached a peak of 4.6 hours per day in 2012 but fell to 3.8 hours in pre-pandemic 2020 – a drop of more than 17 percent.[46] Insider Intelligence projected that slide to continue and it has to this day.

Conversely, time spent engaging with digital content, and specifically digital video content, has been on the rise. Over the same 2012 to 2020 period, the number of hours U.S. adults spent on digital platforms increased nearly 80 percent, reaching 7.5 hours per day.[47] Time spent watching

---

[45] Google/Ipsos, Global (U.S., CA, BR, U.K., DE, FR, JP, IN, KR, AU), "How People Shop with YouTube" Study, 18–64-year-olds who go online at least monthly and have purchased something in the last year, n=24,017 (July 2018).

[46] Mark Dolliver, "US Time Spent with Media 2020: Gains in Consumer Usage During the Year of COVID-19 and Beyond," *eMarketer* (April 29, 2020).

[47] Dolliver, "US Time Spent with Media 2020."

digital video increased an astonishing 240 percent in that period, reaching more than two hours per day.[48]

From streaming services, such as Netflix, to media platforms like YouTube, it's undeniable that video viewing has trended away from conventional television. The average number of viewers throughout 2019 for the four largest TV networks, CBS (7.1 million), NBC (6.3 million), ABC (5.2 million), and Fox (4.6 million), is a combined 23.3 million Americans.[49] This total is undoubtedly exaggerated as it ignores that many of those people likely overlap. While the number of Americans watching network television is not insignificant, it's a far cry from Netflix's 73 million U.S. subscribers (182.2 million globally)[50] and nowhere near the 175.5 million Americans who visit YouTube each month[51] (with more than 2 billion people globally viewing videos on YouTube monthly[52]). The overwhelming size of digital video platforms is a clear indication that consumers look favorably on the breadth of content choices, ease of use, and simple access. It's important for analysts to understand the motivations behind such shifts in consumer behavior. By doing so, they can help guide decisions on where brands should place content to reach consumers.

Who is watching traditional and digital video is an equally important question. Apparent demographic differences among consumers are driving the shift from traditional television to digital video. Younger viewers, frankly, don't watch TV like past generations. According to eMarketer, Generation Z consumers (under the age of 23) spent less than one-third as much time

---

[48] Dolliver, "US Time Spent with Media 2020."

[49] *Variety,* Leading ad supported broadcast and cable networks in the United States in 2019, by average number of viewers (in millions) (December 26, 2019).

[50] Netflix, Number of Netflix paying streaming subscribers in the United States from 3rd quarter 2011 to 2nd quarter 2020 (in millions) (July 16, 2020).

[51] Comscore, Most popular online video properties in the United States as of May 2020, ranked by unique viewers (in millions) (July 21, 2020).

[52] We Are Social, Hootsuite, and DataReportal, Most popular social networks worldwide as of July 2020, ranked by number of active users (in millions) (July 23, 2020).

in front of the television as boomers (age 56 and older). Millennials (age 24 to 39 in 2020) and Generation X consumers (age 40 to 55) watch less TV than boomers as well.[53] The trend toward older viewers watching television was clear in a 2018 AdAge analysis:

"If the broadcast networks were living, breathing human beings, they'd be closer to the tomb than the womb. Last season, the median age of the primetime CBS viewer was 61 years old, or a few candles north of the display that illuminates the birthday cake of the average NBC (57 years) or ABC (55) enthusiast. With a median age of 51 years, Fox is now eligible for AARP membership, and even the hip, teen-friendly CW is just a few years shy of aging out of the 18-to-49 demo."[54]

Digital video, on the other hand, exhibits greater usage among younger consumers. More than 90 percent of U.S. teens and adults under the age of 45 used digital platforms (including 98 percent of Americans ages 18 to 24) while fewer than 70 percent of boomers visit such sites.[55] Understanding the demographic makeup of consumers can inform analysts' recommendations on which platforms are ideal for reaching consumer segments.

OLV's influence on shopping behaviors and entertainment choices offers opportunities for brands to create content that influences consumers. Doing so effectively requires understanding how to measure the success of those efforts.

---

[53] eMarketer (April 2020); N.B.: Includes live, DVR, and other prerecorded video (such as video downloaded from the internet but saved locally); includes all time spent watching TV, regardless of multitasking; Gen Z are individuals born between 1997 and 2012; millennials are individuals born between 1981 and 1996; Gen X are individuals born between 1965 and 1980; and baby boomers are individuals born between 1946 and 1964.

[54] Anthony Crupi, "Sleepy, Hollow: What You Won't Hear at This Year's TV Upfronts," *AdAge* (March 15, 2018).

[55] eMarketer, Digital video penetration in the United States as of March 2019, by age group (February 18, 2020).

Key OLV Measures

Brands can evaluate success in using online video platforms through a blend of traditional methods that are used to measure television (the original video platform) and new metrics that measure OLV's unique capabilities.

Reach

Reach is a measurement of the size of the audience that watches an ad. This is a classic metric used as a key measure of success for most traditional media, particularly television, and is calculated as Reach (%) = Gross rating points (%) / Frequency.

Frequency

Frequency is the number of times the ad was exposed to an average person or household during a given period. For example, if the ad reached 30 million households in an audience or region that has 10 million households, its frequency would be three. Frequency is also used to assess television and other traditional media.

X+ Reach (Effective Reach)

Effective reach is a target detailing the number of people who see an ad with a frequency at or above the number of times deemed to be most effective. For example, "1+ Reach" means everyone who saw the ad at least once. This is also a measure used extensively to track traditional media channels.

Rating Points

Expressed as a percentage, a Rating Point is 1 percent of the potential audience. For example, if 25 percent of all targeted viewers saw an advertiser's commercial, the advertiser has achieved 25 rating points. Rating Points were conceived to track the effectiveness of traditional television campaigns but are used increasingly to track OLV.

Gross Rating Points (GRPs)

GRPs measure the total of all Rating Points an advertiser earns during a campaign. The measure is calculated by simply summing the Rating Points of all ads run during the campaign. Alternatively, GRPs can be calculated by multiplying a campaign's reach by its average frequency. For example, if a campaign reached 30% of the market and the consumers reached saw the ad an average of 4 times (i.e., a frequency of 4), the campaign earned 120 GRPs. As you can see, this metric can be greater than (even much greater than) 100.

In-Demo Gross Rating Points (also known as TRPs)

In-demo GRPs represent the percentage of the total GRPs earned from an audience that fits the advertiser's target (e.g., women aged 35 to 64). For example, if an advertiser's media plan reached 10 percent of its in-demo audience, it has 10 in-demo GRPs. This metric is also used to gauge television effectiveness.

Completed Video Views (or Rate)

Completed video views is the number of times a consumer watches a video to completion. This metric can also be expressed as the percent of consumers who are served the video and watch it all the way through (i.e., completed video view rate). Consumers who watch the video to completion, as well as those who don't, give brands important insights into their videos' effectiveness.

Engagement Rate

Often, brands want consumers to do more than watch videos. Engagement rate – the percentage of consumers who engage in additional behavior (e.g., sharing the video, clicking a link in the video, etc.) – can provide insight into the video's ability to encourage those desired behaviors.

Measuring a brand's relevance to consumers provides a sense of awareness, interest, and many other key brand attributes. Share of audience (SOA) is one way to quantify relevance. To calculate SOA, divide the number of subscribers to an OLV channel by total subscribers for brand channels in the category. SOA is inexact – after all, the same person can subscribe to any number of OLV channels – but it can provide a directional idea of a brand's popularity.

In Summary: Online Video

OLV is an important way for brands to engage with consumers. OLV's blend of sight, sound and motion provides brands with unique opportunities to craft consumer experiences in a rapidly evolving marketplace. While YouTube is the world's largest online video platform, streaming services from traditional video creators and new entrants are adding new content choices for consumers. These services seek to realize benefits created by the significant shifts in consumer behavior in the way video content is enjoyed, its role in entertainment choices, and the influence it has on purchase decisions. Measuring successful online video campaigns requires new metrics, as well as traditional video measures that have been adapted for online video delivery.

In the next lesson, we'll turn our attention to what could be the greatest marketing channel – online search.

Online Search

Five things discussed in this lesson:

- Online search provides insights into consumer intent like no other marketing platform
- Google is the largest search engine in the market, contributing more than 90 percent of consumer searches conducted worldwide
- Brands' management of online search marketing typically has one goal: improving search rank for critical consumer searches
- Recent increases in "near me" searches indicate new online search opportunities for brands
- Measuring the success of online search marketing typically depends on a handful of critical metrics

Online search could be the greatest marketing channel of all time. Where else is an advertiser given the opportunity to "talk" with consumers one-on-one and provide answers to uniquely personal questions? Think of the last time you were in a store and a sales associate approached you. How guarded were you? Did you withhold information to maintain negotiation leverage? Did you withhold information because you didn't feel comfortable discussing it with a stranger? Now, compare that to the last time you visited an online search engine. Most likely, the difference in transparency is significant.

The degree of transparency that consumers show when searching online is one of the clearest signals of their intent. Incorporating that intent into an advertiser's marketing efforts requires a thoughtful approach to online search advertising.

Search Engine Market Share

A significant number of search engines operate online, each working in the same general way: People show up with questions, and the search engines find the answers they see as most relevant, and then present the answers.

Each search engine has its own methods for collecting information from the web and determining relevance, which can vary significantly. But one thing that's consistent in the world of search engines is that most people choose Google to conduct their searches. Recent StatCounter data show Google had the largest search engine market share worldwide in May 2023:

Figure 2.2: Search engine share of page referrals[56]

Engine	Global Share	Notes
Google	93.1%	World's most popular search site founded in 1998
Bing	2.8%	Search engine that Microsoft owns and operates
Yandex	1.2%	Largest search engine in the Russian market today
Yahoo!	1.1%	Search network that Verizon Media owns
DuckDuckGo	0.5%	U.S. search engine that emphasizes user privacy
Baidu	0.5%	Dominant search engine in the Chinese market

---

[56] StatCounter Global Stats, "Worldwide Data for Search Engine Referrals" (May 2023).

Before we go too deep into online search as a marketing platform, we need to talk about two important concepts: search engine optimization (SEO) and search engine management (SEM). Each concept is important for brands and means different things for them.

Search Engine Management Versus Search Engine Optimization

Search engine management is about brands investing in paid search to reach consumers. Although the placement of paid search results changes as search engines frequently redesign their search engine results pages (SERPs), paid search ads can generally be seen at the top and alongside search results and are distinguished through a Federal Trade Commission-mandated symbol.[57] Here in Figure 2.3 are those ads and symbols:

Figure 2.3: Sample SERP from Google

---

[57] Lesley Fair, "FTC Staff to Search Engines: Differentiate Ads from Natural Results" (June 25, 2013).

How paid ads are returned is a complicated system based on a number of factors. Hal Varian, Google's chief economist, published a video in 2014 that expertly simplified that process.[58] Varian described the elements that go into determining the order of paid search results on the SERP as:

→ The advertiser's bid in Google's ad auction.

→ The click-through rate (i.e., the percent of people who see the ad and click on it) that Google expects that result to earn.

→ How well the page linked to the ad (i.e., the "landing page") is organized to create a good consumer experience.

→ The relevance of that ad to the question the searcher asked.

→ How that search ad uses the various ad formats (e.g., additional links, descriptions, etc.) that Google offers advertisers.

An advertiser's management of these factors across search engines is SEM.

Meanwhile, SEO is related to organic results. Those organic results are presented on the SERP below the ads, which generally land at the top of the results. Search engine algorithms trigger organic results similar to the way they present paid search results; however, organic results don't have a bid component. In other words, brands can't use money to influence how and where search engines display organic content, which effectively levels the playing field for big and small content owners.

SEM and SEO differ significantly in the way they promote internet content, but they have similar objectives. Advertisers want their content to be where consumers are when they're searching for something relevant to advertisers' brands.

---

[58] PPC, Hal Varian, "Pay Per Click Management - Insights on the Google AdWords Auction System" (October 24, 2014).

In 2007, InquireO published a study that demonstrated the importance of brands being at the top of the SERP. By overlaying a Google search page with a graphic of where consumers' eyes fell on the page, InspireO visualized this idea perfectly. The majority of consumers look at the first couple of results before clicking a link.

A recent study from Travel Tripper makes this clear. The online travel site and technology provider, which recently merged with Pegasus, worked with research company Sticky to test consumers' interaction with a SERP for a hotel-related query. A sample size of 100 users had 15 seconds to look at each page. Sticky recorded eye tracking and the results can be seen here:

Figure 2.4: Sticky's Google SERP eye tracking results[59]

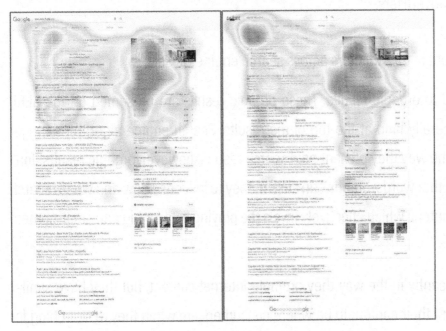

---

59 Tris Heaword, "Eye Tracking in 2017 for Google Hotel Searches: Why the Old Rules Don't Apply," Pegasus (March 17, 2017).

Some studies say consumers expect the best brands to be at the top of that list, whether through organic results or paid search engine management advertising. If a brand's objective is to be relevant to consumers when they're searching for something the brand can offer, a high search rank – the position the brand's website or page is returned on the SERP – is important to success.

Consumer Behavior and Search

The way consumers engage with online search engines is evolving. Recent trends in queries demonstrate shifts in consumer interests, needs, and intent. Google reports that near me searches are increasing across almost every category, with people combining locally sensitive searches with other intent signals.

In 2018 and 2019, "where to buy" + "near me" mobile queries increased more than 200 percent.

Examples include "where to buy flowers near me," "where to buy stamps near me," and "where to buy pumpkins near me."[60] During that time, mobile searches for "store open near me" ("grocery store open near me" and "auto parts store open near me"), and "on sale" + "near me" ("tires on sale near me" and "houses on sale near me") increased more than 250 percent year over year.[61]

Key Search Measures

As we've seen, understanding what consumers look for as they search online is an important component to a brand's success. But how can the brand understand what works (and what doesn't) in search marketing? Every brand online should track a few critical metrics:

---

[60] Google, 2019 Research Review: New Media Channels Are Emerging (December 2019).

[61] Google, 2019 Research Review.

Click-Through Rate

Click-through rate is an important metric that identifies the percent of consumers who saw a search ad and clicked on it. The number can help gauge the effectiveness of search strategies that target consumers, as well as the design's effectiveness in engaging consumers.

Conversion Rate

Conversion rate is the percent of consumers who, after clicking on a search ad, take action on the linked page. Tracked actions include making a purchase on the page, downloading a file, or any number of activities the brand deems to be positive.

Cost Per Action

Another metric that's important to assessing search marketing success is cost per action (CPA). This measure takes the cost invested in a search campaign and divides that cost by the number of a tracked consumer action. Those actions could be clicks – cost per click, or CPC – or any other conversion actions the brand deems important.

Impression Share

Impression share is the number of impressions a search ad received divided by the number of impressions the ad was eligible to receive. Effectively, impression share measures the percentage of times an ad showed up in a SERP when a consumer entered a search on which the advertisers placed a bid. Eligible impressions are estimated using many factors, including targeting settings, approval statuses, and quality. Impression share is a good way to understand how well an ad has been optimized to achieve campaign goals (i.e., whether an ad might reach more consumers if its bid or budget was increased, its targeting was set a different way, etc.).

Measuring a brand's relevance to consumers' online searches provides a sense for awareness, interest, and many other key brand attributes. Calculate share of search (SOS) by dividing the number of searches for a brand by total searches conducted for brands in the category. For example, auto manufacturers can gain great insight into the popularity of their vehicles by comparing the searches conducted for one of their sedans against all searches for sedans. Analysts can conduct SOS at a company level, brand level, or product level, and can compare the item being searched against the entire market or a select group of key competitors.

In Summary: Online Search

In this lesson, we saw how online search provides brands with insight into consumer intent like no other marketing platform. Google is the largest search engine in the market, with more than 90 percent of consumer searches worldwide. Brands' management of online search marketing typically has one goal: improving search rank for critical consumer searches. A recent increase in near me searches indicates new online search opportunities for brands. Finally, measuring the success of online search marketing typically depends on a handful of critical metrics.

In the next lesson, we'll take a look at how brands can use display media to connect with consumers at various points along their decision journeys.

Display Media

Five things discussed in this lesson:

- Display ads have evolved significantly since the format debuted in 1994
- Digital display ads come in many formats, including banners, video, rich media, and sponsorships
- Each category of display ads grew consistently and steadily from 2015 to 2019
- Display ads have evolved primarily in their ability to target specific consumers across the internet, but privacy concerns have cast doubt on how effective display ads will be in the future
- The effectiveness of display strategies, campaigns, and creative is measured similarly as search media

The display ad of today hardly resembles the banner ads of 25 years ago.

Introduced in 1994, display ads are one of the oldest forms of digital advertising and signaled a change in the way brands could interact with consumers online. Display ads contributed to the rise of data analytics as we know it today. But the static ads of yesterday have been updated to include video, dynamic content, and other forms of immersive experience that are designed to engage consumers at key moments in their purchasing journeys. Coupled with remarketing technology, the display ad can play a critical and efficient role in a brand's advertising and marketing efforts.

Digital display ads come in many formats. The primary types of digital display ads include banners and similar executions, video ads that aren't in a player, rich media ads that integrate streaming activity (often through the use of Flash or JavaScript to allow users to interact with content), and sponsorships in which advertisers pay for custom content and/or experiences presented in a display format.[62] According to data from Statista Market Insights, there's no slowdown in sight for digital display ads' most common format, the banner ad.

Figure 2.5: Worldwide banner advertising spend ($Billions)[63]

Ad Format	2022	2023	2024	2025	2026
Desktop Banner Ads	$44.55	$46.44	$48.21	$50.05	$51.98
Mobile Banner Ads	$102.60	$115.40	$126.20	$135.80	$144.50
Total	$147.20	$161.80	$174.40	$185.90	$196.50

Placing digital display media has increasingly shifted to programmatic purchases because of the format's straightforward nature. Programmatic media buying is the data-intensive algorithmic purchase and sale of advertising space in real time. Software automates the buying, placement, and optimization of media inventory via a bidding system. The efficiency of programmatic media buying has had a positive effect on display ad spend.

---

[62] *IAB Internet Advertising Revenue Report,* 2018 Full Year Results, prepared by PwC (May 2019).

[63] Statista Market Insights (March 1, 2023).

Evolution of Display Ad Formats

Display media has evolved with new formats and features aimed at increasing consumer engagement. Video, rich media, and custom-constructed sponsorships are examples of formats that build on the static banner concept by introducing attention-grabbing motion, sound, and content. Display ads have primarily evolved, however, in how they can target specific consumers on the internet.

You've probably experienced display ads' targeting capabilities. After visiting a retailer's page to check out a pair of shoes, you likely noticed those shoes popping up in display ads on nearly every page you subsequently visited. This is because digital data placed on your device when you checked out the shoes (in the form of digital cookies, which we'll discuss later in this book) can inform the bidding strategies of sophisticated display advertisers, ensuring they remind you of the items. A recent study by *Washington Post* technology columnist Geoffrey A. Fowler found that in one week of browsing the internet with Google Chrome, more than 11,000 tracking cookies were deposited into his browser.[64]

For the analyst, tracking cookies can help identify consumers who exhibit an intent to purchase products and services based on behavior across digital properties. As Fowler's report makes clear, however, the use of tracking cookies tied to display advertising is at the center of the privacy issue being debated in the digital marketing industry today. We'll explore the intricate topic of privacy in Part 3 of this book. At this point, it's more important to understand that display ads' ability to target consumers in the future – and therefore, their usefulness to analysts – is less than certain.

---

[64] Geoffrey A. Fowler, "Goodbye, Chrome: Google's Web Browser Has Become Spy Software," *Washington Post* (June 21, 2019).

Key Display Media Measures

As an interactive media unit, display ads are measured by metrics that gauge the effectiveness and efficiency of consumer engagement. Typically, analysts would assess display media using the same metrics found in a search campaign.

Click-Through Rate

As with search ads, click-through rate is an important metric for display media. Tracking the percent of consumers who saw a brand's display ad and clicked on it gauges the effectiveness of display strategies that target consumers, as well as the effectiveness of the display ad's creative to engage consumers.

Engagement Rate

Similar to the metric used to gauge video engagement, the engagement rate of a display ad tracks the rate by which consumers interact with the ad.

Conversion Rate

Conversion rate is calculated as the percent of consumers who, after clicking on a display ad, take action on the linked page. Tracked actions could be making a purchase on the page, downloading a file, or any number of activities the brand deems to be positive.

Cost Per Action

Cost per action (CPA) takes the cost invested in a display campaign and divides that cost by the number of tracked consumer actions. As with search, the action could be clicks on the display ad (cost per click, or CPC), or any other action the brand deems important.

Display ads have evolved significantly since they debuted in 1994, adding a number of features to increase consumer engagement. Today's digital display comes in many formats, including banners, video, rich media, and sponsorships. Each category of display ads grew consistently and steadily from 2015 to 2019. Display ads have primarily evolved in their ability to target specific consumers across the internet, but privacy concerns have cast doubt on how effective display ads will be in the future. Measuring the effectiveness of display strategies, campaigns, and creative can be done in much the same way as with search media.

In the next lesson, we'll discuss how brands can use social media to develop consumer relationships and earn important insights into consumer behavior.

Social Media

Five things discussed in this lesson:

- Social media usage continues to grow, with usage reaching 4.9 billion worldwide in 2023
- Which social media platform a consumer uses varies significantly with age and need
- While each major social media platform offers unique positioning to consumers, Facebook is the largest player
- Brands most frequently use social media through sponsored posts that seek to influence consumer decisions authentically and organically
- Measuring the success of a brand's social media efforts requires metrics that are unique to each platform and those that apply across a brand's marketing channels

Since its founding in 2004, Facebook has been the dominant social media platform in the world. It's changed the way people communicate, maintain personal relationships, and investigate brands for the 4.9 billion users of social media today in 2023.[65] Behind Facebook and its image-based social media property, Instagram, stands platforms that include Pinterest, Twitter, Snapchat,

---

[65] "Top Social Media Statistics And Trends Of 2023," Forbes (2023).

and LinkedIn. Combined, these six players represent the majority of social media engagement, and each has carved a unique niche in the social media landscape.

Despite the recent privacy and data challenges social media platforms experienced (Facebook, in particular), social media remains a critically important channel for brands. Analysts can mine tremendously robust information and deep insights from social media.

Social Media Market Share

Social media use is increasing around the world. Without a doubt, it's one of the most popular online activities for people of all ages. According to Statista, in 2022, 60 percent of the world's Internet users visited a social media platform at least once a month, and that number is growing.[66] That equates to about 4.6 billion people.

Facebook dominates the social media landscape. Young Americans, especially those ages 18 to 24, stand out for embracing a variety of platforms and using them frequently. Who else uses social media? Active users include 90.4 percent of millennials, 77.5 percent of Generation X, and 48.2 percent of baby boomers.[67]

---

[66] Statista. Number of Social Media Users Worldwide from 2017 to 2027 (June 15, 2022).

[67] "Here's Why You Need Social Media," Yapmedia (2019).

Figure 2.6: U.S. share of social media visits as of March 2023[68]

Network	U.S. Share	Notes
Facebook	53.09%	World's largest (and original) social network
Twitter	16.25%	Unique value proposition due to intensity of sharing
Instagram	13.85%	App-focused photo and video site that Facebook owns
Pinterest	12.77%	Image-based social site with robust integration to Web

Consumer Behavior and Social Media

The social platform a user chooses typically depends on need. For business connections, a person turns to LinkedIn, while someone who wants to connect with others on a personal level is more likely to fire up Facebook. Age also affects platform choice. Approximately 78 percent of 18- to 24-year-olds use Snapchat and a sizeable majority of these users (71 percent) visit the platform multiple times per day.[69]

Furthermore, social media has matured to become a strong influencer in buying decisions. Social media channels give customers an easy way to contact brands. Customers can learn about brands' organizations and browse their friends' opinions. In late 2019, Lyfe Marketing documented three facts that support the power social media has on the consumer decision journey:

→ **81 percent** of customers make buying decisions based on their friends' social media posts (Market Force). In other words, when followers engage with an advertiser's page, they not only connect with those consumers, but also potentially influence all of their connections.

---

[68] StatCounter, Leading social media websites in the United States as of March 2023, based on share of visits (April 1, 2023).

[69] "Here's Why You Need Social Media," Yapmedia (2019).

→ **71 percent** say social media referrals make them more likely to purchase an item (HubSpot). When people refer a brand on social media, the advertiser boosts its sales potential with everyone who sees that post.

→ **133 percent** increase in conversions when shoppers on mobile see good reviews about a brand before they buy an item (Bazaarvoice). Great reviews on Facebook and other social media sites can help convince people to try a business.

How Brands Use Social Media

A sponsored post integrated into a user's feed is the most common ad product social media platforms sell. These posts can feature all types of digital advertising mentioned thus far: display ads, video ads, and even search ads from a social media platform's search page.

Social media ads tend to gravitate toward common appearance. "Sameness," in this sense, is by design as the platforms monitor one another for innovations and optimizations. Snapchat – with its young consumer segment – has produced less traditional (perhaps more innovative?) ads than other platforms, although the benefit is questionable. In a similar (albeit, antithetical) way, LinkedIn has crafted advertising that serves specific purposes for specific consumer segments. Other social media platforms tend to copy innovations they believe will have a positive effect on consumer behaviors.

Advertisers can use each social media network to realize a unique objective, despite the commonality in ad formats. Facebook's enormous reach and consumer data allow brands to connect to a great number of consumers in a highly targeted, personalized way. Twitter's connectiveness and unique format (i.e., limited character content delivered in short bursts) enables brands to reach targeted segments of consumers quickly and efficiently through rapid sharing. Pinterest's use of "image pinning" reveals internet browsing behavior. Instagram works in conjunction with Facebook's social network, allowing advertisers to connect with consumers in different ways while complementing simultaneous Facebook campaigns.

Guiding an advertiser in the successful use of social media – including the leading networks mentioned here and those that weren't discussed – requires a clear understanding of each network's position in the social media market. Through this understanding, the analyst can design objectives that fit each network while carefully weighing its pros and cons.

Key Social Media Measures

How brands measure return on social media investments is a function of brand focus and the chosen social media network's measurement offerings.

Audience Growth

When tracking audience growth, analysts look at how many people are connected to a brand on social media. "Followers" are a common designation on social media platforms for people who have agreed to receive content updates from brands (e.g., Twitter followers). Picking two points in time and measuring the increase in followers provides audience growth. Clearly, the faster a brand increases its audience and the bigger the audience is, the better for that brand.

Amplification Rate

Amplification rate measures the advocacy that consumers show toward content on a brand's social media platform. For example, if consumers share videos or comments from a brand's social media feed on their social channels, that's amplification. Amplification rate tracks the volume of "shares" for a piece of content, or the rate at which those shares are collected (i.e., the number of consumers who shared the content / the total number of consumers who saw the content). Amplification is important for many reasons – namely, when brands talk to consumers, brands want consumers to relay their messages to others. A brand gains credibility when consumers share the brand's words. In addition, consumer endorsements are perceived as being more credible than marketing messages. The higher the amplification rate, the better for the brand.

Applause Rate

Applause rate is different from amplification rate. Applause rate measures the degree to which consumers react positively to a brand's work. Positive reactions can come from a "Like" on Facebook, a favoriting of a tweet on Twitter, or saving an image to a Pinterest account. Applause rate is calculated as the percent of users who see the content that has the desired positive reaction. Applause is not sharing the content, so this measure stops short of quantifying brand advocacy. Applause rate can still be an effective measurement for identifying the content that does or doesn't work for consumers.

Click-Through Rate

As with search and display ads, click-through rate is an important metric for social media ads and campaigns when a consumer can click on an ad and be sent to another destination, such as the advertised company's website. Tracking the percent of consumers who saw a brand's ad and clicked on it gauges the effectiveness of display strategies that target consumers, as well as the effectiveness of the display ad's creative to engage consumers.

Engagement Rate

In the context of social media, engagement rate measures the percentage of consumers who engage in additional behavior (e.g., comments on Facebook, re-pins on Pinterest, brand mentions on Twitter, etc.). Similar to the way this metric works with OLV, engagement rate can provide insight into the video's ability to encourage those desired behaviors.

Reach

As with OLV, reach, in the context of social media, is a measurement of the size of the audience that sees an ad. Reach applies to video ads, sponsored posts, and any other ad types on a social media platform.

Share of Voice (SOV)

Similar to SOS (see Lesson 2: Online Search), brands can measure their relevance by conducting a share of voice (SOV) analysis. To calculate SOV, divide the number of social mentions for a brand by total social mentions for brands in the category. SOV can be conducted at a company level, brand level, or product level, and can compare the item being mentioned by consumers against the entire market or a select group of key competitors.

In Summary: Social Media

The role social media plays in the consumer/brand relationship has evolved significantly since Facebook's founding in 2004. Social media usage continues to grow, with more than 3 billion users worldwide. The emergence of other social media platforms has offered consumers additional choices. Each platform plays a unique role in the market and, therefore, enjoys a unique role in creating consumer relationships for brands. Which social media platform a consumer uses varies significantly with age and purpose. While each major social media platform offers unique positioning to consumers, Facebook and Instagram are the dominant players in the market. Brands most frequently use social media through the use of sponsored posts that seek to influence consumer decisions authentically and organically. Measuring the success of a brand's social media efforts requires metrics that are unique to the social media and those that apply across a brand's marketing channels.

In the next lesson, we will explore a framework analysts can use to organize and make sense of the consumer data collected from digital platforms, McKinsey's Consumer Decision Journey.

The Consumer Decision Journey

Five things discussed in this lesson:

- Consumers' digital lives are complicated
- Making sense of consumers' digital data requires a framework that organizes the data and makes it easier to understand
- McKinsey & Co.'s "Consumer Decision Journey" (CDJ) is an effective framework for understanding how consumers research and buy products
- Each CDJ step triggers new questions that brands can investigate to improve their understanding of consumers
- Data can provide answers to those questions

The Zero Moment of Truth (ZMOT), the period from when consumers experience a stimulus that produces the recognition of a product need (i.e., trigger) until they stand at a shelf and choose a product, is a vitally important time for analysts. In that ZMOT, consumers transmit significant information that would be beneficial for brands to collect. The problem is that the data is messy.

Consumers are bombarded by information from all types of sources online. Product reviews can shed insight into others' experiences with items that consumers are thinking about buying. Discussion groups can offer an intricate web of opinions and frustrations. Advertisements in the form of display ads or sponsored social posts can detail product benefits, while unboxing videos can reveal true quality.

In turn, consumers create their own information. When they ask questions on social media, conduct searches, watch (or skip) video ads, and engage with brands on their websites – including filling out forms – consumers generate rich digital data. Brands would love to collect this information to learn about consumers and their interests.

Collecting data points for one consumer may seem manageable. A recent Luth Research study found that consumers who perform research for a prospective automobile purchase – a significant investment for anyone – experience a few hundred digital interactions before making a decision.[70] But when one considers that most large brands would need millions of consumers to reach a meaningful scale for a product, those hundreds of interactions quickly number in the billions. Analysts need a framework to turn the data that flies around at that moment into useful information for analysis.

The Introduction of McKinsey's CDJ

In 2009, consulting firm McKinsey & Co., introduced the Consumer Decision Journey (CDJ) to help analysts make sense of the contemporary consumer path to purchase. The CDJ offered a view into the consumer experience as an alternative to the traditional funnel idea that the path to purchase is a straight line that begins with a great number of brands and progressively pushes brands out of consideration until one brand (i.e., the one purchased) is left standing.

I've found McKinsey's CDJ to be a great framework for organizing this data and creating actionable insights. I learned the framework at the consulting firm I joined after graduate school. After I left consulting for an advertising agency, I was delighted to find the agency's planners and data analysts used the CDJ extensively. When I joined Google, I found that it, too, had embraced the

---

[70] "Auto Correct: The Marketing of Car-buying Is Changing" Luth Research (July 7, 2017).

McKinsey framework. The CDJ is a broadly used approach, and chances are, you've worked at a firm that used it.

McKinsey's CDJ illustrates the variety of influences on consumers through the purchase process. It identifies a number of critical moments that consumers experience before they buy and enables advertisers to use digital analytics to improve how they position and sell brands and products.

The Steps of the CDJ

The CDJ is comprised of six elements, inclusive of the initial action that kicks off the journey. Each step represents a distinct phase of the decision-making process and is traversed in the same logical order, no matter what product a consumer is evaluating. At each step, brands have a different set of questions they can ask to gain insights into their consumer/brand relationships, as well as data that analysts can use to provide answers.[71]

---

[71] N.B.: If you are, as I expect, a dutiful analyst reading this book, you'll want to understand how you can collect and analyze data to answer the questions in the CDJ. Fear not! While we'll simply identify those questions in this lesson, Part 4 of this book will explore how we pursue and find those answers in greater depth.

Figure 2.7: McKinsey's CDJ framework in visual form

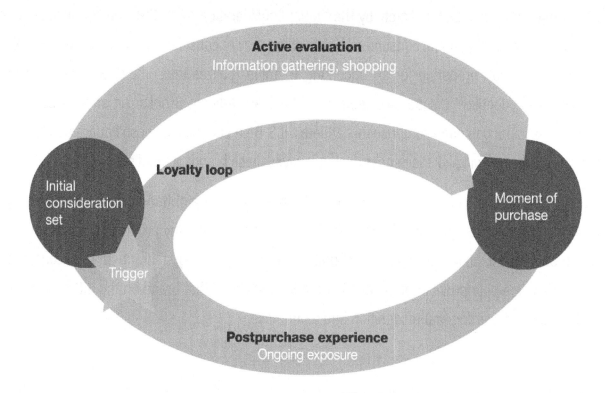

Trigger

The CDJ begins with a trigger, similar to P&G's three-step model of marketing. It's the point when consumers realize they need to begin shopping for a new home, or they see an ad that makes them want to buy a pizza, or any stimuli that starts a consumer on a purchase path.

At the point of the trigger, brands want to know what creates that consumer need. Why do consumers suddenly feel like they need their product or a competitor's product? Was an ad the impetus? Was it an environmental issue that popped up? The answers to those questions can provide insights into when brands should interact most urgently with consumers, and how they should position messages in later stages of the decision journey.

That trigger is followed immediately by the "Initial Consideration Set" (ICS). The set includes the relevant brands that pop into consumers' heads when they're considering products. For example, a consumer who's preparing for an upcoming triathlon realizes their shoes are too worn for training and identifies prospective replacements: Nike, Adidas, Brooks, or any brands that immediately spring to mind comprise this athlete's ICS. Being on the list doesn't guarantee brands that the consumer will pick their shoes. It simply gives those brands a head start.

Questions around the Initial Consideration Set for brands are straightforward: "Am I part of that list? Do customers recognize my brand? Are they aware of me and my products?" To get on that ICS, brands must build awareness, recognition, and trust. Being a brand that a consumer recognizes as a poor provider of the needed product may land that brand on the ICS but doesn't bode well for converting that recognition into a purchase.

'Active Evaluation'

A period of "Active Evaluation" follows the ICS. Essentially, this time is Google's Zero Moment of Truth (ZMOT). It's when consumers evaluate what products to buy, what brands to invest in, and where to purchase them. Significant amounts of information flow to and from consumers during this point. It's a critical part of the decision journey and a key battleground for brands.

All is not lost for brands that don't make a consumer's ICS because during Active Evaluation, they have the chance to get into the consumer's head. To do so, it's important for brands to understand consumers' needs and how their products satisfy those needs. A brand should answer the question, "Am I positioned in a way that makes my products attractive to consumers?" Understanding what consumers are evaluating during that process is vitally important and a way for brands to win during ZMOT.

Next is the "Moment of Purchase." This is the time when a consumer makes a decision and buys a product. McKinsey's Moment of Purchase equates to P&G's First Moment of Truth.

At the Moment of Purchase, brands will ask a number of questions, including, "Are my sales efforts resulting in wins for my brand?" Brands should determine if the things they do at the shelf, in the store, and during checkout facilitate sales, so they can win at the Moment of Purchase.

'Postpurchase Experience'

The "Postpurchase Experience" is the next step in the buying journey. It occurs when a consumer takes a product home and uses it. Effectively, this period is P&G's Second Moment of Truth. As with SMOT, the brand's challenge is to live up to the expectations it sets with the consumer.

In the Postpurchase Experience, the primary question brands ask is, "Does the experience I deliver fulfill the expectations that consumers have for my product?" Understanding how the brand can help consumers is an important insight this phase can reveal. This is where customer service comes in. In addition, it helps to have a solid product, and a reputable name behind it.

The 'Loyalty Loop'

The final component of the CDJ is the "Loyalty Loop." This is where every brand wants to be. The Loyalty Loop is basically a shortcut from a trigger to the Moment of Purchase. When traveling along the Loyalty Loop, a consumer experiences a trigger, and rather than going through an Initial Consideration Set and Active Evaluation, invests in a trusted brand straightaway.

An example of the Loyalty Loop in action is my experience with Apple Inc.'s Macintosh laptops. My last several computers were Macs. The next time my Mac laptop dies, I will – as I have done in the past – willingly enter this Loyalty Loop and buy a Mac immediately. I don't have to think about it, consider other brands, or evaluate my options. I trust Apple, and the brand is an important part of my life.

The Loyalty Loop's benefits are obvious for a brand. Bain & Company research shows it can be five to 25 times more expensive for a brand to earn a new customer than to keep a current one.[72] But the benefits to the consumer – expedited decision-making from not having to do research, an absence of stress that's often associated with buying a brand for the first time, and enhanced service through brand-sponsored rewards programs – can be just as powerful.

Regarding the Loyalty Loop, an important question brands need to explore is, "Do customers advocate for my brand?" Often, people in a brand's Loyalty Loop are highly motivated supporters of the brand – known as brand evangelists – who influence others toward the brand. When consumers advocate for brands, it can indicate the brand is well-positioned to earn a customer's loyalty during the next trigger.

Applicability of the CDJ

One of the things I love about the CDJ framework is that it takes something that's extremely complicated and makes it simple and flexible. While the time it takes consumers to make decisions and the number of sources they use during their evaluations may vary, the CDJ accurately describes the decision-making process for consumers who are buying a car, or standing in line at a grocery store and looking at candy bars on display. The highly involved category of car shopping may fit the CDJ more intuitively, but the framework also applies to consumers who eye candy bars.

What can seem like a knee-jerk decision can more accurately be broken into several important steps. Standing in the checkout line, consumers may notice the candy and reason that they could go for a treat. That moment of recognition is the trigger. The candy that immediately comes to mind is their Initial Consideration Set. As they look at the candy and weigh their options, they're engaged in Active Evaluation. Choosing a treat, dropping it on the conveyor belt, and paying for it is the Moment of Purchase. And what Postpurchase Experience could be better than the first bite of a

---

[72] Fred Reichheld, "Prescription for Cutting Costs," Bain & Company (September 2001).

candy bar? A consumer who eats only one kind of candy bar will go from the trigger of being hungry for a candy bar through the Loyalty Loop to a specific brand before making that purchase.

The CDJ applies to small products as well as it does to big purchase decisions. The only variable is the amount of time consumers will spend on their journeys. The decision journey that ends in a checkout aisle candy bar may be completed in a few moments, while recent research suggests consumers who shop for automobiles take an average of 96 days to make their purchases.[73] In either case, the CDJ is an effective tool for mapping consumers' thought processes and important moments for brands.

How Ad Blockers Affect Digital Measurement

While frameworks like the CDJ can help analysts make sense of consumer data, technology complications can inhibit these models. One such disruptive technology is the ad blocker.

Ad blockers rank among the most common categories of installed software in the United States with approximately 30 percent of consumers having some form of the technology installed on their computers or phones. First introduced in 2002 as an element of Mozilla's Firefox browser, the major ad blockers today (Adblock, Adblock Plus, and Ublock) are all based on browser extensions. In general, these blockers prevent ads from appearing by inspecting each element of a webpage as it loads, cross referencing each element against rules that include a list of known ads, and preventing known ads from appearing. Ad blockers typically use default ad identification rules from easylist.to and have historically blocked display ads and pop-ups from rendering on webpages and social media feeds. More advanced technologies like Adblock Plus claim to be able to block video ads on platforms like YouTube.[74] The history of ad blocking is an interesting game of cat-and-mouse, as ad revenue dependent digital platforms and advertisers work to find tactics that

---

[73] "2019 Car Buyer Journey Study," Cox Automotive (June 4, 2019).
[74] Adblock Plus (2020).

undermine the ad blocker and allow ads to show. Ad blockers have reacted quickly to shore up their rules when a workaround is discovered, and the pattern continues.

Ad blockers' implications are far-reaching. Digital advertising, as we've seen, is a fundamental element of the internet, and ad blockers pose a serious threat to digital marketers. Google, Facebook, Twitter, Snapchat, Tik Tok, and nearly every digital platform operating today depend on the revenues earned from serving digital advertisements to consumers. It's been estimated that a platform like Facebook generates 98 percent of its revenue through the ads.[75] Digital advertising is the reason visitors to these platforms aren't required to pay for each video they watch, or search they conduct, or message they post. Yet, ad blockers impede this revenue stream for platforms.

Ad blockers have the further consequence of complicating an analyst's ability to measure the effect of digital advertising as they threaten to create a class of consumers who cannot be reached through digital advertising. While advertisers often view ad blockers with ambivalence (after all, when ads are blocked in most models, it means the advertiser isn't charged) this growing segment of "digital unreachables" should give advertisers pause and motivate marketers to produce creative advertising consumers want to view. Achieving this objective places even greater emphasis on the role of analysts to test and optimize digital advertising. For more about analysts optimizing digital ads, see the discussion of Creative Optimization in Part 3, Lesson 3.

In Summary: The Consumer Decision Journey

Consumers' digital lives are busy and complicated. To make sense of consumers' purchase journeys, analysts need a framework that will allow them to organize associated data. McKinsey's CDJ is an effective framework. At each step of the CDJ, brands have relevant questions and unique ways they can use data to answer them. The CDJ applies to all consumer purchase decisions and is an invaluable tool for analysts. Technology complications can inhibit these models. One such

---

[75] J. Clement, "Facebook: Advertising Revenue Worldwide 2009-2019," Statista (Feb 28, 2020).

disruptive technology is the ad blocker, which introduces even greater need for the analyst who can account for and work to counter this disruption.

In the next part of this book, we'll explore the technical ways brands collect data that feed frameworks such as the CDJ.

PART 3
The Science of Analytics

Lesson 1   Digital Data Infrastructure

Lesson 2   Digital Measurement

Lesson 3   Analytics and Dataviz Tools

Lesson 4   Digital Marketing Maturity

Part 3 focuses on understanding digital data creation, how brands use that data to measure digital marketing effectiveness, and the tools and skill sets analysts need to work effectively with data. While the contents are lightly technical, this section veers into the colloquial as I dive into multitouch attribution models, media mix models, incrementality studies, and other ways analysts conduct marketing measurement today.

Part 3 also provides a useful framework for evaluating data analysis and visualization ("dataviz") tools and explains the critical importance of digital marketing maturity to analysts and the companies for which they work.

Digital Data Infrastructure

Five things discussed in this lesson:

- First-, second-, and third-party data are the three primary categories of data brands use
- Digital cookies, tags, and sign-in requirements have provided the technical foundation of digital data collection for decades
- Data value was inversely related to data availability in the internet's early days, but that relationship has changed in modern data analytics
- Recent changes in data privacy regulations and browser strategies have affected data collection and use
- Analysts can still make informed decisions based on available data, even if that data isn't as robust as it was previously

We've seen the explosive growth in consumer-generated data and the way brands can make decisions from that data using helpful frameworks like McKinsey's CDJ. But how is data collected?

The basic tools that brands use to collect consumer data have been around for more than 25 years. Brands have come to depend on these data collection tools, whether they collect data themselves or work with partners, such as Comscore, IRI, and Nielsen.

These tools are experiencing great change today as a result of regulatory reform triggered by privacy concerns. The future for these long-used tools is uncertain. But before we investigate industry changes that threaten their viability, let's look at the basic categories of data and the data collection tools that help brands understand consumers.

Categories of Data

Brands obtain three primary categories of data to help their marketing efforts. Typically, a brand will collect data in all three categories to learn more about consumers who purchase their products and those who don't.

First-Party (1P) Data

An organization collects first-party data through a direct relationship with a consumer. This data could be earned through the company's sales process (e.g., sales data), its own digital properties (e.g., web traffic data), its offline connections with consumers (e.g., in-store data a retailer collects and imports online), or other systems that record the company's direct exchange of data with consumers (e.g., customer relationship data). First-party data usually includes consumers' personally identifiable information (PII) and is well-guarded by the data owner.

Second-Party (2P) Data

When an organization owns and shares data, the data it shares is considered second-party data to the recipient. Examples of second-party data are survey responses a survey vendor collects and shares with a brand or data a brand collects through its website analytics tool (e.g., Adobe Analytics, Google Analytics, etc.). These approaches allow a brand to collect data through means that are outside its areas of expertise or technical capabilities. A brand typically obtains second-party data through a data-sharing agreement.

Third-Party (3P) Data

Firms collect third-party data when they don't have direct relationships or agreements with the consumers who generate the data. For example, third-party data can be data scraped from public websites, purchased from the original data owners, or inferred (i.e., modeled) from past behavioral data. This data is aggregated across many different sources, matched to a specific consumer and offered for sale. Third-party data often consists of rich behavioral or demographic data that expands beyond a brand's first-party data.

Brands need a system to store, sort, and analyze data before it becomes useful, given the vast amount of data available to marketers across the categories mentioned above. This is where a data management platform (DMP) can be valuable. Examples of DMPs include The Trade Desk, Adobe Audience Manager, and Oracle DMP (formerly BlueKai). A data management platform can help brands use data to target specific consumer audiences and can measure campaign performance across segments and channels.

Digital Data Collection: Cookies, Tags and Sign-Ins

How do brands (or systems working on behalf of brands) collect consumers' digital information? Historically, the three important tools are cookies, tags, and sign-in processes. These are probably familiar terms so I will be brief in my descriptions.

Digital Cookies

Digital cookies are text files that sit in an internet browser's cache on your device, typically a desktop computer or laptop, and allow websites and servers to identify you through a unique cookie ID: a string of characters that is associated with the browser storing the cookie.[76] Think of a digital cookie as a name tag. Lou Montulli, a 24-year-old programmer, invented cookies in 1994 and

---

[76] N.B.: On mobile devices, such as phones and tablets, digital cookies can be used on mobile web browsers just like they're used on desktop and laptop computers. Cookie technology, however, doesn't work in apps, which comprise the majority of mobile device internet usage. Mobile cookie data is, therefore, viewed as less comprehensive and less reliable than cookie data from laptops and desktops. As a result, a unique "device ID" is created to allow websites and servers to identify your mobile device.

digital cookies have played a central role in the collection of digital data since then. They are particularly relevant in the collection of third-party data.

Tags

Tags are strings of code that initialize when someone performs an action in a browser, such as loading a webpage or clicking an object displayed on that page. When activated, tags allow analytics tools or marketing partners to collect data related to consumer behaviors on the tagged website. Analytics platforms, such as Google Analytics and Adobe Analytics; testing tools, such as Adobe Target and Optimizely; market research companies, such as Comscore, IRI, and Nielsen; and marketing partners, such as Google and Facebook, use tags. Tags are critical for the collection of second-party data.

Sign-Ins

Giving consumers the opportunity to create accounts and sign in is a common practice among online content providers. From the *New York Times* to Travelocity to Facebook, digital accounts are everywhere. Sometimes, those sign-ins are required and used to control access to subscriber-only information kept behind a sign-in paywall (think NYTimes.com's premium content), sensitive financial information, such as credit card numbers (think Travelocity), or private personal data (think Facebook). Other content providers, including Google, give consumers the option to create accounts and sign in or access content without those steps.

By tying activities to accounts, content providers can connect consumers to behaviors on their platforms without cookies and tags. Sign-ins are an important tool in the collection of first-party data.

Data Availability and Value

In his 2004 book, *Web Analytics Demystified,*[77] Eric Peterson introduced the "Pyramid Model of Web Analytics Data." He believed in an inverse relationship between the volume of available data and its value. At the bottom of Peterson's pyramid are readily available web traffic data points like "hits." While easy to collect, this data tells us little about consumers and is "mostly useless," he concluded. At the top of the pyramid are more elusive, yet more insightful, data that point to "Uniquely Identified Users."

The data revolution that's been underway since the time of Peterson's writing has significantly affected the availability and accessibility of data. The biggest effect has been at the top of Peterson's pyramid: data for Uniquely Identified Users. From social media posts to location histories, data related to the behavior of identifiable consumers has exploded in volume. While expanding the usefulness of data for advertisers, this increased ability to understand consumer behavior has prompted meaningful data privacy concerns.

Data Collection and the Effect of Privacy Concerns

Privacy concerns are popping up on every corner of the internet. High-profile data breaches, hacker attacks on corporate data stores, and cases of data misuse by digital platforms have produced an expected backlash of mistrust. This mistrust is particularly deep in the area of third-party data collection. As a result, regulatory bodies have stepped in to provide protection for consumers. Many companies – some at the center of consumers' privacy concerns – have taken steps to improve data security.

How regulatory reform will play out in the digital space is unclear. A few things are coming into focus, however, as new directives around the world are raising the bar for privacy. For example,

---

[77] Eric T. Peterson, *Web Analytics Demystified: A Marketer's Guide to Understanding How Your Web Site Affects Your Business* (2004).

the European General Data Protection Regulation (GDPR) that became effective in 2019 requires advertisers to clearly identify each party that may collect, receive, or use data from their sites, apps, and other properties. They must also obtain consent for that collection and for personalized advertising. Policymakers continue to advance legislative proposals around the world, with many focusing on privacy. I expect action around privacy and data protection to continue to grow.

In addition, companies in the digital realm have worked to enhance privacy, reflecting consumer demand, and, often, taking advantage of the market opportunity that shift in consumer awareness creates. Web browsers are adding features to limit digital cookie and tag use, including those used for personalization and measurement. For example, the latest Safari browser included "Intelligent Tracking Prevention" (ITP), which immediately rendered unusable digital cookies that can track users across multiple sites, eliminating content providers' ability to track and measure consumer behavior. Firefox recently announced plans to implement an enhanced approach to anti-tracking, and I expect other platforms will make similar decisions in the future.

Some common themes are emerging from privacy-related regulation: Users should know who is collecting data about them, how that data is being used, and have the opportunity to opt out. At the heart of the issue is the idea of user control. If consumers can't disable data collection technologies, a claim of users agreeing to allow companies to collect that data rings hollow. The permission to amass data buried inside long, nearly incomprehensible user agreements doesn't give consumers transparent control over the collection and use of their personal data. Indeed, without control, there can be no consent.

Opaque tracking and profiling techniques that don't provide user controls, such as the practice of "digital fingerprinting," whereby unique attributes of computer/browser/user behaviors are used to identify consumers, are increasingly popular as cookie technology has become less reliable. Browsers, however, are reacting to such insidious tracking by offering consumers enhanced control. Apple's Safari browser limits fingerprinting and other probabilistic methods of tracking. It also blocks social media "Like" and "share" buttons and comment widgets from tracking users without their permission.

The regulatory and market responses to this shift in privacy awareness have had a dramatic effect on digital measurement by reducing the availability and accuracy of collected data (primarily third- and second-party data, but also first-party data to a degree). Yet, analysts can still make informed decisions based on available data, even if that data isn't as robust as it once was.

Analysts can account for the loss of data and bring more accuracy to their analysis through a thorough understanding of privacy limitations' impact on data collection. Moreover, a strong understanding of the brand's operations, objectives, and environment (think Data Strategist skills) will sharpen the analyst's intuition and ability to separate truth from lies in the data.

In Summary: Digital Data Infrastructure

First-, second-, and third-party data are the primary categories of data brands use to better understand their customers and consumers who have yet to purchase their products. Digital cookies (and mobile device IDs), tags, and sign-in requirements have provided the technical foundation of digital data collection for decades. While data value was inversely related to data availability in the internet's early days, that relationship has changed thanks, in large part, to this important technical foundation. While recent changes in data privacy regulations and browser strategies have affected the collection and use of digital data, analysts can still make informed decisions based on available data.

In the next lesson, we'll explore the categories of digital measurement analysts can use to evaluate a brand's marketing efforts.

Digital Measurement

Five things discussed in this lesson:

- Assessing the effect of digital marketing programs across platforms has long been a challenge for analysts, but recent regulatory changes have introduced additional uncertainty
- Tools still available to analysts, including multitouch attribution models, marketing mix models, and incrementality studies, can help brands answer marketing effectiveness questions
- The degree to which today's uncertainty has affected each category of measurement, as well as each tool and provider, varies
- Leading advertisers use the concept of "Measurement Multiplicity" to clarify their decision-making
- A test-and-learn mentality is also critical for marketing (and measurement) success

Think of the role measurement plays in marketing as sailing with a compass. That compass can give analysts the most efficient, expedient path to their destinations. Although the compass's dial may flicker from time to time, analysts can trust and depend on its guidance. Unfortunately, uncertainties introduced in the wake of regulation and data privacy initiatives have smashed that compass. While it's still readable, it's hard to know if its guidance is accurate. Yet it remains – just as it has always been – easy to know which way the wind is blowing.

The marketer's instinctive ability to read the wind and tack toward a destination has become more important than ever. Regardless of the challenges in the digital environment, a variety of measurement techniques can confirm wind direction with great accuracy, even if their guidance toward the best path forward must be taken with a grain of salt.

In this context, digital measurement minimizes uncertainty in evaluating marketing performance and fuels instinctive decision-making. Specifically, measurement does three important things for a brand:

→ **Establishes a source of truth** – Ensure stakeholder trust in data reliability across data sources to measure what matters by defining clear customer value and key performance indicators.

→ **Allows for insight discovery** – Understand consumer behavior and the effect of marketing efforts in the context of the customer journey.

→ **Enables the activation of insights** – Allocate scarce marketing resources optimally across channels, initiatives, and partners.

Analysts' measurement plays an important role in any organization by enabling business growth through a combination of understanding and accountability.

The Four Categories of Digital Measurement

Digital measurement covers a wide variety of objectives, platforms, and tactics, making it necessary to use a simple framework of categorization. The framework presented in Figure 3.1 classifies digital measurement in four categories:

Figure 3.1: The four categories of digital measurement

Brand Impact

How well does marketing improve the way consumers perceive your brand?

Insights into brand health allow marketers an idea of their digital marketing performance as a complement to sales lift measurement

Consumer Outcomes

How well does marketing drive value for you across each / all sales channels?

Valuing outcomes that range from sales to the important actions leading to a sale informs tactics to manage consumer behaviors

Customer Value

How well does marketing help you maximize value from your consumer?

Optimizing profitability is a key benefit of programs rooted in lifetime value (LTV), calculated using sophisticated methods or simple models

Attribution

How well do you measure and value the impact of your media across channels?

Marketing Mix Models (MMMs) are a traditional approach being complemented by Mutitouch Attribution (MTA) using new data and methods

Making the Intangible Tangible: Brand Impact

Companies can use several methods to value what has been an inherently intangible asset: their brands. Each approach differs in its perspective regarding value and the inputs in its calculations, but each can provide valuable insights into brand impact.

Assessing Attributes

This subjective means of assessment assigns values to attributes, such as satisfaction, loyalty, awareness and market share, which are tracked separately or weighted according to industry. Advertising agency Young & Rubicam has developed a "Brand Asset Valuator," which is an attribute assessment approach that's based on differentiation, relevance, esteem, and knowledge. Other approaches exist, but the concept remains the same. Such methods often use an assigned value, rather than a measured value, and are subject to challenges.

Brand Equity

The brand equity approach combines three elements: effective market share, which is the sum of market shares in all segments, weighted by each segment's proportion of total sales; relative price, which is a ratio of the price of goods a brand sells, divided by the average price of comparable goods in the market; and durability – the percentage of customers who will buy that brand in the following year. While thorough in its design, this data-intensive approach relies heavily on modeling for its calculation.

Brand Valuation

Brand valuation methods seek to take the most robust financial data available to model a plausible valuation of a brand. While the assumptions underlying these methods are also subject to challenges, they at least strive to create an objective-as-possible marker or view of a brand's strength.

Algorithmic

Advertising holding company WPP performs an annual valuation published as "The BrandZ Top 100 Most Valuable Brands" report. This approach uses an advertiser's financial data, market dynamics, and an assessment of the brand's role in income generation to forecast brand value. Other similar "blended" formulas are used to quantify elements that most influence a brand's strengths and risks. Though certainly detailed, this method provides a once-per-year snapshot of brand value due to the annual nature of required data inputs.

'Royalty Relief'

Brand Finance publishes its annual *Global 500* study using a "royalty relief" approach that calculates the net present value of the hypothetical royalty payments an organization would receive if it were to license its brand to a third party. As a hypothetical approach, the assumptions underpinning a royalty relief calculation are open to challenge. Yet the system of royalty payments is well established so assumptions can be rooted in practical experience and applications.

A popular measure is "net promoter score," or NPS, a metric Fred Reichheld, Bain & Company, and Satmetrix developed. Its power is its simplicity. It asks customers, "How likely are you to recommend company/brand/product X to a friend/colleague/relative?" and scores their responses from zero to 10. "Promoters" give a nine or 10 score, "passives" a seven or eight, and "detractors" a zero to six score. The NPS score is the percentage of promoters less the percentage of detractors and ranges from −100 to +100. Although largely qualitative, this method is straightforward.

Each method for quantifying brand impact has strengths and weaknesses that analysts should consider and manage accordingly. When analysts apply these methods properly, the insights can show analysts how their digital marketing performance complements (or replaces) measurement of more tangible assets, such as sales lift.

Measuring Sales Levers: Consumer Outcomes

The desired outcome of nearly every marketing program in the for-profit world is more sales for the brand. Indeed, the result of increased sales is a diligently tracked consumer outcome. Vast networks of point-of-sale solutions and internal tracking systems exist for the express purpose of tracking sales. Analysts can mine these outcome data for insights and, frequently, provide greater context through sophisticated measurement techniques, such as incrementality studies (detailed later in this lesson).

Ever-present consumer outcomes stop short of an ultimate sale, but are valuable, nonetheless. Such outcomes happen along a consumer's decision journey and the path toward a sale and, therefore, should be measured. In this context, the small presale steps (e.g., visiting an auto dealer website) are called microconversions, while the final conversion (e.g., buying a car) is the macroconversion. Microconversion outcomes occur in online and offline consumer behaviors.

Analysts can measure a plethora of microconversions in consumers' online interactions. As data are created online, analysts can access and track the information with tools in Google Analytics. Activities that could qualify as examples of microconversions from consumer actions on a website include:

→ Viewing a page
→ Watching a video
→ Commenting on a blog post
→ Sharing a post through social media
→ Creating an account
→ Signing up for an email newsletter
→ Downloading an app
→ Placing an item in an online shopping cart

Analysts can earn insights that will inform marketing strategies that are designed to drive these microconversions by assigning dollar values to each outcome. Typically, the assigned values should be based on the likelihood that a consumer fulfills a macroconversion after the microconversion (and, of course, the calculated dollar value of that macroconversion). Outcomes more highly correlated to a macroconversion (e.g., placing an item in an online shopping cart) should have a higher assigned value than those that exhibit less correlation (e.g., viewing a webpage).

Measurable offline behaviors can also be thought of as microconversions. Store visits, which measure consumers who enter a defined physical location, are an important microconversion outcome for most advertisers. This is especially true for brands that interact with consumers offline (e.g., retail shops, movie theaters, auto dealerships, etc.) and build online relationships to influence behaviors in the physical world. Although a store visit outcome is a step short of a sale, advertisers that value store visits typically see a high correlation between a consumer who visits a location and then buys an item at that moment or in the future.

The mobile location industry began as a way to customize apps and target ads but has, in the words of the *New York Times'* Jennifer Valentino-DeVries and Natasha Singer, "morphed into a data collection machine."[78] As of Valentio-DeVries and Singer's report in late 2018, at least 75 companies receive precise location data from hundreds of apps whose users enable location services for benefits such as weather alerts.[79]

The *New York Times* revisited the topic of location tracking in December 2019 when Stuart A. Thompson and Charlie Warzel wrote an article that demonstrated how easily they were able to obtain from a company a database of "50 billion location pings from the phones of more than 12 million Americans as they moved through several major cities, including Washington, New York, San Francisco and Los Angeles."[80] Data such as this is at the heart of the consumer privacy concerns discussed in the previous lesson. Thompson and Warzel make this clear, as the issue of consumer consent is central to their investigation.

Typically, companies collect, use, store and sell location data to help advertisers, investment firms and others. Apps most popular among data companies are those that offer services keyed to people's whereabouts – including weather, transit and travel – because users are more likely to enable location services on them.

Location data can be tremendously important to advertisers who seek to optimize their marketing strategies (and, more specifically, their media bidding strategies) to consumers' locations. For

---

[78] Jennifer Valentino-DeVries and Natasha Singer, "Your Apps Know Where You Were Last Night, and They're Not Keeping It Secret," *New York Times* (December 10, 2018).

[79] Valentino-DeVries and Singer, "How to Stop Apps from Tracking Your Location," *New York Times* (December 10, 2018).

[80] Stuart A. Thompson and Charlie Warzel, "Twelve Million Phones, One Dataset, Zero Privacy," *New York Times* (December 19, 2019).

example, my local frozen custard shop in Chicago's Roscoe Village may want to answer a "best ice cream" query from someone searching in the neighborhood, but chances are, the shop is less inclined to bid on a consumer searching from Pittsburgh. Location tracking is the data that enables such differentiated strategies.

Perhaps even more importantly, location data helps analysts assess advertisements' effectiveness. Online retail advertisements should be assessed by the degree to which they drive consumers to stores. Used in this way, location data provides transparency for investing advertisers while holding platforms, agencies, and others involved in media sales accountable for ad performance.

Digital ad platforms, including Google and Facebook, offer important store visit measurements to advertisers. As the *New York Times* noted, however, a growing number of independent third-party companies offer this data as well. Analysts should carefully consider the use of location data as a means of measuring marketing effectiveness, assuming providers can ensure consent and privacy, and limit data quality issues.

Understanding What Is Important: Customer Value

Scott Kirby, formerly president of American Airlines, gave Wall Street analysts a peek into the lopsided economics of his airline on an October 25, 2015, conference call, saying half of the company's 2014 sales came from 87 percent of customers who flew on the airline once.[81] What this means, of course, is that a paltry 13 percent of travelers contributed 50 percent of American Airlines' annual revenue.

The idea of differentiated customer value isn't unique to the airline industry. Every business earns different economic value from different consumers. By understanding what their valuable

---

[81] David Yanofsky, "Half of American Airlines' Revenue Came from 13% of Its Customers," *Quartz* (October 27, 2015).

customers look like (and what they don't resemble), advertisers can affix differing levels of value to nearly every consumer they could pursue in the market.

The key to unlocking this insight is understanding valuable attributes for prospective customers. Advertisers can build "best customer" profiles based on analyses of demographic, psychographic, and behavioral data they collect. "Look-alike analyses," that is, identifying consumers who demonstrate similar attributes, can reveal new high-value targeting opportunities.

The importance of understanding valuable consumer attributes goes beyond acquisition opportunities. Applying relative values to each characteristic, attitude, and action that comprises the value calculation can deepen customer understanding while providing the foundation for marketing strategies that target consumers, engage with messages, and incentivize behaviors.

Assessing Marketing Effectiveness: Attribution

Measuring lift on a marketing campaign seeks to isolate the effect the campaign had on consumer behaviors. Online behaviors are easier to measure than offline actions, but online and offline conversions are important to lift measurement. At its core, this pursuit seeks to answer whether an intervention (e.g., the ad campaign) compelled a consumer to act, or would the consumer have acted anyway.

Well-designed studies can help answer this question, but they don't address an advertiser's complete marketing investment, which can be spread across a number of campaigns and platforms. Indeed, one of an analyst's most critical challenges is measuring total marketing effectiveness by determining which media investments drove sales, calculating returns, and optimizing future investments.

The rapid pace of change leaves analysts reeling from reshaped consumer behaviors, data, and partnerships. And yet, no single digital solution measures the full journey a customer will take to evaluate brands and make an ultimate purchase. Facebook, for example, remains the only solution that rigorously measures consumer behavior on Facebook pages, as the platform maintains an exclusive list of partners that receive valuable Facebook data. But when those consumers are on YouTube, Facebook is just as unlikely to know their behaviors as Google is to collect behavior data while consumers are on Facebook.

Analysts can plug gaps in understanding with highly tuned and data-rich models, but the results are estimates of consumer behavior. This situation leaves analysts in the uncomfortable position of feeling tremendously empowered, but unable to answer questions related to digital campaign performance. Several solutions available today, however, can help them piece together an assessment of marketing effectiveness.

Multitouch Attribution

Multitouch attribution models (MTAs), also known as marketing attribution solutions, promise to provide actionable insights by collecting real-time customer behavior data. Through sophisticated models based on collected data samples, MTAs measure the relative benefit of specific digital media to influence consumers. Where actual data on consumer behavior exists, the models are termed "deterministic," while models that plug gaps in consumer behavior data are termed "probabilistic." A blend of deterministic and probabilistic models forms the inner workings of any MTA solution.

Traditional MTA solutions attempt to measure consumer interactions across the full spectrum of media channels (e.g., from TV to radio to out-of-home to all digital ad exposures). In contrast, digital platforms offer single media channel attribution solutions to measure and optimize consumer interactions exclusively on their own sites. Each attribution solution faces challenges in today's measurement environment.

Figure 3.2: Comparison of single channel and cross-channel attribution solutions

As with any measurement system that relies on third-party cookies, MTAs are limited in their ability to measure and reach users because of changes in privacy and browser technology. These solutions will see reduced effectiveness in the form of limited match rates or even sample biases for surveys and testing. The lack of insight into consumer behavior has forced MTAs to be more probabilistic in their modeling, making it difficult to validate findings and base decisions on MTA results.

Content providers' collection of consumer behavior data on their own digital properties has been largely unaffected by moves to enhance privacy. As we've seen, these content providers can rely on user sign-in as a mechanism to connect behaviors to consumer profiles, rather than digital cookies. As a result, the attribution solutions these providers offer – single media channel attribution solutions – can be seen as reliable predictors of how marketing efforts affect consumers on those platforms. Advertisers can use attribution solutions on their media platforms to help optimize investment.

However, single media channel attribution solutions have drawbacks that are important for analysts to understand:

→ **No cross-platform view** – Single media channel attribution solutions are good at helping advertisers optimize media within the channel but have serious flaws when it comes to evaluating holistic advertising efforts.

→ **Bias** – Single media channel attribution solutions can only see the media placed on that channel, and hence, no matter which attribution calculation (last click, position-based, or data-driven), these solutions are biased toward themselves, taking more credit than they deserve.

→ **Data discrepancies** – The data each channel collects fluctuates constantly, as should be expected. As data accumulates on platforms at different rates, certain media types are more effective with a product type or audience, etc. This necessitates fixed weighting to try to match a single media channel attribution solution to a specific data source. Otherwise, collected data that's related to the platform will be incorrect in different ways at different times of the year, month, week, or even day.

→ **Varying methodologies** – Every single media channel solution has a different methodology and, thus, can't be used for apples-to-apples comparisons. For example, the way view-through conversions (i.e., a conversion that follows a consumer simply seeing – and not clicking on – a digital ad) are valued in Google attribution solutions for YouTube or display ads is different from how Facebook attributes credit for view-through. This means that if an analyst were to use the same approach for every digital channel where they believe view-through has significant value, some platforms could come out ahead unfairly based on methodology versus performance.

Marketing Mix Modeling

Marketing mix modeling (MMM) is a time-tested method for measuring the effect of marketing and media investments. Many leading brands use MMMs to determine what's working across different channels. The MMM can be a crucial tool for guiding budget decisions as a periodic analysis to measure the effectiveness of each media type and channel (offline and digital). Typically, MMM studies are run quarterly, but a recent trend has been for brands to increase the frequency of MMM, up to a monthly cadence.

MMMs attempt to determine how media spend has affected KPIs – such as brand perception or product sales – by isolating the broad factors that can influence consumer behavior to calculate a media channel's return on investment (ROI). This is a tremendous undertaking, as everything from advertising to recommendations from friends to the weather can affect nearly any KPI an advertiser adopts as its metric for success. As a result, MMMs are built upon vast amounts of data and have been refined over long periods. Many can trace their roots as far back as the 1960s.

Many MMMs struggle with the nuances of digital advertising as they attempt to evaluate all channels of consumer connection through a consistent currency (e.g., impressions). Search advertising, for example, poses a particular conundrum for MMMs as the idea of a search ad impression betrays the true value of the channel. Search ads, after all, are to be clicked on and not simply seen.

Furthermore, most of the time, an MMM isn't set up to provide actionable insights when it comes to digital channels. Many brands are stuck treating digital ads the way they would traditional advertising platforms, including television, with one ROI for TV, one for search, and another for online video. On the surface, that might seem fair, but it doesn't capture the variety of ad formats and tactics available in digital marketing.

MMM providers can improve their models by embracing the nuances of digital measurement. To do so, analysts should advocate for their MMM providers to follow the five steps described below to get more accurate and actionable reads on the effect of their digital efforts.

Figure 3.3: The five steps to more actionable MMM digital reads

Segment	Distinguish	Differentiate	Validate	Test
Evaluate your media by geography and market to help get additional data points that make the model more representative of actual media performance	Break out video by platform so the model provides an individual read on each as key metrics (and behaviors) can differ widely and will have a different effect on media effectiveness	Assess different elements of the media plan by channel, including ad formats, audience segments, and frequency to reveal stronger connections between online efforts and offline results	Run sales lift tests or other isolated experiments to validate the effect of a change in strategy recomended (i.e., estimated) by MMM modeled results	Measure the effect of creative elements on sales by testing various message and visual tactics to optimize media performance

A more detailed look at these steps reveals their importance to and effect on actionable measurement insights:

→ **Evaluate media by geography and market** – Big television buys may run nationally, but digital ads deliver on demand locally and offer granular reporting. Collect and model the data by market to get additional data points that make the model more representative of reality. Jeff Shatz, vice president of marketing effectiveness at Nielsen, explains why this is critical: "The more granular the data, the more variability the statistical model is able to pick up, and the greater ability to tease out true drivers. If only national-level marketing data is used, the model will not be able to account for critical market-level influences that impact whether a purchase is made."[82]

→ **Differentiate video platforms** – Ditch the generic digital buckets that treat all online video impressions equally. Instead, break out video by platform, so the model provides an individual read on each. Qualities like watch time, audibility, and viewability vary widely across video platforms and, depending on what you're trying to achieve, will have a

---

[82] Kevin Hartman, "How to Bring Your Marketing Mix Modeling into the 21st Century," *Think with Google* (June 2019).

different effect on the effectiveness of media. Recent research from Nielsen supports this, finding that when advertisers' MMMs evaluated video platforms independently rather than aggregated, return on ad spend varied by as much as 48 percent.[83]

→ **Consider the various elements of your media plan** – Assess different elements of the media plan by channel, including ad formats, audience segments, and the campaign's reach and frequency. From there, the analyst can find stronger connections between online efforts and offline sales. The Hershey Co. marketing team does this by asking media partners and their media agencies to supply data directly to their marketing mix modeling measurement partner, helping ensure the data is accurately broken out by brand and ad format. On YouTube, this level of granularity helped the team establish that a specific mix of YouTube TrueView, Google Preferred, and six-second bumper ads was most effective in driving sales for Reese's Peanut Butter Cups. As measured by marketing mix modeling, the retail ROI for The Hershey Co.'s portfolio of brands increased 40 percent year over year from 2017 to 2018.[84]

→ **Validate model outputs through experiments** – MMMs are inherently complex models – and they're not perfect. Before making major changes to the media strategy based on marketing mix modeling results, run sales lift tests or other isolated experiments to test the effect of a single change in strategy. For example, Frito-Lay North America, a division of PepsiCo, uses MMM, along with sales lift and brand lift studies, so it can evaluate three points of measurement before changing its media strategy. The results of all three methodologies won't always align, but this validation helps guide future media planning and justifies increased investments in a platform or strategy over time.[85]

---

[83] Nielsen MMM Meta-Analysis, U.S., n=20 studies from CPG clients, 2016–2018.

[84] Hartman, "How to Bring Marketing Mix Modeling."

[85] Hartman, "How to Bring Marketing Mix Modeling."

→ **Test your creative tactics** – Telling the brand story on digital is possible in infinite ways. That's why the savviest advertisers remove the guesswork from these decisions by using marketing mix modeling to measure the effectiveness of their creative. Frito-Lay North America uses MMM – complemented by isolated experiments – to test the effect of the more personalized creative it developed for YouTube. For example, as its marketing team creates customized videos at scale, they're seeing indications in their MMM results that more personalized creative is driving higher incremental sales than a message designed to have broad appeal. "We want to provide consumers with the most relevant content based on what makes them tick," says James Clarke, senior director of portfolio media, analytics and customer relationship management at PepsiCo. Clarke added that as the company measured the effect of creative elements on sales, surprises arose. "Sometimes, creative elements we thought would be meaningful don't have an impact; other times, things that seemed trivial really move the needle."[86]

With the flexibility and customization that digital marketing offers, traditional measurement methods must evolve. Setting up the right data inputs in an MMM at the outset of campaigns means more actionable measurement in the output.

Getting to True Lift: Incrementality Testing

Incrementality tests are on-demand experiments that measure the incremental effect of a specific campaign or tactic, as needed. Most often, incrementality testing is done using traditional test and control designs and demonstrates benefits by comparing observed results to those one would expect if the stimuli being tested (e.g., a digital advertisement) hadn't happened. A well-designed

---

[86] Hartman, "How to Bring Marketing Mix Modeling."

incrementality test will assess any Marketing Objective effectively, whether the objective is related to brand impact, consumer outcomes, customer value, or attribution.

Incrementality tests fall into two categories: experimental and observational. According to Facebook's guide for implementing incrementality tests, these approaches differ in important ways, including their requirements for upfront resources and the robustness of the results they produce.

→ **Observational** – Begin with an existing set of data that resulted from exposing people to a certain ad or ad variable, and then apply a model or statistics to estimate how much value a treatment may have had. Common methods involve using synthetic experiments to attempt to replicate a real experiment by "finding" a control group within a group of people who were not exposed to the ad or ad variable the analyst is trying to evaluate. For example, one could evaluate the effect of a technical issue that only affected some users by finding a "similar" group of people who were unaffected. This method doesn't require upfront work, but it may be less accurate and subject to bias on unknown factors. It also requires advanced methods and support from data scientists later in the process.[87]

→ **Experimental** – Begin by developing a hypothesis about the effect a change in strategy will have. Next, designate a group (or groups) of people who will be exposed to the treatment, and a control group that won't. By isolating the exposure of a variable, such as creative or audience, and then comparing it to the control group, an analyst can understand the true incremental value of the strategy. The quality of experiments may vary, but they're still the ideal and most accurate way to measure incrementality. True experiments are often the benchmark for other methodologies. Despite their benefits,

---

[87] Alex Esber, et. al., "Measure Marketing Effectiveness: A Guide to Implementing Incrementality," FacebookIQ (September 11, 2018).

experiments require upfront setup, as well as the opportunity cost of withholding treatment from the control group.[88]

To determine the most effective way to collect evidence in the assessment of interventions, we can turn to a field with a long history of testing: the medical sciences. Clinical trials that assess the effects of treatment strategies and pharmaceutical products are a hallmark of modern medicine. In much the same way marketing incrementality testing seeks to identify the effect of an intervening advertisement on consumer behavior, clinical trials in the medical sciences attempt to isolate the effect of medical interventions on health and well-being.

In assessing various methods for collecting evidence, pediatric gastroenterologist Dr. A K Akobeng found a class of experimental incrementality tests, known as randomized controlled trials (RCTs), to be the gold standard for evaluating the effectiveness of interventions.[89]

---

[88] Esber, et. al., "Measure Marketing Effectiveness."

[89] A K Akobeng, "Understanding Randomised Controlled Trials," *Archives of Disease in Childhood* (2005).

Figure 3.4: Akobeng's Hierarchy of Evidence

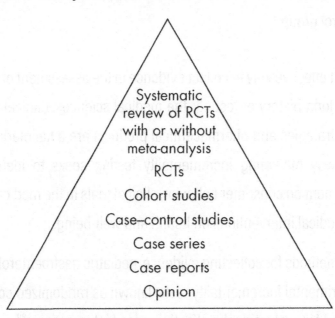

An RCT is a type of study in which participants are randomly assigned to one of two groups (most commonly called the "treatment" and "control" groups). RCTs that use large geographic locations to assign participants to treatment and control groups discourage potential hidden biases by ensuring that fundamental, yet unknown, differences between samples are balanced among treatment and control groups. After a representative sample of the population of interest is randomly allocated to one or another group, the two groups' behaviors are observed in an identical manner for a specified period of time called "the pre-test period."

During the pre-test period, a factor can be calculated that equates the treatment group's behavior to that of the control group before the intervention. Once the intervention has been introduced (i.e., the "test period"), this factor can then be applied to the observed control group behavior to estimate how the treatment group should be expected to behave. This expected behavior pattern from the treatment group is called "the counterfactual." Truly measuring the incremental effect of the intervention means comparing the observed behavior of the treatment group to the counterfactual during the Test Period – not the observed behavior of the control group during that time.

Figure 3.5: Proper incrementality test design

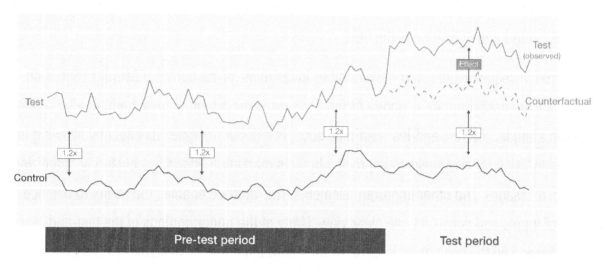

Although incrementality tests can be time- and resource-intensive, they remain the most accurate way to measure marketing's effect.

A Word on Clarity through Measurement Multiplicity

As we have seen, the present state of digital marketing measurement is fraught with uncertainty. The vastness of consumer behaviors online presents an overwhelming number of important behaviors that should be conscientiously observed. Data limitations have added complexity to measurement tools that are already excessively sophisticated. Traditional measurement techniques that struggled to evaluate digital media channels accurately still have this problem.

Given this predicament, no single measurement tool or technique should be viewed as gospel. Instead, a combination of tools applied concurrently or in a planned cadence clarifies a brand's performance and market environment. This is a practice I call "Measurement Multiplicity." Today, leading advertisers apply this idea by cross-checking brand impact and customer lifetime value measures with single media channel attribution reads or supplementing quarterly MMM reports with incrementality tests run as campaigns launch. In the case of the most sophisticated advertisers, all available measurement techniques described in this book are employed, each providing context and validation of the next.

This approach requires time and considerable investment of resources. Ensuring that such a robust measurement program is done efficiently requires the adoption of something else: a test-and-learn attitude. The test-and-learn attitude accepts risk but mitigates its effect by allowing for programs to "fail fast," and seeks to improve a brand's marketing efforts by constantly optimizing targeting, messages, and other important elements. This attitude enables the ability to balance a number of inputs and construct one clear view. Many of the underpinnings of the test-and-learn attitude depend on the company's level of digital marketing maturity, described in Lesson 4.

It's important for analysts to adopt the practice of Measurement Multiplicity and a test-and-learn attitude. In doing so, analysts will ensure the most effective and efficient approach to measurement.

A Word on Digital Measurement Challenges

Digital measurement is a challenging endeavor. From the need for tedious precision in study design (and implementation) to the trial of accounting for inevitable irregularities in collected data, digital measurement poses several problems for the analyst. Obvious issues (e.g., a poorly designed study, bias in the data, etc.) sometimes produce the flickering dial of the marketer's measurement compass described at the beginning of this lesson. Such glaring imperfections can be easily rectified.

More frequently, however, intrinsic challenges to measuring digital activity complicate the analyst's work. For example, in the previous lesson, we learned about the use of digital cookies to track consumer behavior. Cookies operate at a computer level, however, and a number of people can use any given computer (think of the shared family desktop found in many households). Consumers also frequently access websites from multiple devices: their work desktops one day, their personal laptops on the next, and their mobile phones during the time between. In addition, as consumer identification data passes between a brand and its marketing partners, the degree to which consumer IDs are linked across different datasets to the same person (i.e., the "match rate") affects the accuracy of the data and the brands' ability to provide consumers with personalized experiences.

Multiple people using the same computer profile, cross-device measurement, and cookie matching are some of the challenges that obscure the clear and consistent picture of an individual's digital behavior. Analysts can account for these challenges by clearly understanding their measurement objectives and the effects such challenges have on the data they collect. In this way, analysts can offer the grain of salt along with insights to bring more accuracy to the marketer's instinctive decisions.

In Summary: Digital Measurement

Assessing the effect of digital marketing programs across platforms has long been a challenge for analysts; however, many measurement techniques provide data and insights to guide marketers' decision-making. Tools, including multitouch attribution models, marketing mix models, and incrementality studies, can help brands answer questions regarding marketing effectiveness. While regulatory shifts and privacy initiatives have affected each category of measurement, the effect on precision varies from category to category. Leading advertisers use a combination of measurement techniques and a test-and-learn mentality to bring clarity to their decision-making, a practice and attitude that analysts should adopt. Finally, analysts must account for the inherent (and obvious) challenges posed to digital measurement to ensure the marketer's decision-making process is rooted in accuracy.

In the next lesson, we'll explore the data analytics and data visualization tools that analysts can use to help them find the answers brands need.

Analytics and Dataviz Tools

Five things discussed in this lesson:

- The market for data analytics and visualization tools is a fast-moving field of established providers and new entrants
- Adopting a way to think broadly about the market is more important than being up to speed on the development of new tools
- Two evaluation criteria – data flexibility and ease of use – provide a powerful framework for the evolving marketplace
- Data flexibility and ease of use make it clear which tools analysts should keep in their toolboxes and which they should discard
- No tool, regardless of its cost, is as important as the analyst who uses it

Tools play an important part in the analyst's work. They aid in data collection, cleanse data of errors, and allow for sophisticated analysis techniques. They can scale insights across companies large and small. In a very real sense, tools enable analysts.

The market for digital analysis tools is expanding quickly and changing constantly. The growing need for analytics solutions, rampant acquisition activity, and the low cost of tool design have produced a fast-moving field that features established companies and entrepreneurial startups. A quick web search reveals page after page of "Top 10 Analytics Tools" lists, showing the best resources selected from what must number in the thousands, if not tens of thousands, of tools.

In the vastness of the digital marketing analytics tool market, analysts will find a few critical categories that are particularly important. Tools in these categories are required to unlock insights that are unique to consumers' online behavior.

Social Listening

Social listening tools connect to various social media networks to extract consumer data. These tools provide direct access to content consumers create and allow marketers to learn about interests, actions (e.g., likes, favorites, etc.), and thoughts in consumers' words.

Some social listening tools, such as Brandwatch (brandwatch.com, formerly Crimson Hexagon), Meltwater (meltwater.com), and Hootsuite (hootsuite.com), connect to multiple platforms at the same time. In addition, analysts can use several free tools to gain insight into how consumers interact with a brand on social networks. Tools that include BrandMentions' free real-time social tracking tool, SocialMention (brandmentions.com/socialmention), collect publicly available information about a brand across social media posts, website blogs, news, videos, articles, and other content and are particularly valuable tools when conducting SOV analysis. Also, social media networks often provide detailed analytics about who's interacting with content through native social listening tools, including Facebook's analysis tools.

Content Analysis

Content analysis tools help analysts use collected data in meaningful ways by studying digital text, photos, audio and visual formats of communication. These tools can reveal otherwise unrecognizable patterns in data. Term relevance (i.e., the relative number of times a term is used in a body of text data) and consumer sentiment (i.e., the tone of consumer mentions of a company, brand, or product typically categorized as "positive," "neutral" and "negative") are two of the more popular and useful types of content analysis.[90]

Many free tools, including the R package Quanteda, provide quantitative text analysis by analyzing keywords, representing text visually, applying sentiment analysis frameworks, and more. Commercial tools, such as Linguistic Inquiry and Word Count (LIWC), interpret text to reveal thoughts, attitudes, feelings, personality, and motivations of the author. Another tool, BuzzSumo (buzzsumo.com), provides insights into the types of content that resonate with specific audience groups and can be a valuable tool for targeting content and competitive analysis.

Search Trends

Internet search trend data reveals the issues that are on consumers' minds. Search analysis tools aggregate and visualize that data to show analysts the popularity of specific topics, which can offer insights on demand for new products, consumer response to marketing campaigns, and brand awareness.

Google Trends (trends.google.com) provides free access to indexed search volume from Google.com, Google Images, Google Shopping, and YouTube. Using Google Trends, analysts can collect data about topic and search term interest over time (ranging from the last hour to 2004) at various geographic levels (ranging from worldwide to a specific city) and download the data into raw files for further analysis. Google Trends is a particularly valuable tool when conducting SOS analysis. Bing and Yahoo offer services similar to Google Trends to analyze search behavior on their properties.

---

[90] N.B.: In some cases, social listening and social media network analytics tools will provide content analysis – term relevance, sentiment analysis, and other modules – which can complement results earned from standalone content analysis tools or be used as a substitute.

Several other free tools – including Searchvolume.io (searchvolume.io) and a search analysis tool found on the *New York Times* website (nytimes.com/search) – offer simple keyword research through online interfaces, while commercial services like Moz ([moz.com](moz.com)) analyze search volume, report metrics and suggest actions.

Website Analytics

Website analytics tools provide information about visitors to a website, including the number of visitors and how they behave on the site. These tools let the analyst gauge traffic and the popularity of content on the site, which is useful for market research. Say the analyst wants to improve a website's design. Clickstream analysis – tracking how visitors interact with the site – can reveal which content visitors believe is most valuable. Metrics, including the number of times people visited the site ("visits"), the specific pages people view ("unique page views"), and the percentage of people who left the site from the first page they visited ("bounce rate") offer valuable insights.

Large, powerful, paid tools, such as Adobe Analytics and Google Analytics 360, can handle this challenge (along with a thousand other challenges) for you. But many lighter-weight tools can perform expert clickstream analysis and visualization at a fraction of the cost of premium platforms. For example, Google's free version of Google Analytics provides many of the capabilities found in the premium tool, including clickstream analysis. The disadvantage of these lighter-weight tools is they can handle less data and have more restrictions than premium website analytics tools.

A/B Testing

A/B testing, also known as "conversion rate optimization" (CRO), is another important category of analysis for the analyst. A/B testing measures the effectiveness of ads, website design, and other forms of digital content by producing two versions of the item being tested, presenting those versions to consumers, and tracking engagement rates. In doing so, A/B testing helps the analyst determine which version is more effective overall and for specific consumer segments.

Online A/B testing is efficient and effective due to the scale of the internet. A tool, such as Google Optimize (optimize.withgoogle.com), offers nearly everything the analyst needs for free. Other premium tools, such as Optimizely (optimizely.com), Visual Website Optimizer (vwo.com), and Evergage (evergage.com), offer a full set of deep capabilities. In addition, the free and paid versions of most website analytics tools offer A/B test and optimization modules.

Creative Optimization

Related to A/B testing is the category of analysis designed to help advertisers optimize the creative effect of their advertising. Creative optimization seeks to maximize an advertisement's effect by using analysis to determine the most effective use of the ad's various elements. Those elements can include tone, the use of color, the use of objects, casting, music, and many others. While creative optimization's objective fits with any type of digital advertising, it's particularly effective in optimizing digital video ads.

Analysts can use a wide range of measurement tools, testing techniques, and technologies to conduct creative optimization. A/B testing optimizes some basic elements of an ad, such as color or even casting. More complex elements require more sophisticated approaches to optimization. One such technique is the use of retention curves for videos. Retention curves visualize the percent of viewers exposed to an ad who are still engaged at each subsequent second through to the ad's completion. Drastic drops in retention (i.e., any point when a large percentage of viewers leave or skip the ad) can reveal elements of the ad that led viewers to disengage. Analyzing retention curves by consumer segments can reveal how elements of the ad appeal to each segment. While retaining all viewers for the ad is an unrealistic goal, analysis of retention curves can help configure ads that have the strongest consumer appeal.

Machine learning techniques can also help to optimize ads. Algorithms can analyze nearly any conceivable element of an ad and correlate that element's effect on any measurable form of consumer behavior. Algorithms can be trained to detect broad sets of categories within a video frame, ranging from logos to animals to the way a room is decorated to visual effects. This allows for optimization of viewer retention on a massive scale that's much larger than the hand-spun analysis an analyst can perform using retention curves. Studies conducted in lab settings that collect dense consumer neurological response data, such as eye movements and brain activity, are an important source of inputs to machine learning algorithms. For a broader discussion of the effect of neuroscience on analysts, see "A Word on the Effect of Neuroscience" in Part 5, Lesson 1 of this book. These data can lead to optimizations that would be imperceptible to the analyst who's unaided by advanced data collection techniques and machine learning.

Perhaps more impressively, machine learning algorithms can analyze ads so deeply that they transcend the "this-or-that" insights offered by A/B testing to reveal patterns in storylines and other artistic characteristics of an ad. In addition to analyzing image attributes in the video frame, machine learning algorithms can detect elements of stage direction, including movement, camera angles, and image cropping.

"Data-driven creative for me no longer means switch this pair of shoes for that one, update that price, or insert logo name here," says Andrew Shebbeare, co-founder and chairman of Essence. "We can do so much more with this kind of technology to bring products to life in ways that are more human. And, in fact, advertising can be more human when it is more data-driven."[91]

While some tools found in these categories have enjoyed long tenures, many more lasted much less time or changed names and/or directions because of mergers and acquisitions in the digital analytics industry. For example, Klout was once the gold standard for measuring social influence but shuttered in 2018 following the influx of simpler and more methodologically sound online tools. Because the digital analysis tool market shifts so rapidly, it's more important for us to characterize and segment this market than it is to stay on top of the newest and "hottest" tools. I like to do this

---

[91] "Why Creativity is Being Liberated By Data and Machine Learning," Think with Google (October 9, 2019).

by thinking about tools in terms of two variables that can be posed as questions: (1) How much can I do with this tool (i.e., data flexibility)? and (2) How easy is it for me to use the tool (i.e., ease of use)?

Evaluation Criteria 1: Data Flexibility

When we look at the first question, we see clear demarcation in the tool marketplace. In fact, three distinct categories of tools emerge:

→ **"Enterprise platforms,"** which are big, powerful solutions that handle lots and lots of data and are packed with capabilities;

→ **"Point solutions,"** which typically center on one primary capability, where they go very deep; and

→ What I call **"analysis gadgets,"** which offer a single, well-defined capability and sit on the low-data flexibility side of the scale.

Let's spend a little time talking about each tool category.

Enterprise Platforms (High Data Flexibility)

The brand names behind today's enterprise platforms are easily recognizable. These tools come from some of the most well-known names in marketing analytics. Companies, such as Comscore, Adobe, IBM, and Google offer premium tools that feature in-depth analysis and visualization capabilities. In fact, these tools give analysts as many capabilities as they could possibly want. The downside to enterprise platforms is their large price tags.[92]

---

[92] N.B.: Many companies that offer enterprise platform products have premium (i.e., paid) and free versions of their tools. For example, Google offers a free version of Google Analytics as well as a premium version – Google Analytics 360 (GA360). Typically, free versions of these tools feature much less data flexibility than their premium counterparts. Free website analytics tools are classified as point solutions rather than enterprise platforms.

It can be a huge benefit if an analyst works for an organization that has an enterprise platform. The analyst will have access to a significant amount of information and – as advertisers that can invest in enterprise platforms typically operate large, complex business models – the ability to handle inputs from a variety of data sources. Benefits aside, not every business has the wherewithal or the need to invest up to six figures a year in an enterprise platform solution.

A number of popular free tools – including R and Python – are included in the enterprise platform solution category as they offer a broad set of capabilities, placing them high on the data flexibility scale. R and Python are open-source tools, with thousands of people contributing to their design by creating help files, building new capabilities, and offering their experience to the user community. Unlike the premium solutions found in this category, however, these free tools lack the slickly packaged and fully integrated feel of premium solutions. This makes them more difficult to navigate and means they may not fit well in every business situation. Still, analysts should become familiar with R and/or Python (see "A Word on R and Python" later in this lesson for insight into the R versus Python debate), given their popularity and low cost to implement.

Point Solutions (Medium Data Flexibility)

Point solutions offer more affordable, but less robust, solutions to analytics problems. If analysts have a single objective or challenge to crack, a point solution can be a viable option. For all analysis and visualization challenges analysts face, they'll find myriad companies that offer valuable solutions.

Examples of point solutions include online survey platforms, such as SurveyMonkey (surveymonkey.com) and emplifi (emplifi.io), that offer insights through "voice of the consumer" data.[93] These tools allow analysts to design surveys, collect responses from consumers as they

---

93 N.B.: The concept of voice of the consumer is also referred to as "voice of the customer," although consumer in this context is used to broaden the surveyed population from people who buy the products (i.e., consumers who are customers) to those who don't (i.e., consumers who aren't customers).

browse the internet (typically, so they can get access to premium content), and analyze results through visualization modules. Promising results in as little as three days – compared to months for traditional surveys – online survey tools can provide consumer insights that help drive important business decisions. Their scope is limited to digital surveys, but they do that job exceptionally well with a deep set of capabilities.

Analysis Gadgets (Low Data Flexibility)

All challenges don't require the depth of capabilities featured in enterprise platforms and point solutions. Low- and no-cost options that I call analysis gadgets are widely available and fit a wide variety of analytics needs.

The analysis gadget market is an exciting, undulating collection of quick-to-market tools born from the minds of experimenting analysts and coders, and community-based open-source solutions. The one characteristic that unites them under the banner of analysis gadgets is that they're extremely lightweight, and the amount of data they can handle pales in comparison to that absorbed by point solutions and enterprise platforms.

These analysis gadgets are available online and usually don't need users to download anything onto their desktops. Some of these tools require users to register and sign in with email subscriptions, while others require nothing. Some analysis gadgets include a request for voluntary contributions to help defray associated hosting or technology licensing costs while others are free.

An example of an analysis gadget is Wordle (wordle.net). When I want to run an analysis of text-based data and need a word cloud, I head to Wordle.net. Wordle works perfectly, making easy-to-generate and beautiful word clouds that lift insights from opaque blocks of words quickly and effectively. While Wordle doesn't do anything more than create simple word clouds, it does the job with such ease, it's become my go-to tool.

Figure 3.6: Word cloud based on discussion topics presented at 2013's "SXSW" digital conference created using Wordle

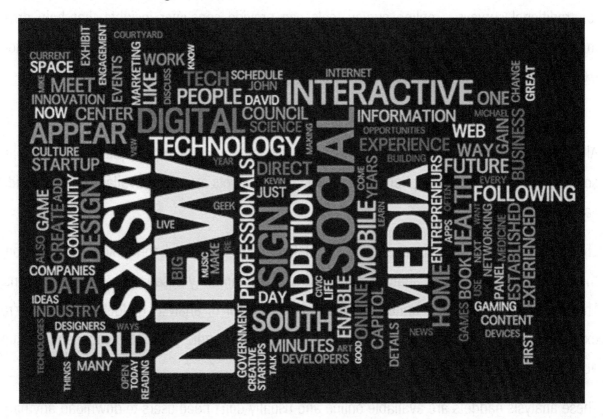

Not every analysis gadget is created by a single developer or even a small company. Google's Google Trends, as well as the search analysis tools from Bing and Yahoo, fit in this category.

New analysis gadgets are popping up all the time. A simple web search is an easy way to find them. Searching on the term "free digital analysis tools" returns a long list of tools that analysts can use for free or a nominal fee and start collecting valuable digital data instantly.

When we address the second question, "How easy is it for me to use that tool?" the market begins to separate into groups of tools we should use for the majority of our analytics challenges and those tools we should discard. The answer to the question of ease of use, of course, is a personal one. A tool that comes naturally to me might not be easy for another analyst. In addition, an analyst's skills will certainly improve, and with training, a tool that's difficult to use today may become easier tomorrow. As a result, how an analyst evaluates tools through this lens should be thought of as a uniquely personal snapshot in time.

Regardless of the temporal and shifting nature of these evaluation criteria, putting together the two questions we've discussed allows for a particularly useful framework with which to view the data analysis and visualization tool market. To illustrate the usefulness of this approach, I'll offer how I would look at the marketplace today (I've included only free, publicly available tools in my evaluation). Four quadrants emerge in this framework. Which quadrant a tool resides in will become important to the role it plays in our practice.

Figure 3.7: My personal 2X2 assessment of the data analysis and visualization tool market[94]

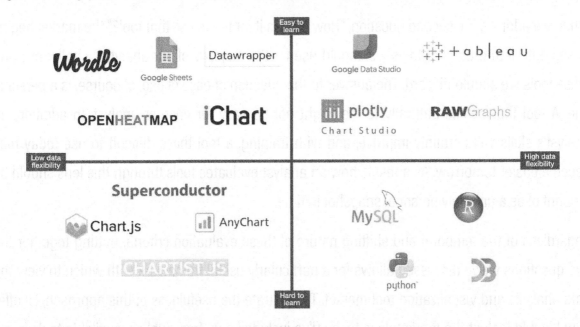

Upper Left Quadrant: Tools to Collect

Tools in the upper left quadrant have limited capabilities but are easy to use. They perform one-off jobs or specific tasks quickly and efficiently. Analysts should keep these analysis gadgets in their toolboxes. In fact, the more easy-to-use tools analysts can master – and, given the inherently low level of complexity, "mastering" tools in this quadrant is often not a challenge – the broader and more flexible their skills will be.

My recommendation is to get hands-on with these tools. When analysts find a tool that comes naturally, they should make it their go-to, with the assurance they won't need to keep up on certifications or training. After all, the benefit of an easy-to-use analysis gadget is akin to learning how to ride a bike: it doesn't matter how long it's been since you've done it – you can pop right on and hit the road.

---

[94] N.B.: This assessment includes a sample of free tools available to analysts and isn't intended to be a complete review of the data analysis and visualization tool market.

On the other side of that ledger, in the upper right quadrant, are powerful and easy-to-use tools. It makes sense for an analyst to settle on one (or possibly two) here and use it as the foundation for data analysis and visualization. The tool(s) analysts choose from this quadrant will do just about everything they need easily and efficiently. This should become an analyst's go-to tool for the majority of data analysis and visualization tasks.

I place Tableau in this quadrant. It's intuitive, proven, and powerful. In fact, Tableau has, in many ways, become table stakes for most data analysts in their role as Data Designers. I use the tools in my upper right quadrant to complete about 75 percent of my visualization tasks.

In the lower right quadrant, we find tremendously powerful tools that have deep capabilities and potential. The downside is that these tools are a tad awkward. Learning them will take a bit more effort and practice. Mastering them can require significant time. Indeed, their power comes with the price of being challenging to use.

Analysts shouldn't avoid these tools, however. In fact, using a tool from this quadrant is extremely important. The explosive creation of data gives analysts opportunities to collect, analyze, and visualize data like never before. Realizing these opportunities often requires tools powerful enough to move through large amounts of data. To do that, a little more sophistication (which often materializes in the form of a sophisticated tool) is required. One of the tools I love most in my lower right quadrant is R. Of course, several other tools in the "High data flexibility/Hard to use" quadrant can serve many purposes as well as R can and even surpass some of the things it can do. But R has become my tool of choice.

The time required to master tools in the lower right quadrant and their overlapping capabilities makes it impractical to learn them all. A better approach is to focus on a single tool in this quadrant.

Analysts should master that tool to complete the sophisticated, data-dense tasks that their go-to tool in the upper right quadrant struggles with.

Lower Left Quadrant: Tools to Avoid

Analysts should avoid any tool that's hard to use and doesn't have strong capabilities. Given the plethora of credible, capable tools that can fit in the other quadrants, there's no reason to waste time on difficult tools.

This approach to evaluating data analysis and visualization tools gives analysts a helpful way to think about the tool marketplace. As the marketplace evolves, so must this evaluation. Think of the quadrant exercise as a view into where the analyst is at the time of the evaluation. Adding new tools to the framework is key. Analysts should shift tools from the "High data flexibility/Hard to use" quadrant to the "High data flexibility/Easy to use" quadrant as their skills progress. Most importantly, analysts should revisit their evaluations periodically to ensure they're using data analysis and visualization tools efficiently.

A Word on SQL

SQL is a programming language designed for managing data held in relational databases. Donald D. Chamberlin and Raymond Boyce developed SQL in the 1970s for manipulating, storing, and retrieving structured data from IBM's original relational database management system (RDBMS) called System R. Today, it's the most popular language the analyst can use to interact with a relational database. For the analyst, collecting and analyzing data at companies that have a relationship database (including MySQL, a free and open-source RDBMS designed by Oracle) requires some use of SQL.

Successful analysts will make it a goal to become very familiar with SQL as they build their Techie skills. In fact, the analyst community largely regards SQL skills as "table stakes," given the programming language's ubiquity and importance.

While the analyst community agrees on the criticality of SQL, there is less consensus on whether the analyst should complement SQL with R or Python (or both). Both R and Python are open-source tools for data analytics that handle exceptionally large datasets. The two have important differences. These differences can help the analyst determine which is the right choice.

Data scientists made R for data-oriented projects. It features a large number of ready-made packages and has built-in ways to visualize data. In addition, R boasts a large community that provides support through mailing lists, documentation, and blogs. R's learning curve, however, is steeper than many languages (including Python), and it's less efficient for general computations.

Python has a growing user community that over indexes in software engineers and programmers. It provides more opportunities to take advantage of artificial intelligence, allows analysts to integrate data analysis with websites and mobile apps more efficiently, and can be adapted more easily for programming tasks besides analyzing data. Python, however, is less efficient for statistical computations, features less-appealing data visualization, and comes with fewer add-on modules and packages.

From my perspective, analysts can boost their productivity with either tool as each is powerful enough to complete nearly any analytics task. Learning the tools and maintaining skills in them can be considerable tasks, so choosing one or the other is more prudent than trying to learn both. The choice between R and Python comes down to personal preference (or the preference of your working group).

I found that RStudio (R's integrated development environment) made programming in R so easy that it quickly became my favorite. I lacked a programming background, and Python didn't have a comparable development environment when I was beginning to learn R. As a result, the choice was simple for me. When making the choice for yourself, consider the pros and cons of each to find the tool that best fits your needs and abilities.

A Word on Tools < The Analyst

One final thought on tools.

While tools are vital to our work, it's important to keep the proper context on that value. As Avinash Kaushik summed up perfectly, "No tool would be useful unless you had a Michelle or an Amir or Enrique or Sasha who understands your business and has the drive to use the tool intelligently to deliver actionable insights."[95] A tool won't solve an advertiser's challenges. When used properly, a tool will do a great job of showing patterns in data that would be undetectable otherwise.

Yet it is you, the analyst, who must first look for and then properly interpret those patterns. Never underestimate your importance and value.

In Summary: Analytics and Dataviz Tools

Data analytics and visualization tools live in a fast-moving marketplace of established providers and new entrants. As a result, it's more important for analysts to adopt a way to think about the market than be up to speed in the development of new tools. Two evaluation criteria – data flexibility and ease of use – provide a powerful framework for the evolving marketplace and make clear which tools analysts should keep in their toolboxes and those they should discard. Remember, no tool is as important as the analyst who uses it.

In the next lesson, we'll discuss the importance of an advertiser's digital marketing maturity.

---

[95] Avinash Kaushik, "Best Web Analytics 2.0 Tools: Quantitative, Qualitative, Life Saving!," *Occam's Razor* (October 19, 2010).

Digital Marketing Maturity

Five things discussed in this lesson:

- Digital marketing maturity is a quantified measure of an advertiser's sophistication regarding digital data and its use
- Boston Consulting Group's view of maturity is based on a robust assessment across a broad array of digital capabilities
- Bain & Company's view of maturity focuses on how savvy an advertiser is in its digital measurement
- Deloitte Consulting and MIT conducted research that found advertisers fall into one of three levels of maturity
- Regardless of the approach to measuring maturity, advertisers found to be more mature saw benefits in sales growth and cost efficiency

The number of touch points along the consumer journey has increased exponentially over the last decade. The tools available to analysts, as we just discussed in the previous lesson, have grown in much the same trajectory as more data created more need for sophisticated analytics and visualization tools. Meanwhile, have the relationships brands maintain with consumers changed?

Some areas of the marketplace have undergone astonishing shifts. An example is how Netflix disrupted the home entertainment market and continues to use technology to optimize its efforts. In contrast, other businesses lag and have yet to realize the full value that digital data can contribute to their marketing. What separates Netflix from the laggards, regardless of their business category or the degree to which their operations depend upon the internet, is digital marketing maturity.

BCG's View of Digital Marketing Maturity

According to Boston Consulting Group (BCG), the path to data-driven marketing maturity is comprised of four stages: nascent, emerging, connected, and multimoment. BCG's research indicates that as of 2021, only a handful of advertisers – just 9 percent, up from only 2 percent in 2019 – operated at the most mature levels by connecting with consumers at multiple moments across the purchase journey through personalized content.[96]

BCG defined the four phases of digital maturity as:

→ **Nascent** – Marketing campaigns are executed, mainly using external data and direct buys, with limited link to sales

→ **Emerging** – Some use of owned data in automated buying with single-channel optimization and testing

→ **Connected** – Data integrated and activated across channels with demonstrated link to ROI or sales proxies

→ **Multimoment** – Dynamic execution across multiple channels optimized toward individual customer business outcomes and transactions

To arrive at its point of view on digital maturity, BCG examined success factors and capabilities of more than 40 European advertisers across eight industries – automotive, retail, financial services, travel, consumer goods, technology, entertainment and media, and fashion and luxury. The study

---

[96] Dominic Field, "Growing Up Digital, Part One: The Four Stages of Marketing Maturity," LinkedIn (Nov 30, 2017).

revealed that digitally mature businesses share a number of success factors. From an organizational standpoint, BCG found that successful advertisers invested in specialist skills, strategic partnerships, agile teams, and fail-fast cultures. In addition, technology at these advertisers is integrated and automated, ensuring the use of connected data and actionable measurement.

Bain's View of Digital Marketing Maturity

Bain & Company's view of digital marketing maturity centered firmly on measurement. Citing opportunities created by the collection of customer information and the technology available to act on it, Bain found measurement is more important than ever. In collaboration with Google, Bain assessed the measurement maturity of 600 advertisers in the U.S., UK, and Canada, and sorted them into four levels on a maturity curve, ranging from "Foundational" to "Best in Class."

Figure 3.8: Bain's perspective on measurement maturity

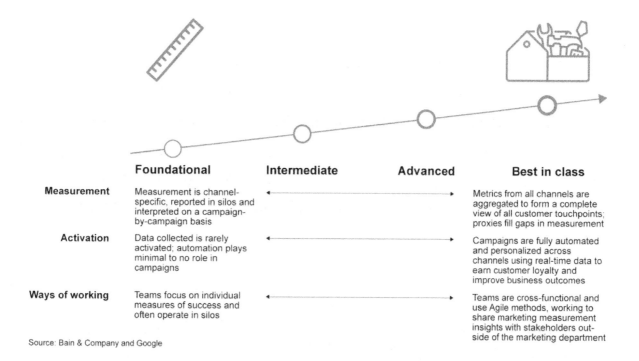

Source: Bain & Company and Google

Bain's look at the digital measurement practices of advertisers found organizations that have realized measurement advantage did three things better than their competitors:[97]

→ **Measurement** – They had a deep understanding of their customers and linked marketing activities to business outcomes

→ **Activation** – They used the latest automation and machine learning tools to reach and connect with customers at scale and personalized their messaging

→ **Ways of Working** – Their agile, customer-centric teams had budget flexibility across channels to understand, test, learn, and act on measurement insights

Advertisers that take control of their marketing and advertising data and technology can respond quickly to customer needs and send personalized messages at the right moment, Bain's research found. This is the ultimate promise of digital marketing and is unlocked through measurement maturity, according to Bain.

Deloitte and MIT Sloan's View of Digital Marketing Maturity

Following four years of research across three groups of advertisers (early, developing, and maturing), Deloitte and MIT's Sloan School Of Business delivered their view of digital marketing maturity. Their perspective was based on the idea that adapting to increasingly digital market environments and taking advantage of digital technologies to improve operations are important goals for nearly every contemporary business. Through their analysis, Deloitte and MIT found many advertisers are beginning to make the necessary changes to adapt their organizations to a digital environment.

---

[97] Bain & Company and Google, *Measurement Maturity Survey* (January 2019); n=622 marketing executives; n=188 leading marketers who grew market share and exceeded top 2017 business goal, n=115 lagging marketers who lagged behind on these two measurements.

Based on a global survey of more than 4,300 managers, executives, and analysts and 17 interviews with executives and thought leaders, the research showed the digital business environment is fundamentally different from the traditional one. Digitally maturing advertisers recognize the differences and are evolving how they learn and lead to adapt and succeed in a rapidly changing market.[98]

Benefits of Digital Marketing Maturity

In the simplest sense, digital marketing maturity helps advertisers identify, acquire, and deepen relationships with high-value customers. Advanced technology and analytics provide a digital measurement foundation to gain a better understanding of the customer lifetime decision journey. We'll delve into how analysts can contribute to customer understanding in Part 4 of this book. Let's close the discussion of digital marketing maturity by reviewing the quantified benefit of each approach.

→ **BCG** found leading businesses that are adding customers, ROI and competitive advantage focus on adopting a path to full data-driven marketing and attribution. Those that succeed are seeing significant benefits – reducing costs by up to 30 percent and increasing revenue by 20 percent. [99]

→ **Bain**'s research found the 100 most measurement-mature advertisers were four times as likely to exceed business goals compared with the 100 least-mature advertisers.[100]

---

[98] Gerald C. Kane, Doug Palmer, Anh Nguyen Phillips, David Kiron, and Natasha Buckley, *Coming of Age Digitally Learning, Leadership, and Legacy* (Summer 2018).

[99] Field, "Growing Up Digital."

[100] Bain & Company and Google, *Measurement Maturity Survey* (January 2019); n=622 marketing executives; n=188 leading marketers who grew market share and exceeded top 2017 business goal, n=115 lagging marketers who lagged behind on these two measurements.

→ **Deloitte**'s work revealed that highly mature advertisers are far more likely to develop the leaders they need for the future.[101]

The benefits of digital marketing maturity are clear in a philosophical sense – after all, it's hard to argue against the benefits of maturity – and, as the research shows, drive business benefits.

Building a Winning Analytics Team

Digital transformation – the process of using digital technologies to modernize business performance – has taken the marketing world by storm. At the heart of digital transformation is data analytics, a practice that helps executives make the best possible decisions based on up-to-date data and insights. Data analytics is (or should be) a fixture at or near the top of every advertiser's executive agenda, but according to the Google / BCG Digital Maturity Benchmark, only 9 percent of businesses use insights and technology to create better consumer experiences effectively.[102]

Companies that build a successful analytics team realize revenue, profit, and market share gains. Those that don't continue to operate inefficiently and fall behind. Building that team can be challenging, though. Through my experience in building industry-leading analytics teams and my work with hundreds of companies, five keys to building a successful analytics strategy and team have emerged:

→ **Get the model right:** Three models – Centralization, Decentralization, and Hybrid (Centralized Decentralization) – unlock analysts' power at different stages of an advertiser's lifecycle. Choosing the right model is the first step.

---

[101] Kane, Palmer, Phillips, Kiron, and Buckley, *Coming of Age Digitally.*

[102] Kristi Rogers, Javier Pérez Moiño, Henry Leon, and Alberto Poncela, *The Fast Track to Digital Marketing Maturity* (September 7, 2021).

→ **Invest in talent over tools:** The right investment balance in tools and analysts tips decidedly toward human capital. Investing in people leads to a flexible analytics capability that can adapt to a changing business environment without locking the organization into an unwieldy system of software and tools.

→ **Understand that culture is king:** Analytics teams thrive in dynamic environments that reward curiosity, encourage innovation, and keep expectations high. By building and reinforcing such a culture, the organization will earn the highest return from its investment in analytics.

→ **Partner with C-suite leaders to grow an analytics culture:** Leaders outside the analytics team can help create an analytics-favorable environment by knowing when to collect data for themselves, presenting business challenges to analyst teams rather than ordering "data widgets," and consistently seeking to quantify goals and objectives.

→ **Be the data-savvy executive:** The data-savvy executive demonstrates commitment by embracing an analytics-centric mindset, asking the right questions of analytics teams, understanding the questions the organization's measurement programs will answer (and those they won't), and supporting in-house analytics teams by holding partners accountable for critical contributions.

Let's explore these ideas further.

Get the model right

When it comes to data's effect on a business, no variable is more crucial than how the analytics team is organized. When analysts are disorganized, analytics innovations won't scale, redundant processes will proliferate, and data's influence on the organization will fade and eventually vanish.

There are three approaches to organizing analytics teams. Each approach is right at a particular time in an organization's existence. Here are the three organizational structures and when they fit:

Centralization

Centralization places the analytics team at the center of the organization. Different company functions or divisions provide their strategies and needs to the central team, and rely on the team for all data needs. The model is good for standardizing tools, scaling best practices, teaching, and aligning everyone in the analytics organization.

The Centralized model works best for small organizations that are starting their analytics investment journeys or focusing on a single brand. In these cases, the organization is better off with analytics resources in one place, executing from one data playbook, and led by a senior executive (such as a chief analytics officer) who's responsible for all elements of the function's performance. Companies that operate a centralization analytics model include Manscaped, Rover.com, Tory Burch, and St. Jude Children's Research Hospital.

As the company grows and the business evolves, centralized organizational structures can become overwhelmed and unable to meet business needs. They resort to standardized deliverables that lack the customization and punch that generate business benefits.

Decentralization

The decentralized analytics organization sees analytics teams built into each business unit, closer to where decisions need to be made, so analysts can focus on the challenges of that business. The results are customized solutions, speed, and agility that are critical for business success.

A Decentralized model is best when disparate parts of the organization are evolving at different speeds, and they all need customized data insights. An example of a company that operates a decentralized approach to analytics is Nestlé, where Nespresso, Gerber, Purina, and nearly every other major line of business has its own analytics team. Others include Clorox (where analytics teams are organized by product category), Nike (organized by geographic region), and General Motors (organized by brand).

Inefficiencies will always7 exist across business units in the Decentralized model, as teams do their own thing. It's difficult to get a cohesive company view because everyone has specific metrics definitions, tools, and testing platforms. Sometimes, decentralized organizations optimize against one another, so an individual division might be winning, but the company, as a whole, doesn't earn economies of scale.

One way to mitigate some of the risk inherent in this model is to consolidate noncore functions that cut across all the decentralized teams, such as data collection or vendor management. Most of the companies mentioned above maintain a team at the center of their analytics functions to take on scaled responsibilities. For example, for years, Nestlé has operated a Consumer & Marketplace Insights (CMI) team that coordinates measuring partners' work and cross-brand programs like Nestlé's MMM. While no formal reporting lines tie CMI to line of business analytics teams, CMI plays an important role in bringing scale efficiencies to initiatives, such as a cross-brand MMM.

Hybrid (Centralized Decentralization)

The Hybrid (Centralized Decentralization) model places a small, experienced group of analysts at the center, directed by an analytics leader who's responsible for every facet of the company's core analytics functions of data collection, data analysis, and data storytelling. This central team works with analyst teams in each business function to ensure a cultural mind meld and efficiencies of scale.

The central team owns:

→ Overall analytics strategy
→ Standards, methodologies, closed-loop decision-making processes
→ Evaluation of new analytics solutions
→ Oversight of centralized data collection and distribution processes or systems

→ Investment in training

→ All of the complex experimentation required when new approaches to tools, data, or analytical techniques appear on the horizon

The central team isn't simply a tools and standards organization. The team is responsible for all company-level analysis to support corporate cross-functional strategy. The purpose of this centralized analysis is to keep everyone focused on what's good for the overall business, and to help fuel strategic business decisions.

Analysts who sit with the business teams are responsible for functional analysis needs (data analysis and storytelling). They ensure data requirements align with business unit priorities, share functional needs with the central team, and provide local training.

For large businesses that have much at stake and a willingness to fund analytics capabilities in the right way, Hybrid is the optimal model. This approach gives organizations a path for improving operational efficiencies and strategic influence. Although it's expensive to build and maintain, the result is a sweet and spectacular business benefit. The Hybrid model fits well with organizations that use analytics across multiple lines of business. For example, this model provides companies with geographically organized teams that are responsible for functional needs inside their regions and report to a central Center Of Excellence (COE). In this way, COEs can oversee all aspects of analytics performance, including best practice sharing, analyst development, and data acquisition.

Which model is best for you?

Here are some questions to help you identify the right model for your organization:

→ Is analytics a loosely structured, organic function that's shared across a number of teams in your organization? Consider building a Centralized model.

→ Do you have an overburdened centralized analytics organization and need customized results across multiple brands or businesses? Consider a Decentralized model.

→ Do you have a complicated, decentralized analytics organization that's turned into a free-for-all of redundancy and chaos? Is the guiding hand of centralized sanity and focus required? Consider a Hybrid model.

Other Considerations

Regardless of which model best fits the organization, the organization must deliver on several important considerations to build and operate a winning in-house analytics team.

Invest in talent over tools (the '10/90 Rule')

While nearly all Fortune 500 companies have made significant investments in web analytics, most struggle to make meaningful data-driven business decisions. That's largely a product of investment strategies that focus disproportionately on tools and vendor professional services rather than people.

These misplaced efforts led Avinash Kaushik, Chief Strategy Officer at Croud and a web analytics trailblazer, to his "10/90 Rule" for web analytics success. The rule states that successful organizations:

→ **Invest 10 percent of the analytics budget in tools:** Packaged software systems and vendor professional services are an important component of a successful analytics team, but they're not a solution unto themselves.

→ **Invest the remaining 90 percent in people:** It's the analysts – not the tools – who transform raw data into actionable insights. Analysts can supplement the company's purchased tools with free, open-source solutions to expand their capabilities.

For example, if you're paying your web analytics vendor $25,000 for an annual contract, you should invest $225,000 in people to extract value from that data. After all, actionable insights don't come from system-generated clickstream reports. Smart analysts produce them. They have the business acumen to frame clickstream data in the context of marketing activities, business decisions, and consumer behaviors to help you improve your performance.

Culture is king

No analyst wants to be relegated to the periphery of decision-making, feeling disregarded and lacking the support needed to fulfill their role effectively. That's why it's imperative that the organization build an analyst culture where top analysts want to work: a dynamic environment that supports learning, growth, and accountability.

The organization establishes such a culture by building an environment rooted in these ideas:

→ **Reward curiosity – not proficiency:** Keep analysts at the forefront of constant change by encouraging them to challenge convention and ask critical questions. A simple way for the executive to create this environment is to lead by example: ask many questions, demonstrating that asking questions is a method to improve quality and reduce risks. Accept "I don't know, but I'll find out" as an answer.

→ **Encourage a test+fail+learn mentality:** Create an environment that constantly tests its marketing effectiveness, identifies weaknesses or blind spots, and pivots to address them. By pushing boundaries through a program of proactive tests, the analytics organization will optimize the metrics that work (and avoid the things that don't) before the rest of the market does. At Google, we celebrated our failures as frequently as our successes. Our analyst team "all-hands" meetings highlighted our wins but gave equal airtime to the stories of projects that went wrong and what we learned from them. In this way, we demonstrated the value of failure while cultivating a culture that recognizes perfection as an unhealthy pipe dream.

→ **Expect robust processes:** Hold analytics teams accountable for delivering processes that mitigate risk and inform marketing programs. Make this a part of performance reviews. At Google, analysts created quarterly "OKRs" (Objectives and Key Results) that detailed what they expected to accomplish. This can be an excellent way to establish performance expectations. Analysts' OKRs are usually so ambitious that analysts can achieve them only when they complete underlying processes. By holding analysts accountable for processes and not just results, the executive can create an environment where process quality improves out of necessity.

Partner with C-suite leaders to grow an analytics culture

The organization can further support the analyst by ensuring that nonanalyst leaders support the analytics team. Nonanalyst leaders must understand the data that drives the decisions they make. Here's how to make that happen:

→ **Democratize data and promote "self-service" as appropriate:** Nonanalyst leaders must understand when it's appropriate to go to analyst teams with problems and when they should collect data themselves, leaving their analysts to attack more significant challenges. Importantly, they must be held accountable for using self-service options when they're appropriate.

→ **Hold nonanalyst leaders accountable for presenting challenges – not requests:** Nonanalysts should be experts in their businesses – not analytics. Train them to present challenges to the organization's data experts rather than request specific analysis techniques or deliverables. We refer to these nonaffectionately as data widgets. Lead by example.

→ **Set quantifiable goals and objectives:** Business leaders understand performance metrics. Set measurable KPIs that align business leaders and analysts in every business unit. Such targets should establish a clear and consistent theme that starts with the C-suite and cascades down through every level, while adjusting to the unique scope of each subsequent layer of the organization. For example, a CEO's KPI of "profit generated by paid advertising" might look like "profit in North America" by the North American region, "lifetime value of customers acquired through paid ads" to the media team, and "profit margin of sales mix" to the organization's e-commerce merchandising team. By doing so, analysts in each business unit will be empowered to prioritize deliveries for nonanalyst leaders and evaluate whether each unit's efforts are delivering results or falling short.

Maintaining a winning analytics capability requires buy-in up and down a company's hierarchy. Nonanalyst leaders will demonstrate this commitment when held accountable for their own analytics acumen. Still, high-performing analytics capabilities can't and won't come to fruition without the full commitment of the organization's chief executive.

Be the data-savvy executive

The analytics team may provide the expertise, but the chief executive provides the leadership required to maximize analytics benefits for the company. The data-savvy executive recognizes data's true value and demonstrably and consistently leads the company's commitment to analytics by:

→ **Understanding the questions measurement can answer (and those it can't):** Holding expectations for measurement solutions requires the executive to understand those solutions. For example, marketing mix modeling is poorly suited to answer the question, "How can I optimize my future media investments?" Executives who expect their analytics teams to use an MMM to answer this question set their teams up for failure. In Part 3, Lesson

2, I discussed how executives can earn this clarity with their MMMs. The data-savvy executive will expand the understanding of marketing mix models detailed earlier to the company's measurement solutions to clarify the answers analytics teams and partners can deliver and those they can't.

→ **Asking the right questions:** The organization should view its analytics team as a group of highly trained, exceptionally skilled experts. Data-savvy executives must feel responsible for deploying their teams against big, meaningful challenges. Analytics resources that focus on questions of media efficiency, such as "How can I eliminate wasted impressions?" may have marginal incremental benefits, but won't produce transformational change. As such, questions stakeholders pose to analytics teams should deliver solutions that benefit their organizations in critical areas, including: ROI ("What did I earn from the investments I made?"); risk mitigation ("How can data reduce uncertainty in my decision-making?"); and hypotheses testing ("I have an idea. How can I use data to test it?").

→ **Holding partners accountable:** Partners should clearly understand, manage, and meet their organizations' expectations. The data-savvy executive must ensure lines of responsibility between in-house analytics teams and vendors are well-defined and that third-party inputs meet timing and quality requirements.

Leading as the data-savvy executive can have real, tangible benefits. Recently, Google helped executives at a global quick-serve restaurant reexamine their approach to media budgeting. This brand spent years basing platform-level investment decisions solely on MMM results. Google helped the executive team take a new look at the measurement tools the group used to make budgeting decisions, and the insights the executives received from their current measurement strategy and partners. This examination led the brand to shift its measurement strategy from using marketing mix models exclusively to employing a blend of MMM, MTA, and experiments. The brand estimated that improvements in channel-level performance generated $45 million in incremental sales (an incremental +2 percent of year-over-year growth) in year one alone.

What You Can Do Today to Build the Analytics Team for Your Future

With minimal investment, you can lay the foundation of your company's in-house data analytics infrastructure immediately. Complete these three steps:

Step 1: Audit your current analytics capabilities

Auditing the organization's current analytics capabilities goes well beyond an assessment of tools and team sizes. Include a gap analysis on the critical areas of analytics best practices shared in this book:

→ **Organizational design:** Does the model of your analytics team – Centralization versus Decentralization versus Centralized Decentralization – fit the current status of the business?

→ **Investment strategy:** Are analytics investments made in accordance with the 10/90 Rule?

→ **Culture:** Does the organization value curiosity over proficiency? Is a "test+fail+learn" mentality apparent among your analytics professionals? Does the organization hold the analytics team to a clear expectation of robust processes, so that the team's outputs meet the highest possible standard?

→ **Analytics acumen among nonanalyst leaders:** Do nonanalyst leaders understand when to pull data for themselves (and do the self-service channels to those data exist)? Is the expectation clearly set that they present analysts with business challenges instead of requests for analytics deliverables? Are nonanalyst leaders held accountable for setting quantifiable goals?

→ **Executive leadership's commitment to analytics:** As the executive leader, do you ask your analytics team the right questions? Do you know which questions your measurement endeavors answer (and which they don't)? Do you demonstrate commitment to your analytics teams by holding your partners accountable for the quality of their work and on-time delivery?

Honest answers to the questions detailed above will reveal gaps in your present approach to analytics. These gaps exist due to leadership challenges – not analytics challenges. No special understanding of analytics is required to address them.

Becoming the organization you want to be requires a change agent who will close your gaps in capability and design by successfully implementing the approaches described in this book. In my experience, the analytics team's organizational model best determines where the organization can find that leader:

→ **Look internally (but outside your analytics team) for the Centralization model**: Shifting an internal leader from outside the analytics team to the role of chief analytics officer or director of analytics works best for the Centralized model. Ideally, this leader will come from the group that's the largest and most important internal customer for the analytics organization. That leader will more than make up for a potential lack in technical knowledge by bringing immediate, built-in influence from a former functional group and a keen understanding of stakeholder business needs.

→ **Find an external analytics expert in your industry for the Decentralization model**: When moving to this model, the organization's subunits face periods of opportunity as analytics teams pivot from delivering the Centralized model's generic outputs to customized solutions that fill specific needs. It's important, therefore, that each person tabbed to manage a subunit's decentralized analytics team has a deep understanding of that subunit's industry. Finding an external analytics leader who has relevant experience is a prudent and effective choice. This gives the new leader permission – as an outsider – to build truly transformative solutions free from the constraints of "how things were done before." And because the scale of each subunit's analytics team is still relatively small, the new leader can make bold moves to bend the team back toward best practices in the face of limited resistance and organizational inertia.

→ **Promote from within for the Hybrid model:** As an organization makes the jump to the Hybrid model, the best choice for its central team's leader comes from within the analytics organization. First, an inside candidate will have the cultural understanding, network, and know-how needed to lead such a complex and demanding organization. Lacking these things, an external candidate will make little to no traction for the analytics team as the new leader "gets up to speed." Losing traction can cause an organization of this size to collapse quickly under its own weight. The implications of such a collapse, even if only for a short time, can inflict irreparable damage to the analytics team's reputation and culture. In my experience, the adage, "once bitten, twice shy," applies perfectly to anyone who was disappointed in the quality of the analytics team's output or underwhelmed by how an analyst performed in a critical client meeting during this period of directionless leadership. Rarely will the analytics team earn a second shot. The team can forge ahead without missing a beat by identifying an internal candidate as part of the Hybrid model. Second, promoting a candidate from within signals to the entire organization the health and durability of the analyst's career path. Moreover, it demonstrates the belief the organization has in its analytics team. This helps ensure the analytics team remains as optimistic for the opportunities that lie ahead as the broader organization is excited about analytics playing a bigger role in the organization's future.

As the analytics industry has matured, now is the time for advertisers and other data-driven companies to implement a more professional, strategic approach to building and operating winning in-house analytics teams. Now is the time for businesses to establish a data-centric culture that will position them to win with analytics today and in the future. Companies that do so realize gains in effectiveness and efficiency, earn important insights from their data, and attract (and retain) top-tier analytics talent.

By following the recommendations detailed in this book, you can ensure your organization will be counted among the winners as a high-performing analytics team.

In Summary: Digital Marketing Maturity

Digital marketing maturity is a quantified measure of an advertiser's sophistication with regard to digital data collection and use. Several firms have defined this concept: Three leading ideas come from BCG, Bain, and Deloitte (in conjunction with the MIT Sloan School Of Business). BCG's view of maturity is based on a robust assessment across a broad array of digital capabilities. Bain Consulting's view of maturity is centered firmly on how savvy an advertiser is in its digital measurement. Deloitte and MIT's joint research found advertisers fall into one of three levels of maturity. Regardless of the approach to measuring maturity, advertisers found to be more mature saw benefits in sales growth and cost efficiency.

PART 4
The Art of Analytics

Lesson 1   Navigating to Your Big Idea

Lesson 2   Planning for Your Analytics Expedition

Lesson 3   Collecting Data, Data Everywhere

Lesson 4   Analyzing for Insights

Every analyst dreams of coming up with the "big idea" – the game-changing and previously unseen insight or approach that gives their organization a competitive advantage and their career a huge boost. But dreaming won't get you there. It requires a thoughtful and disciplined approach to analysis projects. In this part of the book, I detail the four elements of the Marketing Analytics Process (MAP): plan, collect, analyze, report.

Part 4 also explains the role of the analyst, the six mutually exclusive and collectively exhaustive ("MECE") marketing objectives of analytics, how to find context and patterns in collected data, and how to avoid the pitfalls of bias.

Navigating to Your Big Idea

Five things discussed in this lesson:

- Getting to a big idea is hard, but following a process map will help analysts be effective and efficient
- Thorough analysis begins with thorough planning
- Analysts can collect data using three tried-and-true techniques (although one stands out as the most capable technique)
- Finding patterns in data requires analysts to be purposeful in how they investigate the data they collect
- Reporting results is a critical exercise that separates big ideas from simply solid analysis

Analysts desperately want that big idea. They want to uncover the insight that expresses something no one else sees, gives their organizations a competitive advantage, and earns them accolades.

The impossible way for the analyst to reach the insight they seek is to sit alone in a room and think about the problem until they produce the solution. Indeed, analytics is not an individual sport. The *Mad Men* days of three martini lunches and big personalities delivering campaign ideas born from lightning strikes of inspiration are outdated, even if some advertisers cling to the way things were before. Today, a methodical planning process that draws insights from data paves the way for success.

Navigating the analytics journey successfully requires several important and required elements. My friends, Jamie Shuttleworth of mcgarrybowen, Karl Turnbull of Cavalry, and Ross McLean of 20|20 Research, captured this idea very well in a simple visualization. Shuttleworth, Turnbull, and McLean developed the image below, which skillfully places "YOU," the analyst, in communion with your big idea.

Figure 4.1: You sat cozily with your big idea[103]

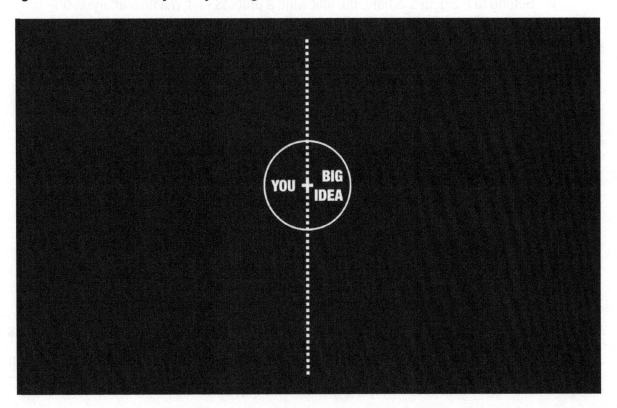

The image was printed on a folded piece of paper. As the paper was pulled out of its folded state, all the inputs required to get you, the analyst, to that big idea were revealed.

_____

[103] Jamie Shuttleworth, Ross McLean, and Karl Turnbull, *Getting to What Matters* (2010).

Figure 4.2: The process of navigating to your big idea[104]

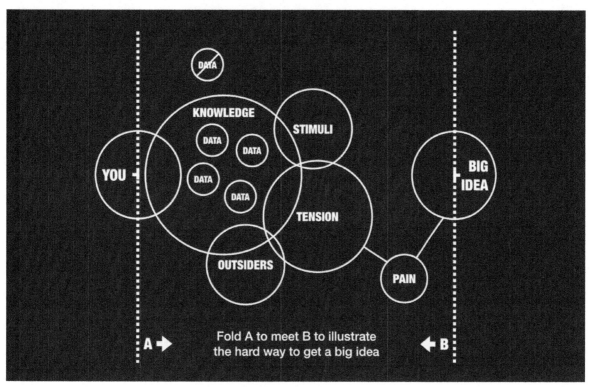

Among the items detailed in the image are the knowledge the analyst will earn, the data the analyst will pull in, the data the analyst will cast out, the stimuli the analyst will want, the tension the analyst will create, the outsiders who will provide context and new perspectives, and the pain that everyone involved in the process will certainly feel. Any good insight, and indeed, any good analysis, will involve some pain. But that pain signifies the growth of ideas.

Luckily for us, we have a map that will guide us along the way and help us navigate to our big idea.

---

[104] Shuttleworth, McLean, and Turnbull, *Getting to What Matters*.

The marketing analytics process (MAP) that guides us along our analytics journey consists of four steps: plan, collect, analyze and report. The four steps are a circular process and each time through informs the next journey. Analysts find data they're comfortable working with. They hone analysis techniques through experience. And as analysts prepare to report their findings, they learn what audiences value and what they don't like. The knowledge analysts build through this process is important. The next time they start a planning phase, they'll have understanding, data, and insights to apply moving forward.

Figure 4.3: The MAP in visual form

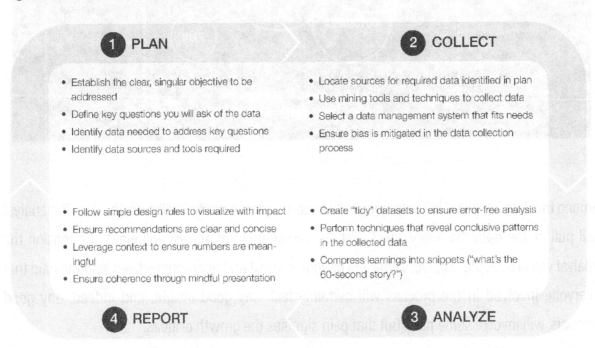

Let's take a deeper dive into the MAP's steps. Analysts start their journeys with thorough planning.

The first item in the plan step is to establish a clear, singular objective for the analysis. Singular is a key word here. The analyst can't tackle multiple objectives with their analysis. It's imperative that the analyst fight for this upfront by getting executive sponsors and stakeholders to align on a singular objective and commit to its pursuit. Taking on too many objectives (i.e., more than one) will scatter resources, analysis, and focus. Being singular in the objective allows the analyst to bring the full weight of their analysis to a specific, identified goal. We'll review the comprehensive set of Business Objectives available to analysts in the next lesson.

The second phase in the plan step is defining the key questions analysts will ask of the data. Approach this by thinking of the three (or more) questions to answer to achieve the objective. For example, if the objective of my analysis is to determine how my company/client can improve awareness for a new product, I might ask questions such as:

→ **What**'s the current level of awareness for products in this category?

→ **Why** have some channels been successful while others haven't?

→ **How** can I use media most efficiently to build awareness among my target consumers?

Questions such as these will dictate the data the analyst needs, as well as the sources for that data. Getting those key questions right is a valuable and important step. We'll discuss the art of question design and explore the Plan step more broadly in Lesson 2.

The final thing the analyst will do in this plan step is to pull it all together in a planning document (a literal plan) that will help guide them through the rest of the analysis. The key elements of this planning document make clear the (1) objective, (2) key questions, and (3) data and sources used to find those answers. This document helps keep the analysis centered as the project works its way through the remaining complex (and distraction-filled) phases of the MAP. We will see an example of such a plan in Lesson 2.

Second Step: Collect

In the collect step, the analyst seeks data to answer key questions. The first step is to find and engage the sources of required data. Frequently, data sources in the plan step don't work out. Data owners could deny access to those sources, access could be too expensive, or the data could no longer exist. This is one of the primary reasons we need to be flexible in our analysis journey. When data proves to be inaccessible, we must refresh our plan with a new dataset that can provide the answers we seek. This is where the experience gained from previous journeys will come in handy, as quickly replacing an inaccessible data source with one the analyst used in the past will preserve the analysis timeline. We will explore data sources in Lesson 3.

Once the analyst identifies and engages sources, the second phase to the collect step is to use data mining techniques and other tactics to pull that data out and get it into a usable form. We'll discuss these techniques at length in Lesson 3, but for now, know there are primarily three: (1) accessing facilitated downloads, (2) tapping application programming interfaces (APIs), and (3) scraping webpages.

The final phase in the collect step is selecting a data management system to house the collected data. Many systems are available, but the key consideration is balancing analysis power with simplicity of use. Usually, those are negatively correlated, as we will see in Lesson 3.

Third Step: Analyze

In this step, we want to uncover powerful, relevant insights that will compel action. We have an objective, we have identified key questions we want answered, and we have collected the data we want to explore. Now, it's time to get into the analysis and see where the data takes us.

The first phase to the analyze step is producing an analysis-ready, tidy dataset. We'll talk about this later in Lesson 4, but beginning with clean, well-organized data will make that process much more efficient and effective.

The next phase of the analyze step is to perform analysis. We'll talk about a number of techniques in Lesson 4. Each has a varying level of depth and, therefore, produces varying levels of insight. Sometimes, a simple analysis with a simple insight is all analysts need. Other times, it's important to go deeper. We'll discuss how those analysis techniques produce that depth of insight.

Step Four: Report

The fourth and last step in the MAP is to report the analysis results. In this step, analysts should feel tension as they compress the story into a tight, digestible packet. Compressing this story means no extraneous information obscures insights that matter, the logical flow of the story is solid, and the story's aperture can be opened wide enough to provide details to low-level stakeholders and focused enough to provide a high-level narrative to a C-level audience. Part 5 of this book is dedicated to this topic.

The first phase in the report step is to design a visual story that reaches audiences effectively and efficiently. The analyst will do this by leveraging preattentive attributes in visual perception, which we'll discuss at length. While that sounds very scientific, we'll talk about how a few simple design tweaks can bring greater contrast to visuals and influence audience understanding significantly.

The second phase is to ensure recommendations are clear and concise. Concepts, ideas, and recommendations included in the analyst's report must be easy to understand. We'll discuss some simple rules to help ensure our message, and all of its elements, is precise.

The last phase in the report step is to ensure the presentation is distraction-free by focusing on details and sophisticated execution elements. We'll review a number of guidelines and tips to help analysts complete this final task successfully.

Open and frequent communication between analysts and stakeholders is a hallmark of any successful analytics journey that arrives at a Big Idea. While communication throughout the process is important, it's never more critical than at its beginning. This is when clear expectations must be set and understood.

One of the greatest complications for the analyst is the discussion of needs and requirements for an analytics project with nonanalyst stakeholders. The analyst is a strategist who applies a specialized set of tools and skills on data to solve problems and find new opportunities. Analysts cannot (and should not) expect their nonanalyst stakeholders to know the solutions that would solve stakeholders' challenges.

Put simply, the analyst is not an order taker. The analyst is not employed to simply produce on-demand analytics products that stakeholders request from a neat, well-defined menu. The sophistication of business today and the complexity of data analytics projects dramatically reduces the shelf life of unmalleable analytics projects. What may make sense for the business today will almost certainly be out of date within a few quarters (if not weeks). More importantly, the carefully prescribed analytics menu constrains analysts and stifles their creativity. This, in turn, leads to suboptimal outcomes for the business as well as the analyst's career.

It's important for analysts to get to what we call "the ask behind the ask" from their stakeholders. In other words, rather than taking a nonanalyst stakeholder's request at face value, the successful analyst will seek to uncover what the stakeholder is attempting to solve. The nonanalyst's requested solution is "the ask," but the real underlying challenge that has motivated the request (the ask behind the ask) is what the analyst must understand. By doing so, the analyst can use their expertise to assess the challenge and craft an appropriate solution.

I recently witnessed a well-intentioned sales leader approach an analyst with a lengthy data request. The sales leader had just received a call from a client during which the client shared plans for a new campaign to take advantage of an unexpected spike in consumer demand.

"The client needs help with their approach to consumer targeting," the sales leader stated, "so there's some data I'd like you to pull." Without any hesitation, the sales leader launched into a review of the long list of data they had hastily scribbled on a notepad. At that point, the analyst interjected with one simple question:

"What are we trying to solve?"

Those six simple words stopped the sales leader in their tracks. What followed was a thoughtful and thorough discussion of the client's market position, the difficulties they faced, and the opportunities before them. This led the sales leader and the analyst to a concise articulation of the challenge facing the planned campaign. In a few minutes, the analyst successfully guided the sales leader to an entirely different analysis path using a different collection of data that would produce a different set of outcomes. These outcomes would provide a clearer and actionable solution to the client's true challenge. When the analyst finished describing their proposed approach, the sales leader stood in amazement.

"I didn't know we could do that," the sales leader said gleefully.

An excited discussion of reasonable turnaround times and deliverables followed. The analyst then set off to do the work secure in the knowledge that they were solving the client's true challenge while working against a set of reasonable expectations.

That the sales leader didn't know the analyst's proposed solution was a possibility illustrates a harmonious system working exactly as it should. In this (as well as any) scenario, the sales leader cannot and should not be expected to know the best way for data to be collected, analyzed, and presented. Such understanding is the responsibility of the analyst and is precisely the reason why the analyst who dutifully rushes off to fulfill orders from nonanalyst stakeholders won't be successful.

By getting to the ask behind the ask, this analyst applied their expertise in data analytics to the client's challenge rather than pursuing the request of a nonanalyst stakeholder. More importantly, the analyst saved the team several rounds of back-and-forth with clients and countless hours of pointless (and, most likely, ultimately rejected) analysis.

In Summary: Navigating to Your Big Idea

Getting to a big idea is hard but following a process map enables analysts to be effective and efficient. That process involves four steps: plan, collect, analyze, and report. We'll use this process to guide us through the remainder of this book. We'll look at the steps in-depth so that analysts can understand them and know how to apply them. As we do, keep in mind how important it is for analysts to get to what we call "the ask behind the ask" from their stakeholders. Only in this way will the analyst ensure the open and clear communication required for a successful analytics journey.

In the next lesson, we'll focus on the planning phase and how to set objectives for analysis.

Planning for Your Analytics Expedition

Five things discussed in this lesson:

- Identifying an advertiser's Marketing Objective is critical for successful analysis, but this process is frequently poorly executed and often goes awry
- Analysts can choose from six primary Marketing Objectives when planning digital marketing analytics
- Finding your Marketing Objective is simple when using the CDJ and asking key questions
- Prioritizing objectives is an important exercise, as the success of an analysis hinges on the objective's clarity and effect
- Design a plan for analysis using a modified scientific research approach

During a November 1957 speech, Dwight Eisenhower famously told military personnel, "Plans are worthless, but planning is everything."[105] This motto applies nicely to how analysts should think about their approaches to developing plans for analysis projects.

The uncertainty that analysts face when starting their journeys means that flexibility is crucial. All too frequently, data deemed necessary is unavailable, errors render data unreliable, or patterns revealed in data contradict the stories analysts believed. Analysts must modify their plans quickly

---

[105] Dwight D. Eisenhower, Remarks at the National Defense Executive Reserve Conference, The American Presidency Project (November 14, 1957).

to keep analyses on track in these situations. The dynamic and shifting nature of the analysis journey means that analysts' carefully laid plans can appear worthless.

The planning process yields insight into an organization's needs, the stakeholders invested (or not invested) in the analysis, and other elements that affect projects and can be taken as important truths. Analysts can use these as "North Stars" to anchor their analyses and guide projects through inevitable twists and turns. One such truth is the objective that acts as a fixed point in the distance for analysts and their analysis journeys. The rigor needed to identify that objective successfully – in Eisenhower's perspective, the "planning" – can keep analysts centered, regardless of how thoroughly they're forced to abandon elements of their plans.

When Objective-Setting Goes Awry

Marketing tends to go sideways for a few recognizable reasons. Too much complexity in a brand's marketing leads to confusing messages that make it difficult for consumers to understand how a product will fulfill their needs. At the other end of the spectrum, marketing without refinement leads to broad messages that lack the punch needed to pierce the consumer's consciousness. More often than not, such debilitating errors enter the marketing process at the early stages. While errors are typically small at the time of introduction, they infect other elements of an analyst's work, rendering a campaign ineffective.

One of the most damaging errors analysts make happens at one of the earliest stages: establishing an objective improperly. Should that objective be off in some way, the effect on the work it guides will ripple through every step. In my experience, three common errors occur during the critical stage of objective setting that an analyst must fight to avoid:

1. Making the objective too broad
2. Confusing an objective with a result
3. Making the objective too complex

Let's take a deeper look at each of these errors and how to correct them through proper objective setting.

Breadth

Focus when setting objectives is critical for success. A well-defined, narrow objective is more attainable than one spanning multiple outcomes. Work hard upfront to ensure the objective is singular. One easy way to make sure this happens is by forbidding the use of the word "and" in the documented objective. For example, the broad objective "build awareness for our new product AND influence consumers to choose our new product" becomes two separate, singular objectives (i.e., "(1) Build awareness for our new product," and "(2) Influence consumers to choose our new product") that must be tackled by two separate analysis paths.

Objectives Versus Results

Too often, analysts incorrectly identify objectives as results. No marketing analysis can yield an insight for an advertiser to "drive sales." Sales are not an objective, but rather the result an advertiser realizes when achieving a different objective. For example, an advertiser whose sales suffer from a lack of awareness must focus on increasing exposure. Therefore, "building awareness" is the appropriate objective that will ultimately "drive sales." In the next section of this lesson, we'll see that the objectives marketing analysis should seek to improve are what we'll call "Marketing Objectives" while sales, volume, and profit are "Business Objectives" that should be viewed as results.

Complexity

When attempting to rally an organization behind an objective, message clarity and conciseness are critical. Likewise, straightforward messages are important when centering stakeholders on the objective of an analysis. To do this, analysts must simplify their approaches to objective setting.

Analysts can feel confident in the soundness of their objectives when selecting from one of six well-known and tested Marketing Objectives.

The Six Marketing Objectives

I submit that six Marketing Objectives can serve as the focus for analysis and the objective of any campaign. Those six objectives are: stimulate demand, build awareness, influence consideration, improve the sales processes, reposition the brand, and increase loyalty.

The six Marketing Objectives simplify the underlying complex systems of consumer/brand connections. They're true objectives that marketing can influence (i.e., they aren't results but are marketing levers that will end in results), and – most importantly – they're mutually exclusive from one another. Marketing Objectives, and their relative position to other categories of important objectives, are presented here in Figure 4.4:

Figure 4.4: A taxonomy of objectives

BUSINESS OBJECTIVES					
Revenue		Volume		Profit	
Increase the amount of money the business brings in		Increase the units sold, number of leads, or capacity of the business		Increase the amount of money the business has after costs	
MARKETING OBJECTIVES					
Stimulate demand	Build awareness	Influence consideration	Improve sales experience	Reposition the brand	Increase loyalty
MEDIA OBJECTIVES					
Reach and frequency		Engagement		Conversions	
CAMPAIGN OBJECTIVES					
Site visits / clicks	Views	View-through rate	Click-through rate	Cost per click	Etc.

The objectives presented in this visual are defined as follows:

→ **Business Objectives** – Broad C-level goals the company wants to achieve, stated in the company's own language and easily measurable. These objectives are the result of the company achieving its Marketing Objectives.

→ **Marketing Objectives** – Measurable department-level goals that support Business Objectives and can be influenced by marketing. Marketing Objectives are the result of the company achieving its Media Objectives.

→ **Media Objectives** – Broad goals affected by various media executions and tactics employed to present consumers with the brand's messages. Media Objectives are reached when Campaign Objectives are successful.

→ **Campaign objectives** – Key performance indicators (KPIs) through which campaign success is measured.

The most important layer of objectives for marketing analysts to understand is the line of Marketing Objectives. These objectives will result in revenue, volume, or profit growth that's critical to business performance. In addition, these are the highest level of objectives that marketing performance can influence. As such, the analyst can most affect the organization by conducting analysis to solve challenges to Marketing Objectives.

There are a few important things to note about the taxonomy of objectives related to the interplay between lines of objectives and their relevance.

First, this visual isn't intended to be read in a vertically linear, one-to-one fashion. In other words, while each layer of objective drives the layer above (and is, in turn, driven by the collection of objectives layered below) nearly any objective on a line can be used to stimulate one of the objectives above. Only the company's unique mix of resources, market opportunities, and competitive dynamics will determine which lower-level objective will move an objective above. For example, while increasing reach and frequency may be the unlock to build awareness for one company, reach and frequency could help another company realize success needed to influence consideration.

Second, an advertiser will most likely face multiple problems across any of these objectives. Advertisers that don't need to build more awareness, influence consideration more effectively, and increase loyalty are rare. Nearly every marketing executive I've met would love to improve all six Marketing Objectives simultaneously. As discussed earlier in this lesson, however, the analyst must focus their analysis to deliver insights related one Marketing Objective at a time.

Let's take a deeper look at each of the six Marketing Objectives now.

Stimulating Demand

Stimulating demand is a curious Marketing Objective. At its root is the idea of convincing consumers they need an advertiser's product. Of course, this idea is not unfamiliar to advertisers. Every brand in the world recognizes the need for consumer demand. The challenging thing about pursuing this objective lies in the need for one critical element: authenticity.

Consumers - and especially consumers of today, with their limitless access to information - can sense inauthentic brand messages from miles away. A brand that simply calls, "Please! Buy my product!" to the market will undoubtedly face consumer apathy or, even worse, distrust. After all, as we've seen in today's consumer/brand relationship, it's the brand that must fit in the consumer's life - not the other way around. Consumers have too many choices for an inauthentic message to drive demand. Brands can use marketing, however, to effectively stimulate demand for their products in a few limited ways.

One way a brand can achieve this Marketing Objective is by providing clarity around how the product is used or the need it fulfills. If consumers are confused about the function or purpose of a product, demand for that product will be hard to earn. By clearing up this confusion - typically through demonstration – the advertiser can reveal the ability of the product to satisfy a need when, often, the consumer didn't know they had that need. When I think of brands that must stimulate demand by offering more clarity around use, myriad products in infomercials (particularly those with the most bizarre appearance) come to mind.

Figure 4.5: I have only one question about the Naväge nose cleaning machine: Why?

A second way brands can stimulate demand is through a high-risk and (sometimes) high-reward approach: creating scarcity. By announcing a dwindling supply of products, brands can try to stimulate demand by effectively manipulating market forces. This approach can have disastrous results for a brand when the message is viewed as a spurious attempt to "trick" consumers. In contrast, creating scarcity can be effective with consumers who are aware of the products and demonstrated affinity for them previously. An example of a brand that successfully stimulated demand through marketing scarcity is Knob Creek's mid-2009 "Thanks for Nothing" campaign.

Figure 4.6: Knob Creek's expertly crafted campaign to stimulate demand

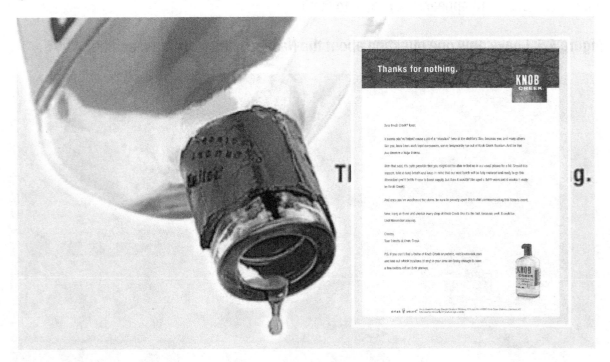

Bill Newlands, president of Knob Creek owner Beam Global, discussed the predicament that led Knob Creek to advertise its low product stock at the time of the campaign's launch. Knob Creek bourbon must age nine years to produce a sufficiently full-bodied taste, Newlands explained. Unfortunately, the company did a poor job of predicting supply in 2000. More accurately, the company hadn't seen the signs of the global economic meltdown that struck in the latter half of the 2000's first decade. The hard times consumers experienced drove unexpected "double-digit growth" for Knob Creek.[106] Anyone who works in the spirit category knows that when times are tough, sales of spirits soar.

Knob Creek ran full-page newspaper advertisements apologizing to its brand devotees, mailed empty bottles to journalists, and even handed out T-shirts bemoaning the "drought of 2009." It also secured demand for the product with a significant portion of its base for years to come.

Stimulating demand is a well-known objective that can be measured easily through market share and rates of sale. In fact, this Marketing Objective is so obviously woven into the fabric of marketing, there's no need to continue its discussion. For the rest of this book, we'll focus on the five remaining Marketing Objectives outlined below.

Building Awareness

Awareness is the percentage of consumers who are familiar with an advertiser's brand or product. Awareness can be measured by the percent of the total consumer population that claims familiarity with the item being measured or against a more specific target population (e.g., awareness among demographic groups like "women 35+" or psychographic groups like "frequent gamers"). General awareness is nice to have, but awareness among key consumer groups is always more important.

There can also be degrees of awareness. "Aided awareness" means the percent of consumers who recognize an advertiser's brand or product when they see or hear either name. "Unaided awareness" means consumers voluntarily mention the brand or product when prompted by a generic question such as, "What brands of automobile have you heard of?" Unaided awareness clearly reveals a deeper consumer/brand connection than aided awareness.

---

[106] Andrew Clark, "Knob Creek Runs Dry," *Guardian* (July 20, 2009).

Consumer surveys are typically the best way to gauge awareness. Survey measurement is particularly helpful for brands that launch new brands, subbrands, products, or features. Tracking awareness can help advertisers optimize their approaches to targeting midcampaign toward consumer groups (e.g., demographics) with the highest awareness lifts.

Influencing Consideration

Consideration is the percentage of consumers who have a positive perception of an advertiser's brand or product. Like awareness, consideration can be measured in terms of the general population or against specific segments of the consumer base. It can also be measured in an aided way ("Which of the following products would you consider purchasing?") or in an unaided way ("Which automobile brands would you consider purchasing?"). Consideration goes beyond awareness to measure consumers who are more than simply aware of the brand or product: They would purchase the item or would consider buying it. Consideration implies a deeper consumer/brand relationship than simple awareness.

To that end, consumers have several layers of consideration. Each represents a different degree of affinity for the brand or product being measured. Basic consideration ("Would you consider buying this product?") indicates the lowest level of consumer commitment to the brand. Favorability ("Which athletic shoe brand do you like most?" – also known as "preference") implies greater brand affinity. Purchase intent ("The next time you buy a personal computer, which brand are you most likely to buy?") measures the deepest degree of the consumer/brand relationship.

Improving the Sales Process

The sales process occurs when a consumer exchanges cash for an item. This can be seen clearly in a digital sense as the online checkout steps that follow placing an item in a digital shopping cart. Offline, the definition of the sales process can blur the lines between improving the sales process and the previous Marketing Objective of influencing consideration. Sales associates in many retail settings are now able to discuss product benefits, close sales, (i.e., influencing consideration) and check out consumers through the use of handheld point-of-sale (POS) systems (i.e., the sales process). Visiting an Apple Store anywhere will bring this concept to life, as Apple has been outfitting sales associates with handheld checkout devices for years.

To keep the Marketing Objectives we're discussing clear and mutually exclusive, we'll define the offline sales process to include only the exchange of money. In other words, from the moment a consumer readies a credit card or other form of payment (e.g., entering a checkout line).

Assessing the sales process is a study in measuring efficiency. In the online sense, cart abandonment rate (i.e., the percent of consumers who place items in their digital shopping carts, but then remove the items or cancel the sales process before completion) is an insightful way for a brand to reveal challenges in its sales process. Hidden delivery fees, exorbitant taxes, and the inability for the company to deliver the product by the time a consumer needs it are all reasons why a brand's sales process can be disrupted. Other challenges, such as confusing or frustrating checkout steps, can also affect a brand's sales process.

Repositioning the Brand

Repositioning the brand is a relevant Marketing Objective when a brand fails to live up to the expectations its advertising sets. Infrequently, repositioning the brand can be an important pursuit when the product provides an unexpected benefit. For example, Pabst Blue Ribbon's sudden and dramatic popularity with the hipster crowd in the 2000s may have been unexpected among the members of PBR's marketing team, but the pivot revived a brand that had reached an all-time low in 2001.

Postpurchase consumer response provides the best insight into the need for repositioning and is trackable through consumer surveys and product return rates.

In rare cases where brands or products have caused harm and the existing brand positioning is no longer viable, repositioning the brand can be worthwhile. Often, it's the only option available without abandoning the brand. Following the Valdez oil spill in Prince William Sound, Alaska, on March 24, 1989, Exxon, the tanker's owner, had no choice but to reposition its brand in a way that demonstrated the company's care and consideration for the environment and sustainable energy practices.

Growing Loyalty

Consumer loyalty for a brand or product is a fundamental component of a brand's success. Measures of loyalty can range from the simple (e.g., the percent of people who own your product and buy that product again, or repeat purchase rate) to the sophisticated (e.g., the highly tuned and complex calculations of lifetime customer values) to the apparent (e.g., social media mentions from people who experience the brand or product). Assessing loyalty for a brand seeks to quantify brand advocacy: the all-important, yet elusive, support for a brand that turns product owners into authentic word-of-mouth advertisements.

Determining Your Marketing Objective

How can analysts determine whether their organizations struggle with one of the Marketing Objectives described above? Some simple questions and a bit of analysis will reveal relevant and irrelevant objectives.

Figure 4.7: Questions to help determine your Marketing Objective

Build Awareness	Influence Consideration	Improve the Sales Process	Reposition the Brand	Increase Loyalty
Do consumer recognize and recall my brand?	Do my products satisfy consumers' needs?	Do my point-of-sale efforts result in wins for my brand?	Do the experiences I deliver fulfill customer expectations?	Do customers advocate for my brand?
Asking whether consumers are aware of the brand or product will quantify the need for greater awareness.	If the products do not, consumers will choose competitors' items, revealing the need to influence consideration.	Leaks in the sales process (e.g., cart abandonment) point to a need for improvement.	Unmet expectations can lead to poor customer experience and a need to reposition the brand.	Customer advocate for a brand will reveal whether a brand can be satisfied with its level of loyalty.

Do You Need More Awareness?

Effectively, the awareness a brand or product earns is reflected in the percentage of consumers who place that item on their Initial Consideration Set when the need is triggered. Asking whether consumers are aware of the brand or product will quantify the need for greater awareness.

The brand can approach these questions by collecting data from a variety of sources:

→ Aggregated consumer search trends from Google Trends or other search trend tools

→ Market share data from industry groups, investor services, and market research companies

→ Product and brand awareness data from voice of the consumer survey tools

→ Social media mentions from social listening or social media platform tools

Do You Need to Better Influence Consumers?

For influence and consideration, analysts should investigate whether a brands' products satisfy consumers' needs. If the products don't, this means consumers are choosing competitors' products, revealing the need to better influence consideration. The analysis of nuanced data, typically collected through market surveys, can point to required solutions. These solutions can include more clear communication of product benefits, better understanding of consumers' needs, and a stronger "challenger brand" position to steal market share away from a dominant brand in the category (think of the "Pepsi Challenge" head-to-head taste choice affront to market leader Coke).

The assessment of a brand's need to influence consumers comes down to measuring shoppers who experience the brand during the active evaluation step of their decision journeys. The brand can approach these questions by collecting data from a variety of sources:

→ A/B testing data to provide insight into consumer preferences from A/B testing or CRO tools
→ Clickstream analysis (focused on how consumers navigate a website to obtain insight into key content as well as content deemed less valuable) from the advertiser's website analytics or clickstream analysis tool
→ Consumer needs data from voice of the consumer survey tools
→ Product and brand consideration, favorability, and purchase intent data from voice of the consumer survey tools
→ Social media sentiment data related to a brand from social listening, content analysis, or social media platform tools

Do Your Sales Efforts Help or Hinder?

For the Marketing Objective, "Improve Sales Experience," analysts must focus on the Moment of Purchase by investigating the sales process for leaks. As mentioned earlier in this lesson, cart abandonment rate is an effective way to quantify the need for changes to a brand's online sales process. In-store customer surveys, observing consumers on their shopping trips (i.e., shop-alongs), and consumer focus groups are among the best ways to assess the efficiency and effectiveness of offline sales processes.

The brand can approach these questions by collecting data from a variety of sources:

→ A/B testing data to provide insight into the effectiveness of various versions of checkout process designs (e.g., messaging, number of steps, page layout, etc.) from A/B testing or CRO tools

→ Checkout process data (e.g., cart abandonment data) from the advertiser's e-commerce system or e-commerce partner

→ Checkout satisfaction survey response data for consumers who buy the products and those who don't using voice of the consumer survey tools

→ Clickstream analysis (focused on experiences of consumers who convert and consumers who don't convert) from the advertiser's website analytics or clickstream analysis tool

→ In-store customer surveys, shop-alongs, and focus group data for offline Moment of Purchase insights

Do You Deliver on Expectations You've Set?

After consumers make their purchases, follow-up is typically the best way to provide the truest view into a need for repositioning the brand. Tracking product returns, monitoring social media, and other measures can also show how well a brand delivered on the expectations set during the decision journey.

The brand can approach these questions by collecting data from a variety of sources during the Postpurchase Experience:

→ Customer satisfaction survey response data for consumers who buy the products using voice of the consumer survey tools

→ Net promoter score (NPS) data from NPS partner or market research companies

→ Product return/refund data from the advertiser's internal systems or an e-commerce partner

→ Social media sentiment data related to an advertiser's products (focused on consumer sentiment of posts that mention the products, implying they own the products or have experience with them) from social listening, content analysis, or social media platforms tools

→ Other data collected related to the customer's response to an advertiser's products (e.g., customer service representative and help desk phone logs)

Do Customers Advocate for Your Brand?

Investigating consumers who advocate for a brand will reveal whether a brand can be satisfied with its level of loyalty. Advocacy quantified through repeat purchase rates, positive social media mentions, and other means can help analysts assess whether the Marketing Objective, "grow loyalty," represents a need.

The brand can approach these questions using many of the same data and sources collected to assess the Postpurchase Experience:

→ Customer satisfaction survey response data from surveys sent to consumers who buy the products using voice of the consumer survey tools

→ Social media sentiment data related to an advertiser's products (again, product-level posts imply consumers own the products or have experience with them) from social listening, content analysis, or social media platform tools

→ NPS data from an NPS partner or market research companies

→ Repeat purchase rate from the advertiser's internal systems or a CRM partner

Prioritizing Objectives

As mentioned previously, most advertisers will have needs across many of these Marketing Objectives. Since we must focus on a single Marketing Objective, it's imperative that we prioritize a brand's relevant Marketing Objectives. An analyst must identify where need exists and find the Marketing Objective that will have the greatest effect on brand performance. One way to do this involves McKinsey's CDJ framework.

The questions we've discussed around the five critical Marketing Objectives layer in well to the CDJ. Brand awareness fits with the Initial Consideration Set. The need to influence consideration can be assessed during the CDJ's Active Evaluation step. The sales process aligns with the Moment of Purchase, just as the need for repositioning ties to the Postpurchase Experience, and the need to increase loyalty is attached to the durability of a brand's Loyalty Loop. A simple econometric model that quantifies the number of consumers at each step will quickly point to areas of critical need (as well as those of less-pressing concern).

Assigning values to each CDJ step allows the analyst to modify inputs at each step to calculate the overall effect of that Marketing Objective. For example, if aware consumers place a brand on their Initial Consideration Set following a trigger, analysts can make assumptions about the percent of consumers who will purchase the product for a certain price. Analysts can, therefore, quantify the value of awareness. Testing different assumption values (i.e., conducting sensitivity analysis) will reveal the incremental effect of driving awareness. Analysts can perform similar analyses at each step of the CDJ. Comparisons of those model outputs across the CDJ steps, informed by the brand's appetite and ability to achieve the assumed levels of success, help to identify the cost/benefit of each Marketing Objective.

Building an Analysis Plan around Your Objective

With the Marketing Objective in hand, the final phase in the plan step is to create a clear, concise document that can help guide analysis journeys. The document format matters little. Analysts should adopt the visual framework that works best for them. However, it's important that the document:

→ **Clearly identifies the Marketing Objective** – This "North Star" truth will guide the analysis and must be succinct in the analysis plan.

→ **Details the connection between the Marketing Objective and key questions** – Identifying key questions that will logically advance the brand toward its Marketing Objective when answered is critical. These questions should be singular (i.e., eliminate the word "and" from all key questions) and distinct from one another.

→ **Clearly identifies the data to be collected and the source of those data** – While the data and sources aren't foolproof, setting them out as areas for exploration is important so that analysts use their time efficiently.

In my experience, designing a plan in a pyramid layout works best to meet these criteria, while allowing for quick modifications to plan elements later on. Analysts can ensure the key questions they pursue explore the full gamut of business challenges tied to their objectives by designing three types of questions: What? why? and how?

Answers to "what" questions (e.g., "What is our brand's current level of unaided awareness?") will typically provide straightforward descriptive facts that can set the foundation of understanding an analyst needs to begin a more robust analysis. An analyst can get to the heart of the matter by answering a "why" question (e.g., "Why did some of our marketing efforts drive awareness while others didn't?") that provides the context, texture, and nuance required of a deeper analysis. Finally, solutions to "how" questions (e.g., "How can our marketing efforts affect awareness levels over the next 12 months?") point to actions required to achieve the chosen objective.

Figure 4.8: The pyramid layout for an analysis plan

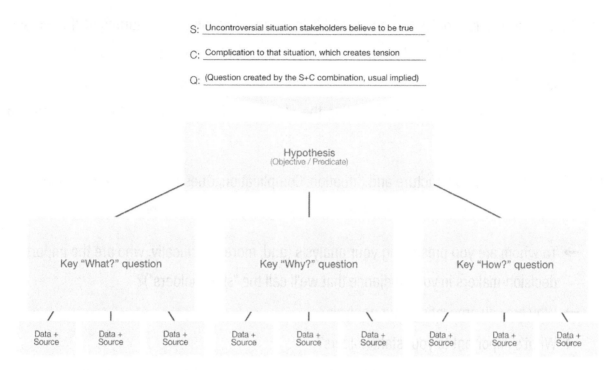

This line of investigation is rooted in the principle commonly known as "The Five W's and How." The Five W's and How is the idea that a complete report must provide answers to questions that start with the interrogative words, who? what? when? where? why? and how? The principle is commonly applied in journalism, law enforcement investigations, and research. The origin of the Five W's and How has been tied to Aristotle's *Nicomachean Ethics*.[107]

For marketing analysis, analysts should provide answers to what? why? and how? questions at a minimum to ensure a complete story. Analysts can expand their analyses to report on the other questions identified in the principle, as needed.

---

[107] Michael C. Sloan, "Aristotle's Nicomachean Ethics as the Original Locus for the Septem Circumstantiae," *Classical Philology* (2010).

Constructing a plan for analysis in a pyramid layout can be as simple as starting at the top and working your way down. You will, however, find that approach a difficult way to build your plan. This is particularly true when facing a complex planning task. A more effective approach involves beginning with what is known and building the plan from that foundation through a series of nonlinear steps.

After drawing a pyramid structure and Situation, Complication, Question (SCQ) introduction lines, take a step back and look at the broad context of your analysis project. Identify:

→ To whom are you presenting your analysis (and, more specifically, who are the important decision-makers in your audience that we'll call the "stakeholders")?

→ Why are you presenting your analysis?

→ What's important to your stakeholders?

→ What level of detail is required to convince your stakeholders of your analysis output?

With this context understood, you can begin drafting your plan. *Phase One* has four steps. Follow these key tasks and use the supporting materials provided.

Step 1: Detail your Main Message hypothesis

Place a short phrase topic for your analysis in your pyramid's Main Message box. This is your "Subject" and the primary area you'll investigate during your project. This is typically the issue you're investigating. Examples of reasonable Subjects marketing analysts take on include "operational inefficiencies," "new product launches" and digital media ROI." The fact that you usually get this information at the beginning of the project doesn't eliminate the need to challenge it. You must ensure that you can point to empirical data that supports the Subject. If you can't find such evidence or you find evidence that contradicts the provided Subject, your analysis will only be successful if you explore the new competing Subject. Build consensus by discussing possible Subjects for your analysis with stakeholders and landing on one that has the most support.[108]

After you've confirmed the Subject, articulate the question you're answering in your stakeholders' minds about that Subject and place it in the "Q" line of your introduction (this is the "Question"). Questions marketing analysts often pursue include:

→ How can we eliminate operational inefficiencies?

→ What ROI have we earned from digital media investments?

→ What's the most profitable market for our new product launch?

As with the Subject, the question you're answering with your analysis is the one stakeholders have presented to you or hired you to investigate. And just as you mustn't blindly accept the Subject your stakeholders provided, you must ensure that the question your analysis will answer is the right one. The criticality of getting the question right can't be understated. Far too often, analysts rush off to answer questions they've been tasked with investigating only to find – after expending too much time and energy – that the answers offer organizations little benefit or don't address their challenges. For more on this idea, see "The Ask Behind the Ask" in Part 4, Lesson 1.

To complete this first step, form a hypothesis that will answer the Question to complete the Main Message box. You can often do this by adding a recommended action to your Subject. For example, say the Subject is "new product launch" and the Question you've identified is "How can we ensure our new product launch is a success?" In this case, a potential Main Message could be "Targeting early technology adopters will lead to a successful new product launch." Your Main Message

---

[108] Marketing Objectives usually make great Subjects. An econometric model that quantifies the effect of each marketing objective on a business goal (such as growing revenue; increasing the units sold, number of leads, or volume; or increasing profit) is an excellent approach for directing stakeholders to meaningful marketing objectives. You could construct such a model for this case study by mapping information to a consumer journey framework, like McKinsey & Co.'s Consumer Decision Journey, and a few key assumptions (e.g., the company's profit margin, number of units sold, etc.).

should read like a recommendation. It's your best guess at the answer to the question your analysis is addressing. But note, too, that this hypothesis is just that – a hypothesis – and you'll have the opportunity to test and refine it as you begin collecting and analyzing data.

The primary purpose of Step 1 is to make sure you know the Question you're trying to answer. Once you have the Question right, everything else will fall into place easily.

Step 2: Add context to your Main Message

Your next task is to add two important ideas that set the frame for your Main Message: the Situation and the Complication. The Situation is an uncontroversial statement of known and accepted fact because your stakeholders know it to be true or because it's historically accurate and easily checkable. The Complication is a threat or opportunity that's creating tension in that Situation. The combination of Situation and Complication is what triggers the Question in your stakeholders' minds. Furthermore, the introduction of the Complication in the Situation compels your stakeholders to seek your help through analysis.

To see these concepts come to life, consider the predicament of a traditional consumer packaged goods (CPG) company whose cereal brands have struggled to be seen by younger consumers as anything beyond "what their parents eat for breakfast." The Situation could be: "Our cereal brand is a cherished breakfast staple for older consumers." The obvious Complication, then, would be: "Our cereal brand has struggled to connect with younger consumers." The combination of this Situation and Complication would lead directly to the Question that would likely be on the executive team's mind at our fictional traditional CPG company: "What can our brand do to build more equity with younger consumers?" That Question, as discussed in the previous step, is what you're there to answer, and your Main Message is your hypothesized answer to that Question when you're building your plan.

After writing down your SCQ introduction, check its veracity by reviewing the following questions:

→ Do your stakeholders accept the Situation? Avoid starting your story with a provocative statement that your audience may respond to with disbelief or suspicion. Eliciting these emotions will put you at a disadvantage.

→ Does the Complication immediately raise the Question? If not, refine your Complication to make sure it leads to your question. If you're sure that the Complication is correct, but doesn't lead to the Question you've outlined in your plan, return to Step 1. Next, refine the Question to ensure your analysis is seeking the right solution for your stakeholders.

→ Does the Situation, Complication, Question, and Main Message present an easy-to-follow, compelling story? If not, refine them until you achieve a tight, logical flow in your SCQ introduction and recommendation.

With a logical introduction and hypothesis documented, your high-level story is in place. Your next step is to plan for the supporting points that will complete your narrative.

Step 3: Document the 'Key Line'

Your next step is to determine the Key Questions stakeholders would expect you to answer after hearing your Main Message. This collection of Key Questions is called the "Key Line" and represents the questions you'll investigate through data collection and analysis. The answers you find to these questions are the statements of fact you must confidently present to stakeholders when your analysis is complete in support of your Main Message. To that end, you must resolve the Key Line to test the hypothesis you detailed. Typically, analysts can ensure the questions they pursue explore the full gamut of business challenges by designing three types of questions: What? Why? and How?

Answers to "what" questions (e.g., "What's our brand's current level of unaided awareness?") provide straightforward descriptive facts that can set the foundation of understanding needed to begin a more robust analysis. An analyst can get to the heart of the matter by answering a "why" question (e.g., "Why did some of our marketing efforts drive awareness while others didn't?") that provides the context, texture, and nuance required of a deeper analysis. Finally, solutions to "how" questions (e.g., "How can our marketing efforts affect awareness levels over the next 12 months?") point to actions required to achieve the chosen objective.

This line of investigation is rooted in the principle commonly known as "The Five W's and How." The Five W's and How is the idea that a complete report must provide answers to questions that start with the interrogative words, who? what? when? where? why? and how? The principle is commonly applied in journalism, law enforcement investigations, and research. The origin of the Five W's and How has been tied to Aristotle's *Nicomachean Ethics*.[109] For marketing analysis, it isn't necessary to answer every question. Often, answers to some questions are too obvious or irrelevant to be detailed in your story. Analysts should provide answers to what? why? and how? questions at a minimum to ensure a complete story. Analysts can expand their analyses to report on the other questions they identified in the principle, as needed.

Getting to the "right" questions in the Key Line involves more art than science. In my experience, the best way analysts can identify a solid Key Line is by placing themselves in their stakeholders' shoes. What questions would your stakeholders expect you to answer once they hear your Main Message? Draw these critical questions from your stakeholders as you discuss the project with them. Listen carefully for stakeholders' areas of concern during your discussions or pull ideas from them by asking broad, open questions (e.g., "What do you believe are the biggest challenges to [insert your Subject here]?").

Regardless of the questions you choose, an important guiding principle for your Key Questions is that they're "MECE." MECE stands for Mutually Exclusive, Collectively Exhaustive and pronounced like "meese" (rhymes with "geese"). This is a powerful concept Barbara Minto introduced in 1987.

---

[109] Sloan, "Aristotle's Nicomachean Ethics."

Mutually Exclusive means there's no overlap across the Key Questions you identify. Each is unique and explores a distinctive element of your Main Message. Collectively, Exhaustive means that no critical part of your Main Message is omitted. You're exploring everything your stakeholders would want to know when you're pursuing answers to your Key Questions.

A second important principle is that at some point, you reach a number of Key Questions that would overwhelm an audience and make it difficult for them to keep your ideas straight in their heads. Conventional wisdom argues that seven Key Questions is a maximum allowable number but, in my opinion, a story that contains as few as five separate ideas can overwhelm an audience. If the number of Key Questions is approaching this maximum, be absolutely sure that your Key Line is MECE. Often, combining and consolidating questions leads to a more concise and powerful story.

Once you form your Key Questions, place each unique Key Question in a box under the Main Message. Remember that at this point, you're still in planning mode and these questions are in no way final. The questions in your plan may evolve as you move through your analysis journey.

Step 4: Identify the supporting data

The final step in building your plan is to identify the data you need to collect for analysis. For each Key Question you've drafted, identify data that you'll need to investigate and a potential source for each data point. Keep in mind the following definitions:

→ **Data:** Metric, Key Performance Indicator (KPI), or measure that you'll collect and analyze.
→ **Source:** Place where each piece of data can be found, such as a database, survey, or report that houses the data.

The most important thing you must keep in mind at this step is to find data that will answer each Key Question. Identifying the right data and data source requires experience. The more you become familiar with data that's available to you, the easier it will become to assemble your list of ideal data quickly. But remember, this is simply a plan at this point. If the data you identify turns out to be unavailable or wrong, you can pivot to other more accessible or valuable data and update your plan.

At this stage, the data and data sources you identify shouldn't be constrained. In other words, this is a "blue sky" exercise, and you're constructing a data wish list. By not constraining your list with factors, such as cost of the data, the time you need to collect it, or current data-sharing agreements, you'll avoid an insidious bias that hinders analysis at the planning stage. Specifically, by identifying the data you *need* – not simply the data you *have* – you'll avoid accessibility bias (see "Countering Bias During Planning" below). As you collect data, you can always refine your data needs to work around constraints. Note that whenever constraints limit your data collection efforts or force you to settle on less-than-ideal proxy data, be sure to let stakeholders know, so that you can manage their expectations.

Countering Bias During Planning

Bias can hamper the planning phase severely. When bias is allowed to creep into the planning process, it can lead the analyst to waste time investigating the wrong set of questions and, more importantly, draw false conclusions. Analysts should be aware of two important biases: accessibility bias and anchoring bias.

Accessibility bias

People tend to make assumptions based on limited information and fail to seek information that's not already known. Analysts can protect against this bias by ensuring they look for the data they need – not simply the data they have. The simplest way for analysts to do that is to look objectively at the question the analysis is answering and compare the data included in the analysis with the data they'd collect in a perfect world. If the current dataset matches the ideal data (or if analysts find dependable proxies for the desired data) analysts can move content forward, knowing they've minimized accessibility bias.

An example of accessibility bias can be seen in a global research company's recent analysis. The company published an article in late 2019 that purported to validate the value of its new MTA model with a headline that boasted, "5 Game-Changing Facts That Prove The Value Of Multi-Touch Attribution." As discussed in Part 3 of this book, multitouch attribution models are under extreme stress from data privacy and cookie deletion policies that limit the consumer behavior data fueling their algorithms. These limits threaten the ability of MTAs to attribute value to media touch points accurately by forcing a heavy reliance on probabilistic models that are less precise than models that use more robust data. The proof points this company offered to validate its MTA, however, were five simple outputs from 109 datasets the company had analyzed using its MTA. Analysts at the company ignored the real question at play – do MTA models accurately attribute value? – and focused on an analysis of the data on hand. While that data may have resulted in interesting insights, it failed to produce the analysis that was really needed.

Anchoring bias

The questions analysts ask are often influenced in the direction of a relevant comparison value or "anchor" found in their experience. In this way, anchoring bias (also known as focalism) disrupts analysis by leading analysts on pursuits informed by their frame of reference, but not the data's full picture. The anecdote to anchoring bias is perspective. By broadening the aperture of the analysis, an analyst can introduce a wider set of comparisons that will challenge the original focal point. A more comprehensive set of data, competing perspectives from outsiders, or new comparisons will achieve this result.

A classic example of anchoring bias can be seen in Pepsi's battle to unseat market leader Coke in the late 1960s. Product analysts for Pepsi repeatedly tried to find a bottle design that would carry the recognition of Coke's iconic hourglass shape. Pepsi wasn't able to move out from Coke's shadow until 1970, when market research from Pepsi's then new marketing vice president, John Sculley (who would later be known for heading Apple), led to the design of the two-liter bottle. By shifting the question analysts pursued to what consumers wanted instead of what would best its largest competitor, Pepsi analysts shed their anchoring bias and successfully reframed their analysis.

In Summary: Planning for Your Analytics Expedition

Identifying an advertiser's Marketing Objective is critical for successful analysis, but this process is frequently poorly executed and often goes awry when complexity, breadth of scale, and confusion between "objectives" and "results" are introduced. By keeping things simple, an analyst can plan for a successful analysis by choosing from six primary Marketing Objectives when planning for analysis. Finding which Marketing Objectives are relevant for a brand is possible by using the CDJ and several key questions.

We saw that prioritizing objectives is an important exercise, as the success of an analysis hinges on the objective's clarity and impact. Analysts should use a modified scientific research approach, commonly known as the Five W's and How, to design analysis plans. Furthermore, analysts must diligently guard against anchoring bias to ensure they are asking the right questions as they set off on their analytics journey.

In the next lesson, we'll delve into the techniques analysts can use to collect data for analysis.

Collecting Data, Data Everywhere

Five things discussed in this lesson:

- Tying collected data to key questions – and to the identified Marketing Objective – is critical for successful analysis
- Data can come in many forms, including raw, processed, unstructured, and structured
- Analysts can use three techniques to collect data: accessing facilitated downloads, using APIs, and scraping the web
- Ensuring data quality requires understanding how bias enters the data and critical points of data handling that frequently lead to errors
- Tools help manage data, but each option has pros and cons

With a nod to *The Rime of the Ancient Mariner* by Samuel Taylor Coleridge[110] ("Water, water, every where, Nor any drop to drink."), marketers frequently bemoan the seas of data that surround them and the frustrating reality that insights are difficult to find: "Data, data everywhere, and not a drop of insight."

Thus far, we've seen the explosive growth of data in today's marketing landscape, the technical process of data collection, and how brands can use that data to make decisions. We'll get to the development of insights through analysis in the next lesson. For now, let's investigate an important

---

[110] Samuel Taylor Coleridge, *The Rime of the Ancient Mariner* (1834).

question: How do analysts get their hands on data? Data collection, which was once fraught with challenges, has become surprisingly effortless.

Before we dive into the data collection process, let's explore the kinds of data analysts should collect.

Unstructured Versus Structured Data

Marketing analysis data comes in two forms: unstructured and structured. Unstructured data doesn't come in a predefined, standardized format. It's usually text-heavy and might contain dates and numbers that don't fit a uniform description, as well as awkward (but increasingly important) data, such as images, sounds, and video.

It's estimated that unstructured data might account for 80 percent of all data in organizations.[111] Understanding unstructured data and how to unlock it is especially important. Collecting and cleaning unstructured data and extracting relevant information from it typically requires a tool (or combination of tools).

What does unstructured data look like? A sampling of Twitter activity gives a perfect example. Basic text, links, videos, and still images appear in tweets. Some tweets include hashtags that can be an important part of the text string. Other times, a tweet's content can appear haphazard and disorganized. Although Twitter confines tweets to a certain number of characters, data length isn't defined. That's what makes it unstructured.

---

[111] Christie Schneider, "The biggest data challenges that you might not even know you have" (May 25, 2016).

Figure 4.9: Unstructured data (and, to the author's point, too many #hashtags)

Mindi Rosser
Systemize Social Selling & Social Marketing Programs for B2B Companies on LinkedI…
now

This is an example of overusing #hashtags on #socialmedia.
#socialmediamarketing #socialselling #sales #marketing #b2bmarketing
#b2bsales #salestip #socialbusiness #socialspam #spamming #toomanyhashtags
#use4-5hashtagsNOTthismany

👍 Like   💬 Comment   ➤ Share

In contrast, structured data is neatly organized and conforms to a clear and consistent data format. Each column is well-defined. After seeing a data sample, an analyst knows the exact format and layout they can expect from the entire data table. Population statistics from the U.S. Census Bureau are structured data.

Figure 4.10: Structured data tables from the U.S. Census Bureau

State Population Estimates: April 1, 2000 to July 1, 2002					
State	**July 1, 2002 Population**	**July 1, 2001 Population**	**July 1, 2000 Population**	**April 1, 2000 Population**	**Census 2000 Population**
United States	288,368,698	285,317,559	282,224,348	281,422,509	281,421,906
Alabama	4,486,508	4,468,912	4,451,975	4,447,100	4,447,100
Alaska	643,786	633,630	627,697	626,931	626,932
Arizona	5,456,453	5,306,966	5,167,142	5,130,632	5,130,632
Arkansas	2,710,079	2,694,698	2,678,668	2,673,398	2,673,400
California	35,116,033	34,600,463	34,010,375	33,871,648	33,871,648
Colorado	4,506,542	4,430,989	4,326,758	4,301,331	4,301,261
Connecticut	3,460,503	3,434,602	3,411,956	3,405,565	3,405,565
Delaware	807,385	796,599	786,512	783,600	783,600

Although structured data comprises a relatively small portion of the data available today, its efficient manner makes structured data tables important for analysts.

Collecting Data

Analysts access data in three ways. We'll refer to these techniques as accessing facilitated download sites, using application programming interfaces (APIs), and scraping webpages.

Accessing Facilitated Download Sites

Through facilitated downloads, a data owner provides a place for others to visit and collect data. These are tightly managed data releases. Typically, a user interface – often called a graphical user interface (GUI) – acts as an access point to this data. When logins are required, access to the data can be monitored and managed, allowing the data owner to determine the level of access. In this technique, I'm including companies' systems that house proprietary data and allow analysts to access the information. For example, when analysts collect first-party sales data from corporate accounting systems, they do so through facilitated downloads. Similarly, accessing DMP-managed second- or third-party data is done through a facilitated DMP-designed download process.

Another example of a facilitated download is the way consumers can access U.S. Census Bureau data. As the principal agency of the U.S. Federal Statistical System responsible for producing data about the American people and economy, the U.S. Census Bureau built the Explore Census Data website (data.census.gov) to encourage access to this data. Analysts will find an easy-to-use and simply designed GUI that facilitates access to census data.

A data owner's facilitated download site doesn't always mean easy access. The Internet Movie Database (IMDb.com) has a facilitated download source, but it's difficult to locate. By navigating to datasets.imdbws.com analysts will find subsets of IMDb data that are available for customers' personal and noncommercial use in a tab-separated-value (TSV) format. The site lacks the clarity and elegance of other facilitated download sites, however.

We live in an era of such plentiful data that an analyst needs to do little more than sign up for a newsletter to earn tremendous amounts of information. For example, Kaggle (kaggle.com) boasts more than 19,000 public datasets to help analysts "conquer any analysis in no time."[112] Signing up for the Kaggle e-newsletter will deliver weekly, interesting, and new datasets that anyone can download from the Kaggle website. The launch of Google Dataset Search (datasetsearch.research.google.com) places almost 25 million datasets at the analyst's fingertips.

Accessing data from facilitated download sites should be the primary method for collecting data today.

Using APIs

A second approach for accessing data is using APIs. APIs let computers connect to other computers to complete machine-to-machine data transfers. An API brings Google Maps data to restaurant websites, weather data to news sites, and real-time financial market information to investment websites. Analysts must understand scripting language and how to collect access tokens API owners grant to build API connections. While accessing data directly via APIs can be valuable, the time required to build those connections often outweighs the benefits.

A number of data analysis tools have simplified API access for the analyst. Many tools described in Part 3 of this book, including Hootsuite and Searchvolume.io, collect second-party data through API connections to social media networks and other data sources. These tools feature easy-to-use GUIs where analysts input criteria for the data they want to collect (e.g., keywords, date ranges, etc.). The tool builds the API query based on the analyst's inputs, establishes the API connection and handles the necessary permissions/token requirements.

In this way, analysis tools simplify data collected through APIs.

---

[112] Kaggle.com website (2020).

A third way analysts can access data is through web scraping, also known as "screen scraping," "web data extraction," and "web harvesting." In the early days of the web, black hat analysts found and collected unique data treasures using web scraping. Open-source datasets and facilitated download sites have largely eliminated the need for web scraping, however.

In my opinion, analysts are rarely required to build web scrapers in R or Python, or use tools like Parsehub (parsehub.com) to scrape data from websites. First, the time it takes to construct the code or configure the web scraping tool can be prohibitive. Second, so much data is now available from data owners, who have created data-sharing processes, that the need for scraping has been greatly reduced. Finally, and perhaps most importantly, if data isn't available through a facilitated download site or an approved API, the owner likely doesn't want to provide access to it. In our current environment of heightened data privacy concerns, it's hard to think of reasons that justify the acquisition of data not intended to be collected.

For these reasons, analysts should think twice before heading down the web scraping path.

Ensuring Data Quality

Analysts must collect data in a way that ensures its quality. An analysis is only as good as the data that analysts collect. Errors are possible at several points in the data collection process. Understanding these points of "data danger" can help analysts avoid common errors and preserve data quality.

Questionnaire Bias

Questionnaire bias can creep in through the questions consumers answer, typically in surveys. Questionnaire bias leads respondents to a conclusion or influences their responses.

For example, a survey that asks, "What words would you use to describe your love of (brand X)?" implies consumers' experiences with the brand have been positive. Analysts can eliminate questionnaire bias by designing surveys that feature only neutral, unbiased questions.

Sampling Bias

Sampling bias, also known as "selection bias," is another way that data can be tainted. When collecting data from a sample of a population, insights from that data are applicable to the larger population only if the sample represents the whole. For example, soliciting opinions on a public official's performance from only high net worth citizens wouldn't provide insight into the views of the entire constituent population. When samples don't represent the whole, sampling bias prevents pattern extrapolation for the entire population. Analysts can reduce the effects of sampling bias by ensuring that surveyed consumers are drawn from all elements of the population, including obvious attributes, such as gender, age, and income, and those more difficult to discern, such as interests, attitudes, and preferences.

Data-Handling Errors

When analysts handle data, they can introduce errors that contaminate the collected information. Understanding these critical points can help analysts avoid data contamination:

→ **Data integration errors** – Joining tables can introduce errors. Data accidentally copied, deleted, or incorrectly matched are examples of integration errors that contaminate datasets and have limited value. Handling data carefully is the best way for analysts to minimize errors.

→ **Data input errors** – Errors typically occur when analysts collect data manually. They can transpose numerals, misread them, and enter them incorrectly. Enacting data quality control methods, such as normalizing data (i.e., allowing data inputters to select from a predefined set of inputs), conducting peer reviews, and using other techniques can help reduce input errors.

→ **Calculation errors** – When analysts use calculations to transform data, they can make common errors. Conducting peer reviews and testing calculations on small portions of the data before rolling out the entire dataset can help reduce such errors.

A Word on Data Tidying

Even if they were to eliminate all errors in their data, analysts must ensure the data is well-organized before they begin their analyses. Ensuring "tidy data" is a standard way to structure a dataset that makes it easy for an analyst or a computer to extract needed variables. Hadley Wickham, the chief scientist at RStudio, has defined Tidy Data as datasets that are arranged such that each variable is a column, each observation (or case) is a row and each value has its own cell.[113] Third-party data and data collected from public sources often lack the structure and organization to meet Wickham's definition.

Tools, such as Tableau Prep Builder (tableau.com/products/prep) and Open Refine (openrefine.org), can help analysts work with messy data by cleaning it, modifying it from one format to another, and transforming it into proper Tidy Data.

A Word on Managing Collected Data

As you move collected data into a management system, you'll have many tools from which to choose. Using Excel or Google Sheets to manage data that's lightweight or limited in scope and scale is acceptable. I've conducted many analyses using only Excel. But if a dataset requires greater statistical capabilities, you can look to a long and distinguished set of viable statistical packages, including SPSS, Minitab, and Stata. From software as a service to statistical packages

---

[113] Hadley Wickham, "Tidy Data," *Journal of Statistical Software* (February 20, 2013).

for the social sciences, a tool is available that will provide the capabilities you need to manage collected data and conduct your analyses.

Balance computational power with ease of use until you find a tool that meets your data and efficiency needs.

In Summary: Collecting Data, Data Everywhere

Linking a singular objective to data is critical for the collection to be conducted efficiently, regardless of whether those data are unstructured or structured. Analysts can use three techniques to collect data – accessing facilitated downloads, using APIs, and web scraping – although the time investment, privacy trappings, and other headaches associated with web scraping should dissuade analysts from pursuing that activity. Regardless of how analysts collect data, ensuring data quality means understanding how bias enters the data and critical points of data handling that frequently lead to errors. Once analysts collect data, they can manage it through a wide variety of tools, each with its pros and cons.

In the next lesson, we'll explore approaches to finding insights in data.

Analyzing for Insights

Five things discussed in this lesson:

- Analysts who seek to reduce large amounts of data into valuable insights will be more successful than those who mine data for rare and undiscovered jewels
- Analysts can choose from five analysis categories, each with its own degree of difficulty and depth
- Context can be the most important element an analyst provides
- Finding patterns in data requires analysts to create views into the data, often from multiple angles
- Even if an analyst's data is error-free, interpretation bias can skew results

We've reached the point where we can begin analyzing data. The proper approach to analysis is more like making diamonds – compressing all the things we learn into tight, consumable pieces of insight – than hunting for gold. Developing "diamond insights" forces analysts to delete extraneous facts that don't contribute to the story that emerges from the data. Such insights will be on display as we attempt to synthesize findings into a concise 60-second story that expresses the true heart of the matter and becomes the yardstick by which we'll measure the value of our analysis. As Fassnacht said, "If there is not a 60-second story, then there is no story at all."[114]

---

[114] Michael Fassnacht, "The Veil of Statistics," *MarketingGeek* (June 7, 2006).

Five primary categories of marketing data analysis reveal myriad insights. Each method features a varying level of sophistication and returns a corresponding depth of insight. Let's take a look at them.

Descriptive Analysis

The first category of marketing data analysis is descriptive analysis. This is typically the initial kind of analysis an analyst performs. The objective of descriptive analysis is to create a summary of the data to yield useful information and prepare the data for further analysis. For example, summing visitors by month from a dataset of daily visits is a way to gain a descriptive understanding of total monthly website visits. Calculating a mean, median, mode, count, and any other standard statistical values also fits this category of analysis. Descriptive analysis will yield clear answers to simple questions the analyst has asked but won't provide much more detail. Monthly website visitors can provide insight into traffic trends but answering more nuanced questions requires more sophisticated analysis techniques.

Inferential Analysis

Inferential analysis is a second category of data investigation. This approach features the use of a small set of data to infer something about a larger set. Inferential analysis is commonly the goal of analysis conducted on survey data that has been modeled to account for sampling bias (discussed in the previous lesson).

Exploratory Analysis

The third category of analysis is exploratory analysis. Typically, visual-based, exploratory analysis seeks to discover connections and patterns in data. This category might not always answer questions, but it reveals interesting connections that lead to deeper investigation and understanding. In this way, exploratory analysis can be a good early step on a broad dataset that points analysts to other techniques.

Causal Analysis

A fourth category of analysis is causal analysis. Causal analysis seeks to determine how the movement of one variable registers on other variables. Typically regarded as the gold standard for data analysis, causal analysis uses correlation and regression techniques to explore the relationship between attributes in a dataset.

Predictive Analysis

Predictive analysis is the final category of marketing data analysis. Closely linked to causal analysis, predictive analysis uses models to predict the future value of data attributes when market forces move some related data. Successful predictive analysis depends on the analyst having the right data and the right data quality. If the model includes data errors, the predictive value will be diminished. Predictive analysis is the most sophisticated method of modeling and analysis.

Media optimization modeling (e.g., MMMs), attribution modeling (e.g., MTAs) and other kinds of response modeling, such as consumer response modeling, are examples of this analysis category.

A Word on the Importance of Context

While conducting analyses, it's important to consider context. A number rarely means much on its own. Unlocking the meaning of a number requires a baseline – a comparative number so that the audience can evaluate the figure's value. Internal or external benchmarks, goals, and comparisons to previous performance add context and insights to data.

Finding Patterns in Data

Often, the best way to find patterns in data is to visualize that data. Visualizing data expresses stories that are unrecognizable when the data is in tabular form. We look for five data patterns.

Figure 4.11: Categories of patterns found in data

Change	Clustering	Relativity	Ranking	Correlation
Trend or instance of observations becoming different over time	Collection of data points with similar (or dissimilar) values	Observations considered in relation or in proportion to something else	Position in a scale of achievement or status	Mutual relationship or connection between two or more things

Change will present as either gradual change or sudden shifts. Clustering represents a collection of data points that are similar to one and yet different from others. Visual techniques that demonstrate relativity allow analysts to identify how two different data points relate to each other. Ranking determines what's at the top of the scale, what's at the scale's lowest point, and everything in between. Finally, how one set of data influences or affects another is revealed through correlation. Each of these patterns indicate the presence of powerful insights that can aid the analyst's story.

Certain visual techniques will reveal each pattern and others will obscure them. For example, a line graph will show change over time, but not ranking. A pie chart might be great at depicting relativity but won't reveal change. In other words, it's important to identify the appropriate visual to answer each specific question and ensure they're in alignment. Figure 4.12 can help guide the analyst to the right visual technique.

It's important to identify the techniques analysts use to answer questions and ensure they're in alignment. Figure 4.12 can help guide the analyst to the right visual technique.

Figure 4.12: Matching pursuit of patterns to visual forms

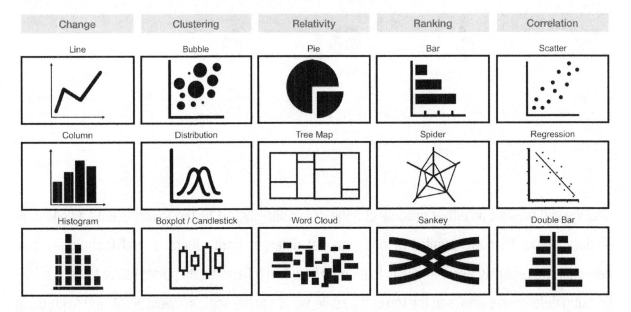

Analysts can use a variety of tools to apply each category of visual patterns to the data they're analyzing:

→ **Change** – Analysts can produce common visual forms, such as line charts and bar charts, using nearly any data analysis or visualization tool they choose – from Excel spreadsheets to more advanced data visualization tools like Tableau.

→ **Clustering** – While Excel, Google Sheets and other tools have cluster analysis capabilities, the process is unwieldy. Statistical software, including SPSS, features more elegant approaches to clustering data. In addition, analysts can execute clustering analysis with R using its built-in K-means command or conduct more robust clustering analyses using fpk, pvclust, and other packages.

→ **Relativity** – Any data analysis or visualization tool will create pie charts and other common visual forms. Analysts can use a tool like Wordle to conduct text relevance analyses to visually quantify relativity in text.

→ **Ranking** – Analysts can use any tool to create bar charts and other simple ranking techniques. More sophisticated visual forms, such as spider charts (also known as radar charts) or Sankey diagrams, require the use of more sophisticated tools such as Tableau, R, or D3.

→ **Correlation** – While analysts can produce simple correlation techniques using spreadsheet tools, they can perform deeper correlation analyses using SPSS and other statistical software or more robust analysis tools like R.

Countering Bias in Analysis

While biases like questionnaire bias and sampling bias can lead to errors that degrade the quality of collected data, biases during analysis can be equally crippling. We can generally classify biases that creep into analysis under the heading of "interpretation bias," but analysts should know about two common varieties: accessibility bias and confirmation bias.

Accessibility bias

People tend to make assumptions based on limited information and fail to seek information not already known. Analysts can protect against this bias by ensuring they analyze the data they need – not simply the data they have. The simplest way for analysts to do that is to look objectively at the question the analysis is answering and compare the data included in the analysis with the data they would collect in a perfect world. If the current dataset matches the ideal data (or if dependable proxies have been found for the desired data) analysts can move content forward, knowing they've minimized accessibility bias.

An example of accessibility bias can be seen in a global research company's recent analysis. The company published an article in late 2019 that purported to validate the value of its new MTA model with a headline that boasted, "5 Game Changing Facts That Prove The Value Of Multi-Touch Attribution." As discussed in Part 3 of this book, multitouch attribution models are under extreme stress from data privacy and cookie deletion policies that limit the consumer behavior data fueling their algorithms. These limits threaten the ability of MTAs to accurately attribute value to media touch points by forcing a heavy reliance on probabilistic models that are less precise than models that use more robust data. The proof points this company offered to validate its MTA, however, were five simple outputs from 109 datasets the company had analyzed using its MTA. Analysts at the company ignored the real question at play – do MTA models accurately attribute value? – and focused on an analysis of the data on hand. While that data may have resulted in interesting insights, it failed to produce the analysis that was really needed.

Confirmation bias

Approaching an analysis with a preconceived idea of what the data will say introduces the risk of confirmation bias. Such prejudice can lead an analyst to draw a conclusion after finding supporting evidence for that conclusion, without reviewing the entire dataset. The analyst will arrive at the answer they seek, but not necessarily the right answer. Analysts can counter confirmation bias by challenging their assumptions and allowing stories to rise from the data organically.

A discussion I had with the chief marketing officer (CMO) of a multinational quick-serve restaurant company illustrates the challenge of confirmation bias. During a three-hour meeting, I presented an analysis that demonstrated the importance of digital media to this brand and substantiated the need to divert money from television advertising to online video. Hard-hitting facts related to demographic shifts, consumer behavior trends, and the ability to achieve more measurable levels of brand engagement build a strong, data-based case for how the brand could achieve greater results with a media plan that increased its online video presence. The executive dismissed my analysis with a simple wave of his hand, saying, "We do our own analysis on our media spend. Each month, I look at the curve of our television ad spend over time and the curve of our sales over time and the two are almost perfectly correlated. TV drives our sales."

What followed was a conversation about correlation and the difference between it and causality. But we also talked about confirmation bias and how the analysis the brand conducted sought to confirm the CMO's narrative rather than reveal the best results for the brand.

While this isn't a comprehensive list of biases that can affect analysis, it does feature the most significant challenges posed at this stage of the analytics journey. The analyst can guard against each of the biases listed above by being able to spot them and dutifully working to prevent them from influencing the analysis.

In Summary: Analyzing for Insights

Finding those patterns requires analysts to create views into the data efficiently, often from multiple angles. They'll be more successful by reducing large amounts of data into valuable insights rather than mining data for undiscovered insights. Analysts use five primary analysis techniques to analyze data, and each one provides a different view into the questions the analysts asked. Regardless of the technique analysts use, context is critical for effective analysis and the identification of patterns in data. Even with error-free data, interpretation bias is a flaw that can sabotage any analysis, and analysts must avoid this bias.

PART 5
Storytelling with Data

Lesson 1   Pictures You See with Your Brain

Lesson 2   Evaluation Framework for the Visual Form

Lesson 3   Sophisticated Use of Contrast

Lesson 4   Ensuring Clear Meaning

Lesson 5   Refined Execution through Visual Polish

Lesson 6   On Your Feet and Getting Your Story
            Across

In Part 5, we dive headlong into the most important aspect of digital marketing analytics: transforming the data the analyst compiled into a comprehensive, coherent, and meaningful story.

I outline the key characteristics of good visuals and the minutiae of chart design and provide a five-step process for analysts to follow when they're on their feet and presenting to an audience. The goal is to equip analysts with the tools they need to tell a compelling and memorable story that "cuts through the noise" of the overwhelming amount of information audiences experience every day.

Pictures You See with Your Brain

Five things discussed in this lesson:

- People struggle to retain information, presenting a big challenge to analysts who want audiences to remember what they say
- Several studies illustrate how easy it is for people to become overwhelmed by information
- Analysts must limit the amount of brain activity their stories require
- Understanding how audiences process visual information can help analysts design better stories
- Using preattentive attributes is an effective way for visuals to "cut through the noise"

Studies show that people forget 80 percent of what they learn within 24 hours.[115] As analysts who've worked so hard to construct stories by working through tons of data to craft perfect diamond insights, we want our audiences to remember what we say. Often, audiences forget information presented because it slips through gaps in attention, or the information isn't introduced in a memorable way. So, how do analysts – as Data Designers eager to present their stories in an effective visual form – do that?

---

[115] Will Thalheimer, "How Much Do People Forget?" *Work-Learning Research, Inc.* (December 2010).

To ensure audiences comprehend and retain our messages, we must understand how they perceive images visually.

Visual Perception and the Door Study

Our eyes are fantastic tools but play a minor part in our system of visual perception. The eyes feed images to the brain and it's the brain's job to perceive the object being viewed. In effect, it's our brains that are seeing. By understanding this, we can better understand how our audiences will experience the data stories we present. When we create images to communicate messages visually, we should think in terms of how those visuals will register in their minds, which can be a complicated and confusing place.

The famous "Door Study" from Daniel Simons and Daniel Levin illustrates the complexity of our minds and how the brain's information processing center, the prefrontal cortex, can be easily overwhelmed. In the experiment, one researcher approaches a subject in a park, hands the person a map, and asks for directions to a nearby place. While the subject is engaged in the map, a pair of researchers carrying a broad door walk between the first researcher and the subject. At that moment, the first researcher ducks behind the door and is replaced by a second researcher. The second researcher, a completely different person in different dress and with a different appearance, continues the conversation that the first researcher started with the subject. In most cases, the study found, the subject didn't notice they were talking to a different person.[116]

---

[116] Daniel J. Simons and Daniel T. Levin, "Change Blindness," *Trends in Cognitive Sciences* (October 1997).

Figure 5.1: The famous "Door Study" from Simons and Levin in action

Source: Simons & Levin (1998)

Subjects in this experiment didn't recognize they were talking to a new person because their prefrontal cortexes were overwhelmed. Processing a map, the location the researcher wants to reach, and the path needed to go from where they are now to where they want to be, require a great deal of highly involved thinking. The part of our brains responsible for this level of thought is the prefrontal cortex. When the prefrontal cortex is engaged in such deep activity, obvious things – like the fact that a different person is now standing in front of the Door Study's subject – can slip through unrecognized.

What this means for us as Data Designers is clear: If we create visuals that require highly involved thinking from our audiences, (i.e., engage their prefrontal cortex), we introduce the risk that they'll miss even the most obvious elements we hope to communicate. Preattentive attributes are tools we can use to communicate messages without triggering the prefrontal cortex.

Preattentive attributes are elements of an image processed in spatial memory without conscious action. In essence, preattentive attributes introduce contrast to a visual that triggers unconscious reactions in our brains. It takes less than 500 milliseconds for the eye and brain to process a preattentive attribute of any image. Analysts can leverage these attributes to make visuals easier to understand while ensuring their audiences' prefrontal cortexes are resting quietly.

Preattentive attributes include size, color, shape, and other design elements that introduce contrast (what I call "contrived contrast"). Below are two sets of figures, each featuring the same number of nines. The set on the right uses the preattentive attribute of color to set the nines apart from the other figures, while the set on the left presents the numbers without contrast. Which of the two sets makes finding the nines easier?

Figure 5.2: The preattentive attribute of color (hue) at work

134244295404913 74630197453O256
458033840583821 72933654963701O
043849501596833 03897464830287G
030293485054019 83938355312910l

Figure 5.2 demonstrates well how color can be used to introduce contrast, but analysts have many other design options. Orientation, size, enclosure, width, and intensity are all ways we can get messages in visuals through our audiences' visual perception systems and into their brains.

A Word on the Effect of Neuroscience

British molecular biologist Francis Crick posited that all actions, emotions and beliefs are the product of physical activity within the brain that's consistent between all people. Marketers can put Crick's assertion into practice by measuring a person's raw initial reactions to something in the form of electrical activity in their brain through electroencephalograms (EEGs), which record the brain's electrical activity, or functional magnetic resonance imaging (fMRI), which measures brain activity by detecting changes associated with blood flow. In this way, data collected from a consumer's neurobiology reveal the nonconscious emotions and responses that affect decision-making. These data allow marketers to determine how a person really feels about stimuli like advertisements, packaging, in-store experiences, or offers devoid of things like social pressure or bias.

Neuroscience has other ways to remove marketers' guesswork. Eye-gaze detection, which reveals the parts of ads consumers are drawn to and those they ignore, can improve ads' effectiveness. By compiling data on where people's eyes are drawn, marketers can highlight attention-grabbing elements of their creative, eliminate distractions, and determine where to place critical information related to products or offers.

Neurobiology can provide clear and consistent insight into human behavior, but today, its technological limitations are throttling its applications. Experiments such as Nielsen's Consumer Neuroscience studies use medical-grade equipment and best-in-class technologies to collect data through multiple EEG sensors that measure memory and attention (at a rate of 500 times per second), facial coding to measure expressed emotions, and eye tracking to measure visual focus on content. The extensive amount of machinery needed to collect these data, however, relegates the application of this equipment to the laboratory setting.

Moran Cerf, a leading neuroscientist, believes that for the practice to reach its full potential, the recording technology must become much less intrusive so that a person can wear it constantly "from boardroom to bedroom." In 2018, researchers affiliated with Ulsan National Institute of Science and Technology in Ulsan, South Korea, introduced a biosensing contact lens capable of detecting glucose levels in patients with diabetes.[117] According to the research team, this innovative "smart lens" featured built-in pliable, transparent electronics that monitor glucose levels from tears in the eye.

Although the device isn't commercially available, less inconspicuous wearable devices have been successfully launched to monitor glucose, heart health (electrocardiography), muscle and nerve control (electromyography), and circulation (photoplethysmography). As such devices evolve to become less obtrusive, their practical applications in marketing become more likely. As discussed previously in this book, however, how marketers navigate consumers' privacy concerns successfully and prove real value for those who would consent to wearing such devices for marketing purposes is unclear.

In Summary: Pictures You See with Your Brain

People struggle to grasp and retain information, which presents a big challenge to analysts who want audiences to remember what they have to say. Several studies illustrate how easy it is for people to become overwhelmed by information. As a result, analysts must try to limit the amount of brain activity their stories require. Understanding how audiences process visual information can help analysts design better stories. Using preattentive attributes is an effective way for visuals to cut through the noise. To this end, it's no wonder that modern marketing has found answers to these questions through the use of neuroscience.

In the next lesson, we'll explore frameworks that answer the question, "How should we define good data visualization?"

---

[117] "New Smart Contact Lens for Diabetics Introduced," *ScienceDaily* (February 22, 2018).

Evaluation Framework for the Visual Form

Five things discussed in this lesson:

- Data visualization is an intricate practice where one misstep can have catastrophic consequences for data stories
- Evaluating the effectiveness of data visualizations can be done through a framework that accounts for each element of the dataviz's complex system
- For dataviz to be successful, analysts must ensure the quality of the data collected, define the objective, design the story, and choose a visual form
- Defining good visual form requires an even deeper analysis and evaluation framework
- Good visual form features a sophisticated use of contrast, clear meaning, and refined execution

Designing effective data visuals is a complicated, difficult task. As we've seen, a long and arduous journey is required to reach the point where we're ready to convey our findings through images. But once we reach this last step in our journey, the work – in many ways – has just begun. It can be a frustrating and beguiling task for even the most accomplished among us. British data journalist, information designer, and author David McCandless captured this idea perfectly:

"Visualisation is hard. I've written books, created software, directed films in my career, but visualisation is by far the most challenging discipline I've ever engaged with. It's something about the precision needed at every level, I think. Concept, data, story, design, style – all are precision arts. In visualisation, they're stacked one on top of the other. If one sags or slips, the entire edifice can collapse."[118]

Where does an analyst begin when facing a challenge that bedevils even world-renowned dataviz professionals? Let's start by understanding what makes for "good" data visualization.

Evaluating the Effectiveness of Dataviz

In a brief post to his *Information Is Beautiful* blog, McCandless offered an idea of what makes for good data visualizations through a simple graphic (or, as McCandless put it, he was simply "thinking aloud in visuals").[119] This framework can be a useful point of orientation.

---

[118] David McCandless in an email to participants in his "Workshops Are Beautiful" seminar (November 29, 2016).
[119] David McCandless, "What Makes a Good Visualization?" (2009).

Figure 5.3: McCandless' take on "What Makes a Good Visualization?"

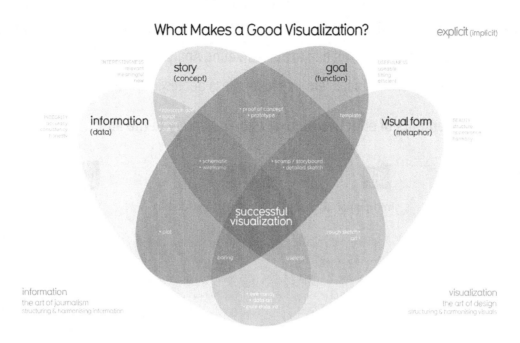

The framework expresses the central idea that constructing visuals is tremendously challenging. Every element must "work" on its own and, more importantly, mesh together in a visual form that an audience understands. By including elements beyond just the "pretty picture" (visual form) to include all the elements of the creative process, the framework puts a fine point on the importance of the analyst bringing all three functional roles they play together – Techie (information), Data Strategist (story and goal), and Data Designer (visual form).

The framework also provides a clear answer to the question, What makes a good data visualization? or, What makes a visualization good? The answer can be elusive. The visual nature of graphs and charts often allows us to know a visualization is "good" without being able to articulate what gives us that feeling. McCandless' visual gives us a language for that evaluation by saying the four major components of any visual – information, story, goal, and visual form – must be present and effective.

I was instinctively drawn to McCandless' visual framework for "What Makes a Good Visualization?" because I instantly recognized how it tied to the Marketing Analytics Process (MAP) that I had been using (and teaching) for years. Each element McCandless details is the direct output of a MAP step.

Figure 5.4: The elements of effective dataviz align perfectly to the MAP

Goal (Plan)	Information (Collect)	Story (Analyze)	Visual Form (Report)
• Establish the clear, singular objective to be addressed	• Locate sources for required data identified in plan	• Create "tidy" datasets to ensure error-free analysis	• Follow simple design rules to visualize with impact
• Define key questions you will ask of the data	• Use mining tools and techniques to collect data	• Perform techniques that reveal conclusive patterns in the collected data	• Ensure recommendations are clear and concise
• Identify data needed to address key questions	• Select a data management system that fits needs	• Compress learnings into snippets ("what's the 60-second story?")	• Leverage context to ensure numbers are meaningful
• Identify data sources and tools required	• Ensure bias is mitigated in the data collection process		• Ensure coherence through mindful presentation

Let's take a deeper look at each element of McCandless' framework and how it aligns with a MAP step.

→ **Goal** – This is the functional purpose of the data we collected and the objective we're working toward, focusing our analysis journey. For all intents and purposes, McCandless' "goal" is the objective we worked so hard to identify and clarify during the MAP Plan step.

→ **Information** – Information is the data we collected; data we hope is accurate, deep, and robust. It was the primary focus of the MAP Collect step. The better that data is, the better our data visualization will be. Information expressed through data is a clear, important element of a successful visual.

→ **Story** – Knitting objective and data together is the story. The story is what takes data and moves it toward our objective. It's a narrative we use to guide our audience and is a collection of the insights we mined from our data. The story is the outcome of the MAP Analyze step.

→ **Visual Form** – The visual form is the image we construct to express our story to our audience, which uses the data we collected to drive toward our objective. The visual form is the ultimate output of the MAP Report step.

We've discussed how to design a clear objective, what makes good data, and how analysis techniques can find patterns in data to produce an effective story. But as we enter the MAP Report step, we have yet to define the required elements of visual form. The McCandless framework provides little insight. To be sure, we know the visual form is important – even critical – to our work as analysts. Yet, how do we know when we've created a good visual?

Understanding the Components of Visual Form

In my experience, effective visual form does three things well. It expresses clear meaning by highlighting its message, it demonstrates a sophisticated use of contrast to direct the audience's attention, and it limits distractions through refined execution.

Clear Meaning

Through an effective use of common elements, including titles, subtitles, and other visual guides, good visual form clearly communicates the insight we intend to convey. Although these elements are familiar (chances are that the first chart you constructed as an analyst included a title), their use can be deceptively elaborate. In Lesson 3, we'll examine the design elements that help convey clear meaning in charts.

Sophisticated Use of Contrast

By leveraging preattentive attributes to create contrast, good visual form separates important data from the rest through visual context. Contrast takes many forms, ranging from obvious to nuanced.

In Lesson 4, we'll investigate each form of contrast and how analysts can use the technique to create immediate, instinctive connections with audiences.

Refined Execution

Finally, and perhaps most importantly, the third essential element of good visual form is refined execution. It's a deep attention to detail: the choice of font we make, the way we apply color, how we allocate space to the page. Each design decision might appear to have a subtle effect on our visual, yet these decisions can mean the difference between an image that conveys its message effectively and one that doesn't. In Lesson 5, we'll delve deeply into the guidelines for refined execution.

Combined, these three elements make for good visual form. We'll use them to provide detailed insight into McCandless' concept of visual form. As Data Designers, these are the elements we can affect, control, and improve.

In Summary: Evaluation Framework for the Visual Form

Data visualization is an intricate practice where one misstep can have catastrophic consequences for a data story. Evaluating the effectiveness of data visualizations is possible through a framework that accounts for each element of the dataviz's complex system. For dataviz to be successful, analysts must ensure the quality of the data they collect, define the objective, design the story, and choose the visual form. Defining good visual form requires an even deeper analysis and evaluation framework. Good visual form features a sophisticated use of contrast, clear meaning, and refined execution

In the next lesson, we'll delve into the first of the three elements of good visual form: sophisticated use of contrast.

Sophisticated Use of Contrast

Five things discussed in this lesson:

- Using contrast in visuals is critical for analysts to communicate insights quickly and effectively
- Size, color, shape, and "contrived" (designed) are methods for contrast that analysts can use when creating visuals
- Using contrast with numbers can be an effective way for analysts to create effective visuals and to improve audience understanding
- Several techniques from FCB's John Kenny can bring contrast and understanding to numbers in an analyst's data story
- Lost art of sketching visuals with pen and paper can help analysts become more efficient in the way they create dataviz

Contrast is an important technique analysts can use to connect with their audiences instantly. Importantly, contrast leverages preattentive attributes to trigger reactions in the brain while leaving the prefrontal cortex quiet and at peace. This allows analysts to deliver information without evoking much thought from audiences, thereby keeping their attention focused. Several types of contrast improve visuals and communicate insights efficiently.

Introducing different-size objects on a page captures attention. The more striking and apparent the size difference, the more attention the objects will attract. The visual displayed in Figure 1.8 of this book, which offers a comparison of daily data-creating human activity by visualizing the amount of data in a collection of different-size boxes, is a good example of size contrast.

The variety communicates the volume of data each activity produces without requiring the audience to digest figures. The graphic below in Figure 5.5 is from David McCandless and captures the shocking contrast between the time American adults spend watching television each year and the amount of time required to create Wikipedia (data from Clay Shirky).

Figure 5.5: "Goggle Boxes," an example of size contrast[120]

Goggle Boxes
Hours spent...

200 billion hours
a year spent watching TV by US adults

100 million hours
to create Wikipedia

---

[120] David McCandless, "Information Is Beautiful," InformationIsBeautiful.net (July 2010), Clay Shirky, *Cognitive Surplus* (2010).

Basic Guidelines	Pro Tips
• Maintain proportional differences in size for accurate representation of data • Keep a consistent scale to ensure accurate comparisons • Keep visuals that employ size contrast simple to avoid confusion	• Pair size contrast with other forms of contrast, like color contrast, to communicate more visual meaning

Color Contrast

Using contrasting colors in an image can be an effective way to attract attention. Using objects in many colors in a chart will convey that each object is unique. Color also helps images "pop" on a page. When analysts select muted colors for chart backgrounds – a gray shade works well – they can draw attention to important elements by designing them in a vibrant color. Different levels of color saturation can achieve the same result. The example in Figure 5.6 demonstrates how a combination of muted and vibrant colors can produce color contrast to "lift" elements off the page.

Figure 5.6: Muted and vibrant colors draw attention to a chart element

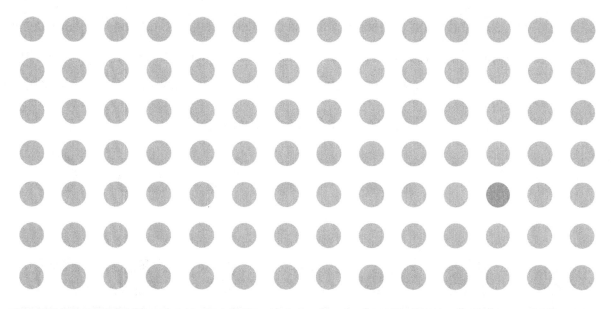

Basic Guidelines

- Balance vibrant colors with muted ones to avoid overwhelming the viewer
- Use consistent color coding across related visuals
- Be mindful of color blindness and accessibility in your color choices

Pro Tips

- Use bright, bold colors to highlight key elements of your chart and muted hues for supporting elements
- Consider the background color of your slide and its effect on color contrast
- Be aware of color psychology and how it influences viewers' perceptions (red typically means something different from green)

Shape Contrast

As they do with size and color, audiences will detect different shapes in images. Differences in shapes communicate the uniqueness of each element instantly. Icons are a particularly effective form of shape contrast as audiences understand that different icons represent unique elements.

Figure 5.7: Icons introduce shape contrast for various data categories

Form submissions	Newsletter sign-ups	Chat contacts	Email contacts	Phone calls	Cross-device activity	Profile fill-outs
Return site visits	Offline dealer lookups	Perception change	App downloads	In-app purchases	Video views	Page visits

Basic Guidelines

- Choose shapes that are distinctively different to ensure clear contrast and easy recognition
- Use the same shape consistently to represent the same type of data or category across visuals
- Opt for simple shapes and avoid lifelike icons as complex shapes can distract and confuse the audience
- Ensure shapes are of appropriate size; not too small to go unnoticed or too large to overwhelm the data

Pro Tips

- Never use 3D shapes, as they distort data perception
- Never use textured shapes for shapes that feature background images because they distract your audience
- Pair shapes with other types of contrast, such as color or size, to add additional layers of understanding

Contrived Contrast

A final category of contrast is what I call contrived contrast. Contrived contrast is the use of boxes, callouts, annotations and other preattentive attributes to distinguish items in a visual. These are purposeful, planned introductions of contrast that attract attention. Use this approach with techniques, including size, color, or shape contrast, or when those more organic techniques aren't an option.

The series of LUMAscape charts from the investment bank, Luma Partners, is a good example of contrast techniques, but the use of contrived contrast is the most effective aspect. The LUMAscapes organize the famously complicated world of advertising technology ("ad tech") by grouping similar companies on one page. The size of the groupings represents the relative number of companies in each area of the ad tech industry. Categories of groupings are set apart from one another using different colored labels. But the introduction of contrived contrast in the form of enclosures placed around each grouping (as well as boxes placed around companies, indicating they were recently acquired or shuttered) is the contrast technique that's the most attention-grabbing.

Figure 5.8: The LUMAscape without (left) and with (right) contrived contrast

 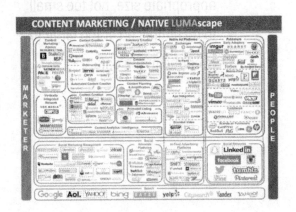

Basic Guidelines	Pro Tips

- Ensure uniform application of contrast elements across all visuals related to the same data set
- Keep visuals clean and focused by avoiding the overuse of too many contrasting elements
- Strive to seamlessly integrate contrived contrasts with the rest of the visualization to enhance rather than distract

- Use contrasts to establish a hierarchy of information, helping viewers understand what's most important
- Learn by studying the work of top data visualizers, taking inspiration from their successful use of contrived contrast

Bringing Contrast to Numbers through Context

Contrast also punctuates figures and facts in presentations. The difference in technique here is that we won't use visual contrast to draw our audience's attention. Rather, we'll introduce context to the figure or fact to lift it from the surrounding chatter or release its meaning.

John Kenny, the head of planning at FCB Chicago, has developed a number of effective techniques, collected in what he calls the "Numerical Comparisons Tool," to bring greater context to numbers using principles of behavioral economics. To demonstrate Kenny's techniques, we'll look at ways to better communicate a large and difficult-to-evaluate figure: The annual consumption of 7,117,500,000 barrels of crude oil in the United States.

This figure is purely fact. More than 7 billion barrels of crude oil (or anything, for that matter) seems like a great amount. But in actuality, we don't know the extent of this figure's value. Millions and billions are strangely familiar, yet foreign, concepts to most people. A quick perusal of any news site will present figures of these sizes in any number of headlines. Yet, throwing out "billions" alone will go right over the audience's collective head. Sure, the figure seems big, but we don't have a point of comparison. We lack the context needed to anchor an evaluation. Kenny's five techniques provide the context needed to frame numbers in a way that makes them understandable.

Let's look at Kenny's techniques and how they can provide context for the figure discussed above.

Translating to Intuitively Understandable Units

The first of Kenny's techniques is to put the number in a unit that people understand. In this case, we can take that idea of 7.1 billion barrels of crude oil and rephrase it in this way: "Americans use enough oil each day to make 36 billion plastic water bottles." We're still using the unit of billions, so we haven't compromised the large scale of American's use of crude oil. But we've tied this figure to an item that's relatable. Everyday objects, like water bottles, are effective units. No doubt as you read this book, you probably have a water bottle near you (but, most likely, not a barrel of crude oil anywhere to be seen). To imagine 36 billion plastic water bottles puts the figure into immediate context and is more understandable.

Using Familiar Comparisons (Like Distance)

Another technique is to use a familiar comparison like distance. In this way, we can translate 7.1 billion: "Each day, Americans use enough oil for 39 trips to the sun and back." We see the sun every day (at least every good day). We might not understand how far away it is in miles, but we clearly understand the sun is a long distance from Earth. To think that Americans use enough oil to make

39 round trips to the sun must require an enormous amount of oil. This rephrasing puts 7.1 billion in a better context.

Using Familiar Comparisons (Like Time)

Another type of familiar comparison can be time. Using this technique, we can rephrase 7.1 billion: "In just two minutes, Americans use 1 million gallons of oil." As we've said, people can't relate to millions and billions, but they know 1 billion (or 1 million) of anything is a significant amount. People also know that two minutes is a relatively short time frame. To say that we use 1 million of anything in two minutes makes the expression of size much easier to comprehend.

Making It Personal

Making the figure personal is another Kenny technique. The 7.1 billion example made personal would play out in this way: "In a year, a typical American family uses 70 barrels of oil." This technique presents the number in a meaningful way. While people might not know what 70 barrels of oil looks like, this technique brings the lofty figure of total American consumption to a personal level that is easier to understand.

Finding the Moral Dimension

Finally, a high-risk, high-reward technique from Kenny is finding a moral dimension to bring context to a figure. In the case of 7.1 billion, we can cast it in a context that elicits an emotional response: "In less than four decades, the world's finite oil supply will be gone forever." Phrasing the number like this will undoubtedly make it more understandable for our audience. It can also polarize people. Before using this approach, an analyst must have some understanding of how the audience feels about the subject to minimize the risk of offending people or turning them off.

The process of identifying a goal, collecting data, and creating a story requires facts and figures. Using Kenny's techniques will help ensure our numbers are relatable, meaningful, and understandable.

Sketching is, unfortunately, a bit of a lost art. Too often, we have the attitude that we must rush to our computer to generate graphics. If we took a moment with pen and paper to sketch our early ideas, however, we could design with much more freedom. We'd no longer be limited by our understanding of the application or its design restrictions.

Through sketching, we're able to explore contrast in a space bound only by the edges of our creativity. The great data visualization artists sketch before placing fingers on keyboards. Sketch your ideas first, then bring them to life using dataviz tools. It's a good practice that will make you more efficient when designing visuals and telling stories with data.

Figure 5.9: My dataviz sketchbook

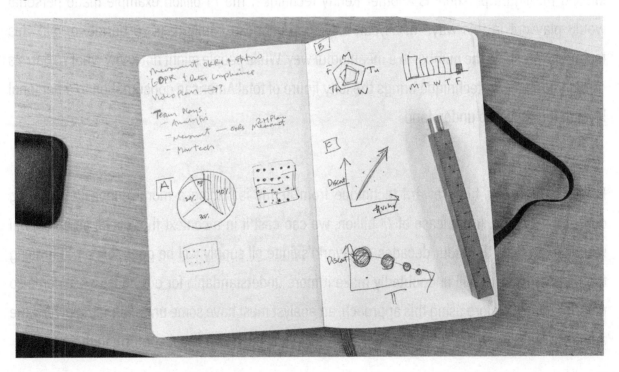

In Summary: Sophisticated Use of Contrast

Bringing contrast to visuals is critical for analysts to communicate insights quickly and effectively. Size, color, shape, and "contrived" (designed) are contrast methods that analysts can use when creating visuals. Adding contrast to numbers can be an effective way for analysts to ensure people understand charts. Several techniques from John Kenny of FCB can bring contrast and understanding to numbers in data stories. The lost art of sketching visuals with pen and paper can help analysts create dataviz efficiently and can reveal new approaches to contrast that analysts wouldn't have thought of while sitting at their computers.

In the next lesson, we'll delve into the second of the three elements of good visual form: how to convey clear meaning through chart elements.

Ensuring Clear Meaning

Five things discussed in this lesson:

- Ensuring clear meaning in our messages hinges on other elements of our visuals being successful
- Using titles and subtitles properly is critical when designing charts
- Highlighting messages visually is the most effective way to convey stories
- Using visual cues, applying annotations, and labeling items directly are simple techniques that help to ensure clarity and reduce confusion
- Eliciting an emotional response from an audience through a story is a high-risk, high-reward approach for ensuring memorable messaging

Most of the building blocks for creating clear messages come early in the data analysis journey. The process of identifying a concise Marketing Objective, collecting data, and finding interesting patterns in data enriches our content. When completing these steps correctly, we have an excellent opportunity to present inherently clear messages.

Design techniques, however, can enhance our messages by enriching visuals. Using titles, subtitles, and other visual guides effectively ensures our designs present insights clearly. These elements are common, but their use can be deceptively elaborate. Let's look at how to apply them properly.

The most important thing analysts can do is to write thoughtful, purposeful headlines and subtitles for their charts. Headlines and subtitles are included on nearly every dataviz, but Data Designers typically take them for granted. Despite this indifference, these are important for audiences. They're typically among the first things audiences will read on a chart. They offer the savvy Data Designer a golden opportunity to start the audience experience positively.

Headlines

Chart headlines should be in plain English and answer, "What am I looking at here?" For example, a headline such as "Product X sales over the past five years" introduces a chart clearly. It orients the audience to the data in the image, importantly sparing them the prefrontal cortex-demanding task of figuring that out for themselves.

In contrast, a chart with the headline, "How have we done recently?" has the opposite effect. While written in plain language, this headline triggers more questions than it answers. How is performance defined? What does 'recently' mean? Should we focus on data from all the years included in the chart, or just those more recent? We lose audience attention when headlines trigger questions.

Place the headline above and left-aligned with the dataviz. Position the headline horizontally and make it bold in a larger font than the graphic so it stands out against other chart elements (e.g., subtitle and labels).

Basic Guidelines	Pro Tips
• Remember that the most important job of the headline is to answer a simple question for your audience: "What am I looking at here?"	• Avoid using acronyms or abbreviations in your headline
• Use clear, concise language in the headline	• Avoid using clever headlines, regardless of how comfortable you are with the data (you can bring personality to your talk through your presentation style)
• Explain plainly and unambiguously what the chart presents	• Flip rapidly through the pages of your presentation, reading only the chart headlines: Did you include all the topics you intended to cover? Are they in the proper order?
• Place the headline above the dataviz, aligned to the left side of the chart	
• Print the headline horizontally, make it bold, and a few font sizes larger than other chart elements	

Subtitles

Every chart should contain a subtitle printed directly below the headline and above the dataviz. The subtitle is a succinct description of the insight an analyst wants the audience to take away from the visual. Through the subtitle, the analyst is effectively telling the audience, "This is what you should think once you have looked at the data in my chart." Like the title, the subtitle should be in plain, unambiguous language and shouldn't contain acronyms or abbreviations.

A subtitle such as "Last year's sales make up for losses suffered in the previous four years" makes it immediately clear what the chart conveys. Conversely, a subtitle that proclaims, "We are doing great!" is simple but doesn't connect to the data in the chart. Such a statement is "intellectually blank," lacking any insight into the chart's underlying message. Like a poorly designed title, this latter subtitle will leave the audience with more questions than answers.

Proper use of subtitles is important for a number of reasons. It allows analysts to control a chart's message. By printing the insight on the page, we're introducing the truth we believe the visual holds. Whether the audience readily accepts that truth or is skeptical of its veracity, we've made the statement plain and clear. In doing so, an analyst can substantiate that insight by pointing to corroborating patterns in the data. In addition, the meaning of the chart is clear to those who weren't at the presentation or didn't hear the narrative that accompanied the visual when the presentation lands on their desk or in their inbox.

The subtitle shouldn't be in a bold font so that it stands apart from the headline. It should be a few font sizes smaller than the headline.

Basic Guidelines	Pro Tips
<ul><li>Include a subtitle on every chart</li><li>Write your subtitle in plain language that concisely conveys the insight the audience should take from your chart</li><li>Place the subtitle directly below the headline, above the dataviz, and aligned to the left side of the headline</li><li>Print the subtitle in a "normal" (i.e., not bold) font a few sizes smaller than the headline</li></ul>	<ul><li>Avoid intellectually blank statements in your subtitles</li><li>Avoid using acronyms or abbreviations in your subtitle</li><li>Flip rapidly through the pages of your presentation, reading only the chart subtitles: Did you include all of your insights? Are they in the proper order?</li></ul>

Highlighting Messages Visually

After properly headlining and subtitling their charts, analysts can introduce other design elements that will guide audiences to data that supports the charts' professed insights.

Using Visual Cues

Visual cues – arrows, boxes, and shaded areas – can be extremely effective additions to visuals. Think of these visual cues as tools that direct audiences to important figures, data points, and patterns. As we learned about visual perception in Lesson 1, these cues stand out to audiences as preattentive attributes. Their brains can't help but notice anything we point out with a tastefully designed arrow (or encase in a box, or place in an area shaded light gray, etc.).

Figure 5.10: Visual cues will direct your audience's attention to the important areas of your chart

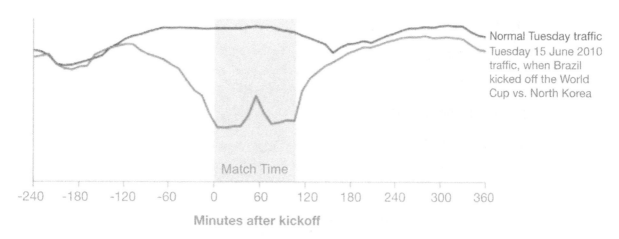

To avoid overloading the visual with "look here!" cues, a good practice is to use no more than one cue on a chart. In this way, we guide our audience to our important data while ensuring that it remains critical. When everything on our chart is called out as important, nothing will be significant. Remember that change – not sameness – catches our audience's attention.

Basic Guidelines	Pro Tips
• Become familiar with multiple types of visual cues • Gauge the need for visual cues by presenting your data with and without them. If the effect is positive, keep them (and remove them if they're unnecessary) • Apply visual cues frequently, yet rarely exceed more than one cue per chart	• Once you find a visual cue that works effectively, reuse it in other charts that benefit from similar attention-grabbing tools

Applying Annotations

Like visual cues, think of annotations as tools that direct attention to important areas of a chart. Unlike image-based visual cues, however, annotations are small bodies of text that inform the interpretation of figures, data points, and patterns.

Write annotations in clear, plain language. They shouldn't appear as labels. Instead, express them through short sentences or phrases. As annotations should be tied to specific areas of the chart data, use a thin line to connect the annotation to the data it explains, whether that data is contained in a single point or a range of points.

Figure 5.11: Annotations on a chart can identify data that supports the subtitle's insight[121]

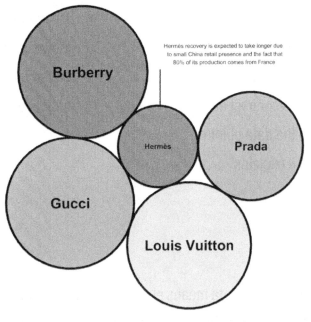

Number of Mainland China Stores in 2020
Luxury brands recover from COVID-19 as China recuperates ahead of Europe

Hermès recovery is expected to take longer due to small China retail presence and the fact that 80% of its production comes from France

Burberry

Hermès

Prada

Gucci

Louis Vuitton

Source: Financial Times

When chart data is dense or insights are subtle, annotations can make clear how annotated data supports the insight expressed in the chart's subtitle. This is particularly important for ensuring consistency or interpretations when people see the chart outside the presentation. In the same way the subtitle acts as a written record of the chart's insight, annotations serve as documentation of the insight's substantiation.

---

[121] Guillaume Cieutat, "Number of Mainland China Stores in 2020" (March 2020).

Basic Guidelines	Pro Tips
• Separate annotations from labels by writing them in short sentences or phrases • Use thin lines to connect each annotation to the data point or range of data it explains	• Use annotations when you know a presentation will be shared outside the viewing audience

Labeling Items Directly

Ensuring audiences focus on chart data means eliminating unnecessary visual elements that draw the eye away. One of the most distracting visual elements, if not the most distracting visual element, is a familiar item Data Designers use extensively: the chart legend. Typically, the legend sits to the upper right of the chart and contains the key to connecting colors, lines, and other visual components of the chart to their names.

While the explanations in the legend seem intuitively helpful, the placement – separate from the visual – creates havoc for an audience. A legend forces people to dart their eyes from each chart element to the legend and back again to understand what the data represents. The mental action of tying a color and label in the legend to its corresponding data in the chart is a task that only the prefrontal cortex can accomplish. As we've learned, engaging audiences' prefrontal cortexes forfeits their attention.

Use direct labeling rather than including a legend on a chart. Place labels at the end of lines, on pie chart slices, or at the base of bars. One- or two-word labels will keep the chart clutter-free. Use color to separate important labels from less critical support data. A label written in an eye-catching red will stand out against gray labels. Coordinating label colors to match the color of the data they describe optimizes preattentive attributes and helps audiences connect labels with data.

By labeling chart elements, we hold audiences' attention, allowing us to deliver clear, distraction-free messages.

Basic Guidelines	Pro Tips
• Use labels instead of legends on your charts	• Coordinate label colors to match the color of the data they describe
• Place labels at the end of lines, on pie chart slices, or at the base of bars	
• Write one- or two-word labels to minimize chart clutter	
• Use colored labels to distinguish important data from support data	

A Word on Leveraging Emotions

Making emotional connections with audiences through the data we describe, the insights we reveal, and the style in which we present them can help ensure our messages are memorable.

Consistently eliciting the same emotion throughout chart presentations will help ensure audiences understand our messages.

Reciting facts won't secure emotional connections with audiences. Plan the emotions you want to elicit with each chart in your presentation and rehearse drawing those emotions from your audience. One caveat: The emotion must be authentic. Eliciting emotions from an audience is a powerful venture, but can alienate people quickly if they don't agree with the emotional response you're trying to manufacture (or, perhaps worse, react with a different emotion). Use this high-risk, high-reward approach when you're comfortable with your material and how an audience will react to your presentation.

Images, icons, and visuals can elicit emotions that will affect audience perception. Ensure that images convey authentic emotions. Avoid stock photos of people in presentations, as these images appear spurious at best and ridiculous at worst. Prohibit the use of Clip Art, because these comically designed images reduce an audience's respect for a presentation. Use icons rather than Clip Art. Icons should be simple; ornate versions lose detail in small sizes.

In Summary: Ensuring Clear Meaning

Being singular in message is one way analysts can ensure clear meaning. Proper use of titles and subtitles in charts is the most important thing analysts can do when designing charts. Highlighting messages visually is the most effective way to convey stories as using visual cues, applying annotations, and labeling items directly are simple techniques analysts can use to ensure clarity and reduce confusion. Eliciting an emotional response from an audience through stories is a high-risk, high-reward approach for ensuring memorable messaging.

In the next lesson, we'll look at the final element of good visual design: refined execution.

Refined Execution through Visual Polish

Five things discussed in this lesson:

- Refined chart design requires particular attention to the details of fonts, labels, lines, and other elements
- Color choice can sharpen an analyst's story, but can cause distractions if not applied properly
- Several well-defined, tried-and-true harmonic color themes are available for analysts
- Analysts shouldn't feel beholden to a single data visualization tool when building charts; instead, they should use multiple tools to ensure high-quality designs
- Several tests can help analysts evolve and improve their data visualizations

If contrast calls attention to items and simple chart elements help convey clear meaning, the role of visual polish is to ensure items that support critical data sit quietly in the background. Refined execution can be best thought of as a collection of rules and recommendations that eliminate distractions from charts. These design guidelines cover everything from color choice to font usage to specific elements of charts (e.g., labels, lines, etc.). By incorporating refined execution In their practices, analysts can ensure their charts are distraction-free.

Let's explore the elements of refined execution.

Color in Charts

Color is often the first bit of data our eyes perceive in visualizations. For this reason, it's critical to examine color's influence on audience perception, as well as its influence on other colors. Analysts must create harmonious visuals by being thoughtful about color choices. To do so, it's first important to understand a few key concepts about color.

Hues

Think of hue as the dominant color of an item. The hue of a cloudless sky at midday, for example, is blue. Hue is technically defined as "The degree to which a stimulus can be described as similar to or different from stimuli that are described as red, green, blue, and yellow."[122] Different hues can be harmonic (e.g., blue and green) and contrasting (e.g., black and white).

Saturation and Value

Color saturation and color value refer to the intensity of color in an image. In technical terms, saturation and value are the bandwidth of light from a source. By increasing (making darker) and decreasing (making lighter) the saturation or value of a hue, analysts can create a variety of color shades that work well together. The difference between color saturation and color value is subtle. Color saturation varies by adding shades of gray (ranging from white to black) to the hue to affect its vibrancy. Value, on the other hand, affects hue by eliminating color from the hue (i.e., making the hue more or less transparent). Color saturation and color value are important and effective tools for Data Designers.

Distinguishing Colors in Tools

Color can be specified in different ways. Each data visualization tool allows analysts to identify, select, and modify colors using one (or more) of three common models.

---

[122] Mark Fairchild, "Color Appearance Models: CIECAM02 and Beyond" (November 9, 2004).

Figure 5.12: Common color models most dataviz tools use

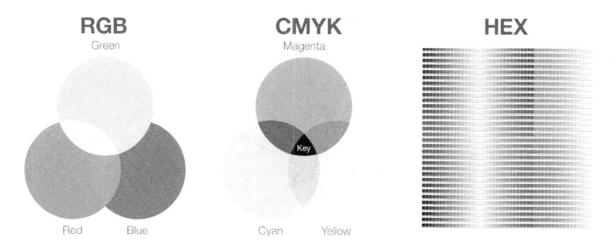

→ **RGB** color model is an additive color model in which red, green, and blue are combined to create a broad array of colors. The name comes from the initials of the three additive primary colors: red, green, and blue.

→ **CMYK** color model (also known as "process color" or "four color") is a subtractive color model, used in color printing, and is also used to describe the printing process. CMYK refers to the four inks used in color printing: cyan, magenta, yellow, and key (black).

→ **Hex** code describes the composition of a certain color in a specific color space, usually RGB. The first value pair refers to red, the second to green, and the third to blue, with decimal values ranging from 0 to 255, or in hexadecimal 0 to FF (#RRGGBB).

The Color Wheel

The color wheel represents the spectrum of primary, secondary, and tertiary colors (more on those later) by wrapping them onto a circle in a logically arranged sequence. Developed by Sir Isaac Newton in 1666, the color wheel allows for the selection of colors in ways that ensure harmony and eye-pleasing themes.

Figure 5.13: Newton's original design for the color wheel

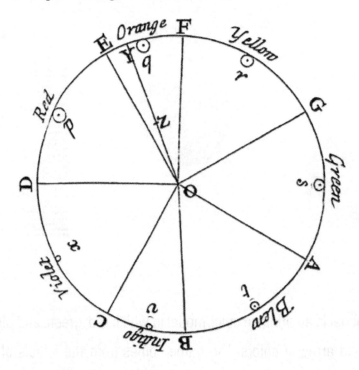

→ **Primary colors** include red, blue, and yellow and are the three primary colors on the color wheel. All other colors are derived from these three hues. The primary colors can't be formed through a combination of any other colors.

→ **Secondary and tertiary colors** include green, orange, and purple. Secondary colors are formed by mixing primary colors. Colors formed by mixing a primary color and a secondary color are the tertiary colors included on the color wheel: blue-green, red-violet, yellow-orange, etc.

Harmonic Color Themes

Two or three colors – plus, the measured use of black, a neutral gray, and white – provide an ample (and manageable) set of hues for any presentation. To ensure harmony in color choice, analysts should choose from several established themes. These themes should include colors that work together to enhance visuals, rather than create distractions.

Figure 5.14: The examples of harmonic color themes

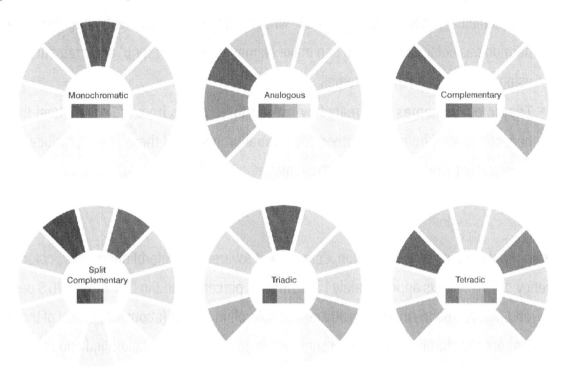

→ **Monochromatic color themes** use one hue to minimize color distraction on the page. Through variations in saturation and value, the selected hue can be expanded to fulfill the color needs of any presentation or visual. Choose one color that has particular relevance and round out the color palette with variances of saturation and value.

→ **Analogous color themes** use Newton's logical order of color properties to create eye-pleasing combinations. Select colors that are next to one another on the color wheel to create color harmony. Three analogous colors will typically provide all the variations a Data Designer will need, but using four colors will expand the theme.

→ **Complementary color themes** use Newton's insights into color properties to create a palette of colors that work well together. Choosing colors that are directly across from one another on the color wheel will produce harmonious pairs of hues to form the basis of the theme. Variations in saturation and value can round out the palette.

→ **Split complementary color themes** are created by using colors on either side of complementary colors on the color wheel. This is another technique for creating harmonious color palettes. You can make elements in a chart "pop" and grab attention by using split complementary themes.

→ **Triadic color themes** are created by picking three colors from the color wheel that are perfectly spaced from one another. The natural properties of these colors produce vibrant contrast that works well in a palette, sometimes surprisingly.

Additional Color Considerations

According to the nonprofit organization, Colour Blind Awareness, colorblindness (i.e., color vision deficiency or CVD) affects approximately 1 in 12 men (8 percent) and 1 in 200 women (0.5 percent) in the world.[123] This means more than 300 million colorblind people (about 4.3 percent of the entire population) are alive today. It's likely that someone in your audience is colorblind and struggles to distinguish different hues (e.g., red, yellow, blue, and green).

Limit your color palette to two or three hues and use different degrees of saturation, as well as black, gray, and white, to round out the palette. These techniques allow analysts to introduce contrast in ways that won't exclude colorblind people in the audience. Analysts can use tools like Pilestone's "Color Blind Vision Simulator" (found at pilestone.com) to simulate how visuals look for those who are colorblind. Analysts need only upload files to the simulator to learn if colorblind people will be able to recognize certain color contrasts and hues. With this understanding, analysts can revise their visuals to ensure greater accessibility.

---

[123] Color Blind Awareness, "Color Blindness" (2020).

Refined execution requires attention to detail beyond color. Every element we place on our charts will affect our audience's ability to understand the visuals. Adopting a set of guidelines that ensures the proper application of these details will result in better charts.

Lines

Whether they're straight or in an arc, lines should be unadorned and distraction-free. Use a maximum of three to four lines and keep the style simple. Avoid shadows, 3D, dashes, and dotted lines. In addition, don't use data markers in lines, as they call attention to specific data points to the detriment of a line's trend. You can use color contrast in lines to capture your audience's attention. Color lines that convey important data in vibrant hues and all other lines in visually muted gray hues.[124]

The most common application of lines in charts is the fonts we use. Fonts, and the letters they convey, are a collection of straight and curved lines. Font choice affects the legibility of graphs. Fonts can help establish a tone and make it easier for audiences to understand chart elements. Comic Sans, Brush Script, and other "fun" fonts don't establish an appropriate tone for a business presentation. It's more important to be seen as credible than it is to express personality. The serious, practical font choices of well-established and respectable organizations, including the New York Times and the Wall Street Journal, are appropriate benchmarks. You'll never find a headline in these publications in Groening.

Unadorned fonts, including Helvetica and Arial, improve legibility. In addition, being consistent in font treatments (e.g., using the same font for every chart headline in the presentation) helps audiences to understand your content.

---

[124] Note that you can harness color's power even more by coloring your labels in the same hue as the data it describes.

Basic Guidelines	Pro Tips
<ul><li>Choose serious, businesslike fonts rather than fun fonts</li><li>Choose unadorned fonts like Helvetica and Arial</li><li>Limit the number of fonts in your presentation to two, possibly three</li><li>Never add shadows or 3D attributes to lines</li><li>Present data with only solid lines (e.g., don't use dashed lines in charts)</li><li>Never add data marker symbols to lines</li></ul>	<ul><li>Adopt a presentation style that mirrors the *New York Times* and the *Wall Street Journal* rather than *USA Today*</li><li>Apply fonts consistently for each chart element throughout your presentation (e.g., headlines are always the same font)</li><li>Color lines that convey important data in vibrant hues and all other lines in visually mute gray hues</li></ul>

Shapes

Shapes are a closed line. Shapes can be geometric, like squares and circles. They can also be organic, like free-form or natural shapes. Shapes are flat and can express length and width.

The best charts should present shapes that are distraction-free and allow readers to compare or contrast the data and draw conclusions. Clean and crisp shapes let readers focus on the data, which is the message of the story, while obtrusions, such as 3D rendering, obscure the data and divert readers' attention from the content.

Basic Guidelines	Pro Tips
• Never add shadows or 3D attributes to shapes • Present data with only solid shapes (e.g., do not place textured designs or images on shapes) • Never add images in shapes (no matter how transparent you make the images) because it will still be distracting)	• Color shapes that convey important data in vibrant hues and all other lines in visually mute gray hues

Space

Space is the area between and around objects. The space around objects is often called negative space: Negative space has shape.

It's important for analysts to make conscious choices about where to place the elements of their charts. Any element on a page can improve or detract from a visual's ability to convey its intended message. Space on a page affects an audience's visual perception. Analysts should place elements consistently from page to page in their presentations. In other words, analysts should use the "position" coordinates in their design tools to ensure that charts are always in the same spot. Analysts can further improve design consistency by ensuring charts, icons, and images are the same size (i.e., height and width) throughout their presentations.

Another best practice will keep a chart clutter-free: Never rotate text in a presentation. All text – particularly axis labels – should be horizontal. Text that's rotated vertically is difficult to read and a distraction. If space is too limited to place a horizontally printed Y-axis label beside a chart, you can move that label to the top of the Y-axis. This technique will maximize the space for a chart and is particularly beneficial when the chart is detailed or contains a great amount of data.

Basic Guidelines	Pro Tips
• Place objects (e.g., charts) in the same spot on your presentation pages to create harmony • Ensure charts, icons, and images are a consistent size (i.e., height and weight) throughout your presentation • For line charts, use a maximum of three to four lines and keep the space uncluttered	• Rather than rotating label text, shrink the chart to allow the label to be printed horizontally or place the label at the top of the axis

Testing to Improve the Visual

Graphics are living, evolving depictions of insights. Every new bit of information and every audience reaction can help inform and improve chart design. To this end, analysts should perform three important tests on their graphics periodically to ensure each iteration improves clarity.

The Spartan Test

To conduct the Spartan Test, examine each element of the graphic to ensure it makes a positive contribution to the visual as a whole. Delete any unnecessary elements methodically. If you need to restore an element you delete, "Ctrl+Z" will undo the delete action and return the element to its rightful place. Keep in mind that every graphic should include the fewest elements possible. The Spartan Test is a great way to see that less is more when creating data visualization.

The 'Peek Test'

To conduct the "Peek Test," set the graphic aside for a few moments. If the graphic is printed on a piece of paper, turn the paper over so the graphic is face down. If the graphic is on a computer screen, switch to a different application or walk away from the computer. You can then return a short time later and look at the graphic. Where do your eyes go? If you're drawn to an area you think is important, you can rest assured your audience's eyes will go there, too. If, however, your eyes pick up some other aspect of the graphic, you should revise it. A recalibration of preattentive attributes could change the graphic's focus. The Peek Test helps ensure the audience will see what you want them to see first.

The 'Colleague Test'

The most important test is what I call the "Colleague Test." In this test, show the graphic to a colleague who hasn't had any association with the project. Make sure your colleague knows little about the data you collected, your objective, and the story you're trying to tell. The less context your colleague has, the more value the test will provide. Show the visualization to your colleague but, ideally, don't say anything about it during the test. Simply ask your colleague for the meaning they take away from the visual. If your colleague understands the design, certainly people who are familiar with the project and stakeholders will also likely comprehend it. The Colleague Test will tell you if your visual is presentation-ready or requires more work.

A Word on Combining Tools to Refine Visuals

A key to producing refined visuals is the design flexibility of the tools we use. When we attempt to design a graphic in a single tool, we're limited to the capabilities of that tool. As Data Designers, we should feel capable of using any number of tools to create the best visuals we can. After all, we want our designs to be based on our creativity rather than loyalty to a tool. You can export basic visuals from desktop applications such as Excel; analysis tools such as R; and online tools, including iCharts, into PowerPoint, Keynote, and Google Slides. After importing visuals, you can fine-tune headlines, subtitles, labels, annotations, and other design elements. To further enhance visuals, consider using sophisticated design tools like Adobe Photoshop or Illustrator, which allow you to change colors, crop images, and resize visuals.

In Summary: Refined Execution through Visual Polish

Refined chart design requires particular attention to the details surrounding fonts, labels, lines, and other elements. Colors can sharpen an analyst's story but can cause distractions if not applied properly. Analysts can choose from several well-defined, tried-and-true harmonic color themes. Other color considerations include how colorblind audiences will experience an analyst's color choices. Analysts shouldn't feel beholden to a single data visualization tool when building charts. Instead, they should use a combination of tools to ensure high-quality designs. Several tests can help analysts improve their data visualizations.

In the next lesson, we'll explore the final step in our communication journey: presenting a data story to an audience.

On Your Feet and Getting Your Story Across

Five things discussed in this lesson:

- How analysts present their data stories can affect an audience's understanding as much as the content can
- David McCandless, the data visualization artist, has an effective approach to data storytelling earned from years of experience
- McCandless' approach to data storytelling can be defined as five distinct steps that I call "The McCandless Method"
- Analysts can apply other elements of presentation style using simple guidelines
- Like every element of marketing analytics, presenting data visualizations is a skill that analysts develop through good habits

The final step in the communication journey is for analysts to stand on their feet and deliver their data stories to audiences. The activities surrounding objective setting, data collection, analysis, and story design led to this point, and its importance cannot be understated. How analysts present their data stories can have as much effect on audience understanding as the content.

Luckily, a simple process helps analysts present data stories effectively. Performing each step in the proper sequence allows analysts to communicate insights clearly, focusing audience attention on their work.

'The McCandless Method' of Data Presentation

The proper approach to presenting graphics can be a learned behavior. Studying dataviz professionals carefully reveals a consistent set of steps analysts can use to lead audiences through data stories. I've developed a process I call The McCandless Method. Named after David McCandless, this five-step process is based on the successful way he has presented data visualization.

Figure 5.15: The five steps in The McCandless Method of data presentation

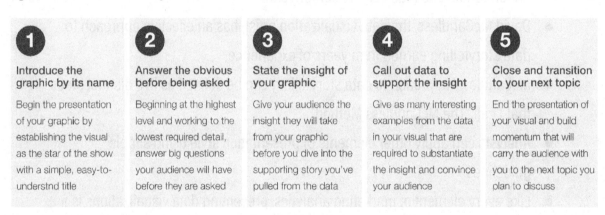

Step 1: Introduce the Graphic by Name

The first step in The McCandless Method is to introduce the graphic by name, allowing audience members to focus their attention on the graphic rather than you. The name should be clear, unadorned, and obvious. Ideally, the name should be the chart headline (see Lesson 4 for more direction on using chart headlines). Often, analysts will give their charts clever names to make them memorable, but the names don't set up the stories. Seasoned analysts can use this technique, but novices should stick to easy-to-comprehend chart names.

Step 2: Answer the Obvious Questions

The second step in The McCandless Method is to answer the obvious questions that will jump to audience members' minds before they can ask those questions. By doing so, analysts can minimize possible confusion and ensure audiences pay attention to analysts' stories rather than try to decode chart elements.

As analysts share their presentations, they can identify the questions people will likely have. The more experience analysts have in presenting charts (formally or informally), the more adept they'll become at identifying elements that require explanation. Obvious questions analysts should address immediately include what contrast – color, size, shape, or contrived – means in the graphic, what data is presented (i.e., the axis labels of the chart), and where the data came from.

Step 3: Give Away the Insight

The third step in The McCandless Method is to state the insight from the graphic. An analyst should reveal their story by telling audience members what they'll see (or feel) before they substantiate the insight. The audience may be curious, even disbelieving, at this point. By sharing the insight before diving into supportive facts, the analyst will benefit in two ways: (1) They can reveal an insight before the audience becomes distracted with facts and figures, and (2) Sharing the insight upfront paves the way for the analyst to deliver the supporting facts the audience seeks. The insight the analyst should reveal is the chart's subtitle (see Lesson 4 for tips on chart subtitles).

For years, I had this step out of order. I presented my evidence patiently and dutifully before revealing (with great aplomb) the insight of my analysis. I believed that by building tension and methodically constructing my story, I was guiding my audience down the primrose path of my logic to its dramatic conclusion.

Eventually, I learned it didn't matter how airtight my story was or how memorable my facts were. The longer it took me to reveal the insight, the less likely it was that I had my audience's attention. Sometimes, the mounting body of evidence overwhelmed people, leaving them unable to concentrate in the critical moment of my big reveal. Other times, someone disagreed with a fact I delivered, causing that person to shut down and disregard what I said next.

When I reversed the order of my story from "evidence → insight" to "insight → evidence" my presentations became more effective than ever.

Step 4: Provide Examples

Once the analyst establishes the conclusion they want the audience to reach, they can provide the substantiation the audience will crave by providing examples. The order in which the analyst delivers their evidence is important and should be done in a way that facilitates agreement from the audience. The analyst can do this by moving hard-hitting facts to the beginning of their narrative when facing a skeptical audience. This will allow the presentation to start off on a high note and earn momentum for the evidence that follows. If the audience is friendly, the analyst has the latitude to present evidence in a way that ends with a dramatic, "no doubt about it" fact that is as entertaining as it is illuminating.

Step 5: Close

Finally, it's important to transition to the next point in the presentation. Foreshadowing the next point (e.g., "on the next slide you'll see something even more amazing"), calling out a fact that links to something on the next slide (e.g., "I've shown you that 90 percent of U.S. adults visit YouTube each month – that will be important context for our next slide"), or telling audience members why the graphic matters to them (e.g., "This is important because it represents a new opportunity for your company to increase household penetration") are all effective ways to transition to the next point while bringing your audience along with you. Close the presentation of your visual in the way that fits your needs and continues the momentum to the next topic of discussion.

The McCandless Method in Practice

McCandless has demonstrated this process repeatedly, but one example of his that stands out is from a *TED Talks* program, *David McCandless: The Beauty of Data Visualization.* You can easily find the video of this presentation on YouTube. Here is the narrative of McCandless' presentation:

This is the 'Billion-Dollar-O-Gram' and this image arose out of frustration I had with the reporting of billion dollar amounts in the press. That is, they're meaningless without context. '$500 billion for this pipeline, $20 billion for this war' doesn't make any sense. So the only way to understand is visually and relatively.

So I scraped a load of reported figures from various news outlets and then scaled the boxes according to those amounts. And the colors here represent the motivation behind the money: purple is fighting and red is giving money away and green is profiteering.

And what you can see straight away is you start to have a different relationship to the numbers. You can literally see them. But more importantly you start to see patterns and connections between numbers that would otherwise be scattered across multiple news reports.

Let me point out some I really like:

OPEC's revenues green box here, $780 billion a year. And this little pixel in the corner (representing) $3 billion? That's their climate change fund.

Americans are incredibly generous people. Over $300 billion-a-year donated to charity every year. Compared with the amount of foreign aid given by the top 17 industrialized nations at $120 billion.

And then of course the Iraq war predicted to cost just $60 billion back in 2003 and then mushroomed slightly after Afghanistan and Iraq now to $3,000 billion.

So now it's great because now we have this texture and we can add numbers to it as well. So we say, 'well a new figure comes out and, let's see, African debt … how much of this diagram might be taken up by the debt Africa owes to the West?' Let's take a look: so there it is to $227 billion is what Africa owes.

And the recent financial crisis, how much of this diagram might that figure take up? What did that cost the world? Let's take a look at that. Dooosh! I think is the appropriate sound effect from that much money: $11,900 billion.

So by visualizing this information we've turned into a landscape that you can explore with your eyes. Kind of map, really. An 'Information Map.' And when you're lost in information, an Information Map is kind of useful.

Each step in The McCandless Method detailed previously is in this narrative.

Step 1: Introduce the Graphic by Name

McCandless begins by sharing the graphic's name. Although the *Billion-Dollar-O-Gram* gives little insight into what the graphic represents, McCandless does a good job of explaining the topic in his introduction. Again, McCandless is a professional, published data visualization artist. Until we reach that rank, we should stick with less colorful names for our charts. What is important is that the audience members can understand what they'll be hearing, and their attention is on the graphic – not on McCandless.

This is the 'Billion-Dollar-O-Gram' and this image arose out of frustration I had with the reporting of billion dollar amounts in the press. That is, they're meaningless without context. '$500 billion for this pipeline, $20 billion for this war' doesn't make any sense. So the only way to understand is visually and relatively.

Step 2: Answer the Obvious Questions

Next, McCandless explains the data's source, what the colors on the image mean, and what the different boxes represent. Given our understanding of preattentive attributes, the elements

McCandless calls out would jump off the screen at the audience. Answering these questions immediately allows the audience members to focus on what McCandless is saying, rather than dividing their attention between the data story and the unresolved questions they have about the chart.

So I scraped a load of reported figures from various news outlets and then scaled the boxes according to those amounts. And the colors here represent the motivation behind the money: purple is fighting and red is giving money away and green is profiteering.

Step 3: Give Away the Insight

McCandless then reveals the insight from his image. He makes his point concisely and leaves no room for interpretation. McCandless has now established a statement of fact that audience members want to have substantiated, thereby setting himself up to deliver the resolution they seek in the next few moments.

And what you can see straight away is you start to have a different relationship to the numbers. You can literally see them. But more importantly you start to see patterns and connections between numbers that would otherwise be scattered across multiple news reports.

Step 4: Provide Examples

Next, McCandless shares examples that illustrate the insight he provided. As discussed earlier, if McCandless had flipped the order of these last two steps, he could have told a masterful story, but the audience would have gotten lost trying to determine where he was headed or, perhaps worse, drawn a conclusion different from his. This would have left audience members confused and impatient when any fact McCandless presented didn't fit the story they'd constructed in their heads. By following the "insight → evidence" approach, McCandless dramatically increases the likelihood that the audience will be receptive to his narrative.

Let me point out some I really like:

OPEC's revenues green box here, $780 billion a year. And this little pixel in the corner (representing) $3 billion? That's their climate change fund.

Americans are incredibly generous people. Over $300 billion-a-year donated to charity every year. Compared with the amount of foreign aid given by the top 17 industrialized nations at $120 billion.

And then of course the Iraq war predicted to cost just $60 billion back in 2003 and then mushroomed slightly after Afghanistan and Iraq now to $3,000 billion.

So now it's great because now we have this texture and we can add numbers to it as well. So we say, 'well a new figure comes out and, let's see, African debt ... how much of this diagram might be taken up by the debt Africa owes to the West?' Let's take a look: so there it is to $227 billion is what Africa owes.

And the recent financial crisis, how much of this diagram might that figure take up? What did that cost the world? Let's take a look at that. Dooosh! I think is the appropriate sound effect from that much money: $11,900 billion.

Step 5: Close

Finally, McCandless takes this graphic and makes it much more personal for the audience, explaining why it's important and ending his presentation.

So by visualizing this information we've turned into a landscape that you can explore with your eyes. Kind of map, really. An 'Information Map.' And when you're lost in information, an Information Map is kind of useful.

These five steps will help ensure audiences understand analysts' graphics. It would be a shame to put so much effort into researching, constructing, and polishing visuals, only to lose people in those last few yards. Analysts must communicate effectively by following The McCandless Method for every graphic they present.

A Word on Presentation Style

The style in which we stand on our feet and present our visuals – the last few yards of our communication journeys – is very important. If we don't present our data stories in a way that conveys confidence and shifts attention from us to the substance of our work, we run the risk of losing our audience and wasting all the work we've done leading up to that moment.

The McCandless Method will set you up for a successful presentation. It will ensure you present data in the right way. It's important for you to build that method into your practice. You should also build other critical habits in your practice of presenting graphics. The basic guidelines presented here will help ensure your presentation is successful. Exceeding those guidelines to include the pro tips detailed below will take your presentation style from good to great.

Basic Guidelines

- Test the room's equipment (e.g., overhead projector, speakers, etc.) thoroughly and have an alternative to your electronic presentation if the equipment fails
- Never apologize in your intro ("Sorry, I'm running late!" or "My flight got in late last night, so I apologize for my low level of energy") because it sets a negative tone for your presentation
- Plan an effective opening and powerful close to your presentation, as the first and last thing audiences hear stick with them the most
- Carefully craft transitions from one slide to the next to ensure continuity in your story
- Be sensitive to your audience's understanding of the subject matter by avoiding acronyms and jargon
- Never expect a visual to speak for itself: Use The McCandless Method for each chart
- Never assume the message is "too obvious:" State your point and ensure it registers on your audience's faces
- Maintain eye contact with your audience by turning to the audience when you speak – not the visual

Pro Tips

- Before your presentation, meet and greet audience members, establishing rapport with them (your audience will give you the benefit of the doubt when they see you're likable)
- Don't be afraid to pause the presentation. Give your audience time to digest the visual or ask questions, particularly when your message is complicated. Being understood is more important than being quick. "I know this is complicated, so I'll pause here and see if anyone has any questions" signals it's OK to "not get it."
- Avoid nonwords (e.g., "um," "ah," "you know") and upspeak (e.g., voice lilt). They don't project confidence.

The Storyteller's Dash: Dashboarding Data Effectively

There are times analysts cannot be with their audience when data is presented. Dashboards have become a go-to solution for analysts who find themselves in this position. In my opinion, however, dashboards are unavoidable in the world of data analytics.

Their ubiquity today makes dashboards a common and frequently used tool for marketers. They can act as interfaces to important data for analysts, marketing decision-makers, partners, clients, and even customers. They can serve an important purpose in the quest to democratize data across stakeholder groups. They can extend the reach of an analyst's work by representing their analysis without the analyst being physically present, on their feet and getting their story across. The dashboards I've seen, however, were poorly designed and sometimes presented data irresponsibly by removing the analyst's voice from the analysis.

Designing dashboards shouldn't be difficult. To this end, follow five simple rules to create what I call the "Storyteller's Dash." These rules help analysts realize the dashboard's power by conveying clear messages, unlocking insights, and expressing patterns previously unseen. Perhaps most importantly, they avoid creating what my friend Avinash Kaushik aptly terms "Data Pukes" by limiting the information presented and representing the analyst's depth of analysis and nuance.

But before discussing how we can create effective dashboards, let's get some basic definitions and details out of the way.

First, a dashboard is a one-page visual interface that people can view fully on a screen without scrolling. In other words, they could print it on a single piece of paper. The interface should be no larger than the resolution of the smallest typical display. This means the dashboard interface is no larger than 1,280 x 1,024 pixels if it's designed for laptops / desktops and 480 Å~ 800 pixels if designed for phones.

A dashboard doesn't have multiple pages or tabs (if the dashboard is presented in a tool like Microsoft Excel), nor does it link to other dashboards. If multiple pages exist or if additional information is required to complement or supplement the data being presented, an analyst has created a report – not a dashboard. When so much information is presented that it requires several steps to view it all, it's nearly impossible for an audience to distill a cogent understanding of what happened and what action should be taken without the analyst there to guide them through the story. And remember: You don't travel with your dashboard.

Finally, a dashboard is a living window into data and is never set in stone. The real-time (or near real-time) nature of the dashboard means that the picture it conveys is in a state of constant change. Like the business world around them, dashboards should evolve to reflect that change.

This is the power of the dashboard and what separates it from a static report. Such freedom allows an analyst to reconfigure the dashboard frequently by swapping out old metrics with new ones that better define performance and success. It also means the analyst has a responsibility to manage the dashboard's story proactively.

Now onto the five rules of the Storyteller's Dash.

Tell a story

A dashboard should never be built as a simple portal to data. That, as we have learned, is the role of the API connection. Rather, a dashboard should be built with a specific purpose in mind and a specific story to tell. That story could be campaign performance, the overall health of a business unit, or any other chronicle that's so dynamic and important that it demands being constantly monitored and told. The dashboard's story answers three questions: (1) What's our performance? (the data); (2) What does that mean? (the insights); and (3) What should we do? (the recommendations). When these elements are understood, the analyst can limit what is presented to the data that tells that story.

Know the audience

It's critical for analysts to know who will use the dashboards they create so they can calibrate the amount of data that displays. If that person is a senior decision-maker, then the dashboard should have a small set of purposeful metrics that combine to tell the story you'd want the senior decision-maker to hear. If the dashboard is designed for a junior or internal audience, then the dashboard can generally feature a bit more data, as these audiences typically require more information in their roles.

Furthermore, an understanding of the audience allows for the thoughtful management of data access. Those who need the data can see it, while those who don't can be denied access. Most importantly, knowing the audience for the dashboard leads the analyst to know what's important to them, what they need to know, and actions within their scope. This information is vital for the dashboard to answer the three questions that make up its story.

Practice "less is more"

An analyst should plan the real estate on the dashboard as carefully as they would plan the attendee list for a meeting with the dashboard's main audience. Only let metrics onto your dash if they have something important to say. Anything that doesn't contribute to the dashboard's story should be omitted as extraneous information that would distract or, worse yet, guide your audience to the wrong conclusion. An analyst should spend significant time trying to understand exactly what critical few metrics drive the business. A general rule of thumb Avinash Kaushik promotes is that a dashboard should contain fewer than 10 metrics. I agree wholeheartedly.

Build in context

No data on a dashboard should appear alone. A metric on a dashboard should ever exist without context because it's how an analyst ensures the dashboard conveys insights rather than creating questions. Context can be a view of the data or a comparison to a target, a competitor, or previous performance. This lets an analyst frame the data that makes up the dashboard's story. Keep in mind that all the rules of sophisticated use of contrast, clear meaning, and refined execution apply to dashboards. The one exception is the use of headlines and subtitles. With static visuals, as we have learned, these lines of text ensure the meaning of a visual is apparent. The limited real estate dashboards provide means that their use isn't practical for every visualization of data. Therefore, analysts must find another way to embed their voices into dashboards. Hence, the final rule of the Storyteller's Dash.

Include the analyst's voice

Never leave data interpretation to the audience. Remember that the dashboard effectively sets the data free: You, the analyst, don't go with the dashboard. To this end, no dashboard should exist without including a cogent set of insights (in written words) that summarize its story by, again, answering three questions: (1) What is our performance? (the data); (2) What does that mean? (the insights); and (3) What should we do? (the recommendations). Without a record of the answers to these questions, dashboards are missing the benefit of all the analysis that went into creating them. A section for text allows the intelligence from the analyst to bubble up to the highest level. This may feel awkward as the dashboard is being designed, as most (if not all) dashboarding tools offer a plethora of dials and charts but no support for blocks of text. But given the importance of the story, savvy analysts will find a way to build text into their dashboards.

Here are some additional best practices of dashboarding to keep in mind.

Basic Guidelines

- Include a visual indicator of the overall theme at the top of the dashboard: a red dot means underperformance, a green dot means on target, etc.
- Put the names of the analyst or analysts responsible for the dashboard on the dash, along with their contact information
- Apply all the rules of contrast, clear meaning, and refined execution in the previous lessons to each visual on the dashboard
- Ensure all text on the dashboard is written in clear, crisp language and avoids jargon

Pro Tips

- Find a champion for the dashboard among your stakeholders, who can ensure it gets into the hands of the right audiences (and out of the hands of the wrong ones)
- Establish a cadence for updates to the text and metrics presented on the dashboard (typically weekly, monthly, or quarterly)

A Word on Building Habits over Time

Building the habits discussed here into your practice will give you the tools to expertly present your work; however, these habits can be hard-earned. While some of the presentation guidelines and tips described in this book are obvious and (relatively) easy to adopt, others might be foreign to you and force you to undo years of habits. The process of bending those behaviors to fit the new approaches introduced here can be tremendously frustrating. And that's OK.

Dona Wong sums up the need for patience in our practice: "We don't start out writing editorials. We start by learning the alphabet."[125] Adopting the presentation guidelines I've discussed in this book will feel awkward at first. If you use them regularly, they'll eventually become automatic. Once you reach that point, you will have truly arrived as a Data Designer.

In Summary: On Your Feet and Getting Your Story Across

How analysts present their data stories affects audience understanding as much as the content does. David McCandless, an expert data visualization artist, has an effective approach to data storytelling earned from years of experience. McCandless' approach to data storytelling can be defined as five steps that I call The McCandless Method. Analysts can learn other presentation style elements by following several simple guidelines. As with every element of marketing analytics, presenting data visualizations is a skill that analysts must build by adopting good habits.

---

[125] Dona Wong, *Wall Street Journal Guide to Information Graphics* (January 4, 2010).

CONCLUSION

Data's road from crude maps to gigabytes of multidimensional information has been a long and winding one. But it is far from over. If anything, the industry finds itself at a critical crossroads that will determine its future for decades to come.

Technology allows us to collect massive amounts of data quickly and comprehensively, use advanced tools to discover previously unrecognizable patterns in behavior, and craft personalized marketing messages like never before. Recent concerns about data privacy and the introduction of regulations designed to address these concerns, however, leaves the industry in a precarious spot. What comes next for digital marketing analytics is unclear, but if history is any guide, it will be fascinating.

GLOSSARY

Following are descriptions of words and phrases that pertain to the concepts in this book.

#

#ferguson – Hashtag used to connect people and filter news on social media during rioting that followed the shooting of Michael Brown, an unarmed teenager, by a police officer in Ferguson, Missouri, a St. Louis suburb.

60-Second Story – A concept Michael Fassnacht introduced that expresses the true heart of the analyst's broader story concisely.

A

A/B Testing – A tactic used to test two versions of an item (e.g., images, creative messages, etc.) by presenting those items to consumers and tracking engagement rates to determine which version is more effective.

Access Tokens – In computer systems, an access token contains the security credentials for a login session and identifies the user, the user's groups, the user's privileges, and, in some cases, a particular application. Typically, one may be asked to enter the access token rather than the usual password.

Active Evaluation – Part of McKinsey & Co.'s CDJ framework. Active Evaluation follows the Initial Consideration Set and is when consumers evaluate what products to buy, what brands to invest in, and where to purchase them.

Adobe Analytics – A web analytics enterprise platform formerly named Omniture. Adobe Systems acquired the platform in 2009.

Adobe Audience Manager – An Adobe DMP that integrates online and offline data from sources to deliver a unified view of audiences.

Adobe Target – A rules-based testing and targeting tool that can integrate with Adobe Analytics and create reports for marketing offers, personalization, and UX testing.

Aided Awareness – The percentage of consumers who recognize an advertiser's brand or product when they see or hear either name.

Akobeng, Dr. A K – Pediatric gastroenterologist and researcher who developed a hierarchy of evidence.

American FactFinder – A facilitated download source for population, housing, economic and geographic information operated by the U.S. Census Bureau.

Amplification Rate – The volume of "shares" for a piece of content, or the rate at which those shares are collected (i.e., the number of consumers who shared the content/the total number of consumers who saw the content).

Analogous Color Themes – Harmonic color themes that use Newton's logical order of color properties to create eye-pleasing combinations by selecting colors that are next to one another on the color wheel.

Analysis Gadgets – Data analysis and/or visualization tools that offer a single, well-defined capability and feature low levels of data flexibility.

Analyze Step – The third step in the Marketing Analytics Process (MAP) during which the analyst analyzes data they've collected to reveal patterns that help explore key questions they're investigating.

Annotations – An element of the concept of clear meaning in good visual form, annotations are small bodies of text that direct an audience's attention to important areas of a chart and provide a written interpretation of the data.

Answer the Obvious Questions – The second step in The McCandless Method of presenting dataviz that provides answers to the questions that will jump to audience members' minds before they can ask those questions. By doing so, analysts can minimize possible confusion and ensure audiences pay attention to analysts' stories rather than try to decode chart elements.

Application Programming Interface (API) – A computer-to-computer interface specific to an application or operating system that allows third parties to extend functionality. Also, a means by which analysts can collect data.

Applause Rate – The percent of users who see the content that has the desired positive reaction. Such positive reactions can come from a Like on Facebook, a favoriting of a Tweet on Twitter, or saving an image to a Pinterest account.

API – Application programming interface is a set of clearly defined methods of communication between various components. It allows a connection between two machines.

ART+SCIENCE – The blend of the art of data visualization and the science of data analysis that produces the successful approach to analytics.

ART+SCIENCE Mind – The mind of the data analyst who successfully balances the three functional skills: Data Strategist, Techie, and Data Designer.

AT&T – American telecommunications company that purchased the first digital banner ad and placed it on hotwire.com.

Audience Growth – Growth in the number of people connected to the brand on the social media platform (as "followers").

B

Banner Ad – A form of internet advertising that embeds an ad into a webpage.

Beck, Henry – English technical draftsman who created the iconic London Underground Tube map in 1931.

Bing – American web search engine that Microsoft owns and operates.

Boldness – The confidence and courage to act innovatively and in a fastidious manner to produce work of the highest quality. One of three characteristics of the successful analyst's mindset.

Booth, Charles – English shipowner, social researcher and reformer, best known for his innovative philanthropic studies on working-class life in London toward the end of the 19th century.

Bounce Rate – A website analytics metric that measures the percentage of visitors who enter a website and leave without viewing other pages.

Boxplot – A graphical method of depicting a group through quartiles.

Brand Advocacy – Observable and measurable public support for a brand, typically expressed through social media platforms.

Brand Asset Valuator – Young & Rubicam developed an approach for valuing brand impact using attribute assessments that are based on differentiation, relevance, esteem, and knowledge.

Brand Equity – An approach to valuing brand impact that combines effective marketing share, relative price, and durability.

Brand Valuation – An approach to valuing brand impact through models based on available financial data and assumptions.

Brandwatch (formerly Crimson Hexagon) – A digital consumer intelligence company headquartered in Brighton, England. Brandwatch sells five products: Consumer Research, Audiences, Vizia, Qriously, and BuzzSumo.

BrandZ Top 100 Most Valuable Brands Report – A report highlighting the 100 brands with the highest brand impact values based on an advertiser's financial data, market dynamics, and an assessment of the brand's role in income generation.

Brinker, Scott – Vice president Platform Ecosystem at HubSpot and editor at chiefmartec.com who has authored the marketing technology landscape supergraphic, the "Martech 5000" since 2011.

Build Awareness – One of six primary Marketing Objectives. By building awareness, the advertiser hopes to increase recognition and recall of a product.

Business Objectives – Broad C-suite goals that a company wants to achieve, stated in its own language, and are easily measurable. These objectives are the result of the company successfully achieving its Marketing Objectives.

BuzzSumo – A Brandwatch-owned content analysis tool that provides insights into the types of content that resonate with specific audience groups.

C

Campaign Objectives – Key performance indicators (KPIs) through which the success of media campaigns is measured.

Cart Abandonment Rate – The rate at which consumers don't complete the checkout process after placing an item in an online shopping cart.

Causal Analysis – One of the five primary categories of marketing data analysis. An approach that seeks to determine how the movement of one variable registers on other variables in the collected dataset or model.

Change – One of the primary categories of patterns found in data. The trend or instance of observations becoming different over time.

Chart Legend – Also known as a "key," the chart legend defines the elements of a chart and is placed on the page near the chart. In this author's opinion, using chart legends is an unnecessary and distracting practice.

Clear Meaning – One of three critical elements of good visual form. Clear meaning expresses the proper use of common elements of a chart (e.g., headlines, subtitles, annotations, and labels) to communicate insights effortlessly.

Click-Through Rate – The percent of consumers who saw an ad (search, display) and clicked on it.

Clickstream Analysis – Analyzing the way consumers navigate websites through the use of tools such as Google Analytics and Adobe Analytics.

Clip Art – Pre-made images used to illustrate concepts or ideas and, in this author's opinion, the hallmark of lazy and subpar visualization.

Close – The fifth and final step in The McCandless Method of presenting dataviz that transitions to the next point in a presentation, continuing the momentum to the next topic of discussion.

Clustering – One of the primary categories of patterns found in data. The task of grouping a set of objects in such a way that objects are in the same group.

Clutter – Untidy data/noise in the data that's insignificant.

CMYK Color Model – Also known as process color or four color, CMYK is a subtractive color model used in color printing and is also used to describe the printing process. CMYK refers to the four inks used in color printing: cyan, magenta, yellow, and key (black).

Colleague Test – A test designed to improve a chart's quality by showing it to a colleague who has no association to the analysis and determining if the chart is effective at communicating its meaning. Passing the colleague test is the bar analysts should set for the quality of their charts.

Collect Step – The second step in the Marketing Analytics Process (MAP), during which the analyst collects data for their analysis through the use of facilitated downloads, application programming interfaces (APIs), and web scraping techniques.

Color Contrast – Differences in color (i.e., hue) in a data visualization that communicate distinct elements in the chart instantly.

Color Saturation (or Value) – The intensity of color in an image. In technical terms, saturation and value are the bandwidth of light from a source. By increasing (darkening) and decreasing (lightening) the saturation or value of a hue, analysts can create a variety of color shades that work well together.

Color Wheel – Sir Isaac Newton's logically arranged sequence of primary, secondary, and tertiary colors wrapped onto a circle.

Completed Video Views (or Rate) – The number of times a consumer watches a video in its entirety (or the percentage of consumers who watch a video in its entirety).

Complementary Color Themes – Harmonic color themes that use Newton's insights into color properties to create a palette of colors that work well together by choosing colors that are directly across from one another on the color wheel to produce harmonious pairs of hues.

Consumer Response Modeling – Also known as "response modeling," this analysis technique improves customer response rates by targeting those prospects most likely to react to a particular treatment, campaign, advertisement, media or promotion.

Control Group – The group in an experiment or study that doesn't receive treatment from researchers and is used as a benchmark to measure how the other tested subjects (treatment group) behave.

Consumer Decision Journey Framework – A journey model designed by McKinsey & Co. that helps analysts understand how consumers research and buy products.

Consumer Outcomes – The set of measurable conversions, macroconversions and microconversions that brands attempt to influence consumers to complete.

Consumer Sentiment – Also known as "sentiment," the tone of consumer mentions of a company, brand, or product typically categorized as "positive," "neutral," and "negative."

Content Analysis – An approach to analysis that reveals patterns in data that are otherwise unrecognizable.

Contrived Contrast – The use of boxes, callouts, annotations, and other preattentive attributes to distinguish items in a visual. These are purposeful, planned introductions of contrast that draw the audience's attention and do not arise from inherent contrast found in size, color, and shape contrast.

Conversion Rate – The percent of consumers who, after clicking on an ad, take an action on the linked page. Tracked actions could be making a purchase on the page, downloading a file, or any number of actions the brand deems to be positive.

Correlation Analysis – An analysis technique used to calculate the statistical relationship between two variables.

Cost Per Action (CPA) – The cost invested in a search campaign divided by the number of some tracked consumer action. Those actions could be clicks (cost per click, or CPC), or any other conversion actions the brand deems important.

Counterfactual – The expected behavior of the treatment group if the intervention during the test period didn't occur. It's calculated by applying the factor determined during the pre-test period to the control group to project treatment group behavior. During the test period, the difference between the counterfactual and the treatment group's actual (observed) behavior is the incremental effect of the intervention being tested.

Correlation – The process of seeing dependence of one variable over another variable.

Curiosity – A strong desire to learn. One of three characteristics of the successful analyst's mindset.

D

D3 – A JavaScript library for producing dynamic, interactive data visualizations in web browsers. It uses Scalable Vector Graphics, HTML5, and Cascading Style Sheets standards.

Data-Driven – The kind of approach that uses data to communicate the message.

Data Designer – One of three roles the analyst must play. Someone who understands how to best express data stories and the ability to use tools to visualize those stories.

Data Flexibility – An assessment of how much an analyst can do with a specific tool. One of two measures (along with ease of use) used to evaluate the fast-moving data analytics and visualization tool market.

Data Management Platform (DMP) – A tool that collects and organizes data, allowing brands to target specific consumer audiences on ad networks and measure campaign performance across segments and channels.

Data Strategist – One of three roles the analyst must play. Someone who can bridge the data and marketing worlds.

Dataviz – Short form for data visualization and represents all the colorful designs that are created to tell a story.

Declarative – Visual form of affirmative data communication.

Deterministic Model – A model that features no unknowns or randomness and thus will always produce the same output from a given starting condition or initial state.

Descriptive Analysis – One of the five primary categories of marketing data analysis. An approach that calculates summary statistics that quantitatively describe or summarize features from a dataset.

Diamond Insights – A concept that communicates the need for analysts to expect insights to come from the compression and distillation of large amounts of data through robust analysis. It discourages analysts from approaching insight development as a trivial process that will reveal insights by sifting through a dataset, akin to a pioneer searching for treasure (i.e., insights are better thought of as diamonds, not gold).

Digital Cookies – Text files that sit in a browser's cache and allow a webpage to identify you.

Digital Fingerprinting – An approach to tracking consumers by analyzing sets of information that can include network protocols, operating systems, hardware devices, and software among other things, thereby avoiding security features and blockers.

Digital Marketing Maturity – The measurable degree to which an organization invests in technology, tools, and analysts to improve the effectiveness of online capabilities for itself and its clients.

Direct Labels – A superior alternative to chart legends, direct labels are placed directly on or next to elements in a chart.

Door Study – An experiment introduced by American researchers Daniel Simons and Daniel Levin to demonstrate a concept they call "change blindness." This is the psychological phenomenon that occurs when an observer overlooks a change in a visual stimulus.

E

Ease of Use – A personal assessment of how easy it is for an analyst to use a specific tool. One of two measures (along with data flexibility) used to evaluate the fast-moving data analytics and visualization tool market.

Effective Reach (X+ Reach) – The number of people who will see an ad the most effective number of times. The most effective frequency (e.g., "1+ Reach" means everyone who saw the ad at least once).

Engagement Rate – The percent of consumers who engage in some behavior (e.g., sharing a video, clicking a link in the video, etc.)

Enterprise Platforms – Big, powerful solutions that feature high data flexibility due to the broad and deep sets of capability.

Enrich – To enhance and improve the quality of data.

Epoch – Periods marked by notable events or particular characteristics.

Evergage – A cloud-based software that allows users to collect, analyze, and respond to user behavior on their websites and web applications in real time.

Evidence → Insight – The incorrect sequencing of a chart's takeaway and the data that substantiates that insight when analysts explain dataviz. In this incorrect approach, analysts present facts from the visual before revealing the insight (see "Insight → Evidence" for the correct sequence).

Excel – A spreadsheet program that's part of the Microsoft Office suite.

Explanatory – An approach to data analysis where visuals created from a dataset are used to search for and explore its patterns.

Exploratory Analysis – One of the five primary categories of marketing data analysis. An approach to analyzing datasets to summarize their main characteristics, often with visual methods.

F

Facebook – American online social media and social networking service based in Menlo Park, California. Mark Zuckerberg founded the service, which launched on September 26, 2006.

Facilitated Downloads – A means of accessing data through a structured process a data owner offers and manages, typically (but not always) involving a graphical user interface (GUI) that guides the data collector through the required steps for access.

FAMGA – An acronym that represents five of the world's largest tech companies: Facebook, Apple, Microsoft, Google, and Amazon.

Fassnacht, Michael – Former CEO and president of advertising agency FCB Chicago, current CMO for the City of Chicago, and an important thought leader in the development of modern data analytics and marketing data strategy.

Favorability – Also known as "preference," the percent of consumers who favor a product over a competitor's product or a set of competitive products.

First Moment of Truth (FMOT) – Part of the three-step model of marketing that Proctor & Gamble developed to describe the process of brand marketing. The time when consumers find themselves at the shelf, are ready to purchase, and have a number of options for the products they want.

First-Party (1P) Data – Data an organization collects through direct relationships with consumers.

Five W's and How, The – The idea that a complete report must provide answers to questions starting with the interrogative words, who? what? when? where? why? and how? The principle is commonly applied in journalism, law enforcement investigations, and research, and its origin has been tied to Greek philosopher Aristotle.

Flooz.com – A now-defunct dot-com venture based in New York City that went online in February 1999, and attempted to establish a currency unique to internet merchants, similar in concept to airline frequent-flier programs. The name "flooz" was based upon the Arabic word for money.

Font Choice – The font or collection of fonts an analyst chooses for their chart.

ForeSee Results – An online survey tool offered as part of the ForeSee CX Suite that Verint acquired in 2019.

Fowler, Geoffrey A. – American journalist and *The Washington Post's* technology columnist, writing from San Francisco.

Frequency – The number of times an ad was exposed to an average person or household.

Full Episode Players (FEP) – Professionally produced, TV-like content that can appear on any device type, across apps and web browsers. The content is typically 30-60 minutes, with commercial breaks.

G

Gates, Bill – American business magnate, software developer, investor, and philanthropist best known as the co-founder of Microsoft Corporation.

General Data Protection Regulation (GDPR) – A regulation in European Union (EU) law on data protection and privacy in the EU and the European Economic Area.

Give Away the Insight – The third step in The McCandless Method of presenting dataviz that reveals a chart's insight. Summarize this insight concisely in the chart's subtitle.

Google – American multinational technology company that specializes in internet-related services and products. It was founded in September 1998.

Google Analytics – A web analytics service from Google that tracks and reports website traffic, currently as a platform inside the Google Marketing Platform brand. Google launched the service in November 2005 after acquiring Urchin.

Google Consumer Surveys – A Google-owned online survey and market research tool.

Google Dataset Search – A Google search engine that helps researchers locate online data that's freely available for use. It launched publicly on January 23, 2020.

Google Optimize – A free, Google-owned website optimization tool that continually tests different combinations of website content.

Google Sheets – A spreadsheet program included as part of a free, web-based software office suite that Google offers.

Google Slides – A presentation program included as part of a free, web-based software office suite that Google offers.

Google Trends – A Google website that analyzes the popularity of top search queries in Google Search across various regions and languages. The website uses graphs to compare the search volume of different queries over time.

Gpairs – R programming language package used for plotting data.

Graphic – Visual form of art that also involves charts (in this context).

Graphical User Interface (GUI) – User interface that allows users to interact with electronic devices through graphical icons and visual indicators, such as secondary notation, instead of text-based user interfaces.

Gross Rating Point (GRP) – Total of all rating points during an advertising campaign.

Groupon – American global e-commerce marketplace that connects subscribers with local merchants by offering activities, travel, goods and services. Based in Chicago, the company launched in November 2008.

H

Headline – A brief description that headlines what the data shows.

Hex Code – A series of coded numbers and letters that describes the composition of a certain color in a specific color space, usually red-green-blue (RGB).

Histograms – A graphical representation of numerical datapoints based on the frequency.

Hollaback! – A photo blog and grassroots initiative to raise awareness about street harassment and combat it by posting photographs and narrative accounts of individuals' encounters.

Hootsuite – A social media management platform created in 2008 and headquartered in Vancouver. Hootsuite's interface is a dashboard, and supports social network integrations for Twitter, Facebook, Instagram, LinkedIn, Google+, and YouTube.

Hotwire.com – One of the earliest travel websites on the internet, launching in 2000.

I

Ice Bucket Challenge – An activity involving the dumping of a bucket of ice water over a person's head, either by another person or self-administered. Video of the activity was typically posted to social media websites to promote awareness of the disease, amyotrophic lateral sclerosis (ALS), and encouraged donations for research.

iCharts – A data visualization tool from iCharts, a company headquartered in Sunnyvale, California, founded on September 9, 2008.

Illustrator – A vector graphics editor Adobe developed and markets for macOS.

Impression Share – The number of impressions a search ad received divided by the number of impressions the ad was eligible to receive.

Improving the Sales Process – One of six primary Marketing Objectives. By improving the sales process, an advertiser hopes to reduce the loss of potential consumers by better facilitating the moment of purchase.

In-Demo Gross Rating Point (aka TRP) – Percentage of the total audience that fits the intended in-demo target profile (e.g., women aged 36-54).

Increasing Loyalty – One of six primary Marketing Objectives. By increasing loyalty, an advertiser hopes to increase the percentage of consumers who repurchase the advertiser's product (i.e., repeat purchase rate) when a need arises that the product can fulfill.

Incrementality Tests – On-demand experiments that measure the incremental effect of a specific campaign or tactic.

Influence Consideration – One of six primary Marketing Objectives. By influencing consideration, an advertiser hopes to increase the likelihood that a consumer will choose the company's product instead of a competitor's product or a substitute behavior (e.g., deciding to not buy anything).

Inferential Analysis – One of the five primary categories of marketing data analysis. An approach that uses a sample of data to infer something about a larger population.

Insight → Evidence – The correct sequencing of a chart's insight (first) and the data that substantiates that insight (second) when analysts present dataviz (see "Evidence → Insight" for the incorrect sequence).

Intellectually Blank – A statement included in a dataviz subtitle that lacks insight into the chart's underlying message.

Internet Movie Database (IMDb) – An online database of information related to films, television programs, home videos, video games, and streaming content online. It includes cast, production crew and personal biographies; plot summaries; trivia; fan and critical reviews; and ratings. The database was launched in 1990.

Initial Consideration Set (ICS) – Part of McKinsey & Co.'s CDJ framework. The set includes the relevant brands that pop into consumers' heads when they're considering products.

Intelligent Tracking Prevention (ITP) – A feature Apple introduced in 2017 that reduces cross-site tracking in Safari browsers by limiting cookies and other website data.

Introduce the Graphic by Name – The first step in The McCandless Method of presenting dataviz wherein the analyst presents the graphic's name. The name should be clear, unadorned, and obvious and be captured concisely in the chart headline.

iPerceptions – An online survey and customer experience management tool founded in 1999.

K

K-Means Clustering – A method of vector quantization that's popular for clustering data into like segments during analysis.

Kaggle – A Google subsidiary that's an online community of data scientists and machine learning practitioners and is a facilitated download source for data.

Kaushik, Avinash – Digital Marketing Evangelist at Google. He's a digital marketing analytics thought leader and the author of *Web Analytics: An Hour A Day* and *Web Analytics 2.0*.

Kenny, John – Head of planning at FCB Chicago. He developed a number of effective techniques collected in the "Numerical Comparisons Tool," bringing greater context to numbers using principles of behavioral economics.

Key Performance Indicator (KPI) – A type of performance measurement. KPIs evaluate an organization's success or the success of a particular activity in which it engages.

Key Questions – Specific questions or hypotheses that an analyst investigates during an analysis. Answering these questions helps the analyst guide a company toward its Marketing Objective.

Keynote – A presentation software application developed as part of Apple's iWork productivity suite.

Klout – A now-defunct website and mobile app that used social media analytics to rate its users according to online social influence via the "Klout Score," which was a numerical value between 1 and 100.

Kozmo.com – A now-defunct dot-com venture that promised free one-hour delivery of "videos, games, DVDs, music, mags, books, food, basics & more" and Starbucks coffee in several major cities in the United States. Investment bankers Joseph Park and Yong Kang founded the venture in March 1998 in New York City.

L

Label – A tag or a marker to any point on the chart.

Lee, Aileen – Cowboy Ventures founder who coined the term "unicorn" to describe pre-IPO tech startups with a market valuation of $1 billion or more.

Legibility – Clarity of what the data/charts say. The graphical representation of the data should be clear enough to read and understand.

Levin, Daniel – American researcher who, along with partner Daniel Simons, introduced the Door Study to demonstrate a concept they call "change blindness." This is the psychological phenomenon that occurs when an observer doesn't notice a change in a visual stimulus.

Lift Measurement – An approach to analysis that measures how a campaign affects an identifiable and measurable metric.

Linguistic Inquiry and Word Count (LIWC) – A commercial content analysis tool that analyzes text.

LinkedIn – American business and employment-oriented service that operates via websites and mobile apps. It launched on May 5, 2003, and became a wholly owned Microsoft subsidiary in December 2016.

Location Data – Information that a mobile device, like a smartphone or tablet, provides about its current physical position.

Logic Tree – A visual technique that divides possible options into branches and makes a decision process visually easy to interpret.

Look-Alike Analysis – A type of data analysis that applies a model of a consumer's attributes to a larger population with the goal of identifying consumers who demonstrate similar attributes.

Loyalty Loop – Basically a shortcut from a trigger to the Moment of Purchase. When traveling along the Loyalty Loop, a consumer experiences a trigger, and rather than going through an Initial Consideration Set and Active Evaluation, invests in a trusted brand immediately.

LUMAscape – A supergraphic Luma Partners created to organize the famously complicated world of advertising technology ("ad tech") by grouping similar companies on one page.

M

Macroconversion – The ultimate goal for a brand of a consumer's journey – most frequently a sale of goods or services – and the culmination of a series of microconversions.

Marbles, Jenna – Jenna Nicole Mourey, better known by her pseudonym Jenna Marbles, is an American YouTube personality, video blogger, comedian, and actress.

Mark I – The IBM Automatic Sequence Controlled Calculator – called Mark I by Harvard University's staff – was a room-sized general-purpose computer built in 1944 and widely regarded as the world's first fully functional computer.

Market Share – The percentage of a market accounted for by a specific product, brand, or company.

Marketing Effectiveness – The effectiveness of a marketer's go-to-market strategy for maximizing positive results in the short- and long-term. It's also related to return-on-investment measures, such as return on advertising spend (ROAS) and return on marketing investment (ROMI).

Marketing Mix Models (MMM) – A statistical analysis, such as multivariate regressions on sales and marketing time series data, that estimates the effect of various marketing tactics on sales and forecasts the effect of future tactics.

Marketing Objectives – Department goals that support the Business Objective, are stated in a company's language, and are measurable. Marketing Objectives are the result of the company successfully achieving its media objectives.

Marketing Technology (Martech) – The term for the software and tech tools marketers use to plan, execute, and measure marketing campaigns.

Martech 5000 – The marketing technology landscape supergraphic that Scott Brinker has created annually since 2011.

Match Rate – The percent of consumer data from a file (e.g., a customer list) that's matched to consumer data in another file (e.g., cookie ID data).

McCandless Method – A five-step process for presenting data stories to audiences that Kevin Hartman developed and named after David McCandless. Hartman's process is based on the successful way McCandless has presented data visualization.

McLean, Ross – Vice President - Mobile Qualitative at 20|20 Research and co-author of the "You + Big Idea" graphic, along with Jamie Shuttleworth and Karl Turnbull.

Marketing Analytics Process (MAP) – The four-step, recursive process that guides an analyst through the journey of an analytics pursuit. It consists of the following steps: plan, collect, analyze, and report.

Measurement Multiplicity – The concept of using a combination of tools applied concurrently or in a planned cadence to bring clarity to the brand's performance and market environment.

MECE – An abbreviation for Mutually Exclusive Collectively Exhaustive. In this context, it means that facts the analyst uses in support of an insight are mutually exclusive from one another (i.e., no overlap) and yet, taken together, represent the full breadth of the insight.

Media Objectives – Broad goals affected by various media executions and tactics employed to present consumers with the brand's messages. Media objectives are reached when campaigns are successful.

Microconversion – An important, measurable step a consumer completes on the way to a macroconversion, such as viewing a webpage, downloading a coupon, etc.

Minard, Charles Joseph – French civil engineer recognized for his significant contribution in the field of information graphics in civil engineering and statistics.

Minitab – A statistics package that Pennsylvania State University researchers Barbara F. Ryan, Thomas A. Ryan, Jr., and Brian L. Joiner developed in 1972.

Moment of Purchase – Part of McKinsey & Co.'s CDJ framework. This is the time when a consumer makes a decision and buys a product.

Monochromatic Color Themes – A harmonic color theme that uses one hue to minimize color distraction on the page. Through variations in saturation and value, analysts can expand the selected hue to fulfill their color needs for any presentation or visual.

Montulli, Lou – A programmer who is well-known for his work in producing web browsers. Montulli is credited with inventing digital cookies in 1994.

Moz – A Seattle-based software as a service company that sells inbound marketing and marketing analytics software subscriptions.

Multitouch Attribution Model (MTA) – A method of marketing measurement that evaluates the effect of each touchpoint in driving a conversion through a sophisticated model, thereby estimating the value of that specific touchpoint.

MySQL – A free, open-source relational database management system. Its name is a combination of "My," the name of co-founder Michael Widenius' daughter, and "SQL," the abbreviation for Structured Query Language.

N

Napster – A pioneering peer-to-peer (P2P) file-sharing internet software that emphasized sharing digital audio files – typically audio songs – encoded in MP3 format. The software was founded in June 1999, and Best Buy acquired it on December 1, 2011.

NASDAQ – American stock exchange founded in 1971 that was the first stock market in the United States to trade online, using the slogan "the stock market for the next hundred years." The Nasdaq Stock Market attracted many companies during the dot-com bubble.

Net Promoter Score (NPS) – An approach to valuing brand impact through a scoring system that gauges the loyalty of a firm's customer relationships.

Nightingale, Florence – English social reformer, statistician, and the founder of modern nursing. Nightingale came to prominence while serving as a manager and trainer of nurses during the Crimean War, when she organized care for wounded soldiers.

Nonwords – Filler words, such as "um," "ah," and "you know" that speakers use during presentations. They can distract audiences and reduce the speaker's professionalism.

Numerical Comparisons Tool – A collection of a number of effective techniques that bring greater context to numbers using principles of behavioral economics. John Kenny of FCB Chicago developed the techniques that comprise the tool.

O

Online Video (OLV) – The general field that deals with the transmission of video over the internet.

Optimism – Hopefulness about the successful outcome of an analysis. One of three characteristics of the successful analyst's mindset.

Optimizely – An American company that provides A/B testing tools, in which two versions of a webpage can be compared for performance and multivariate testing.

Oscars Selfie – A "selfie" photo snapped at the 2014 Academy Awards show. Ellen DeGeneres organized the selfie, which features several prominent film actors. When the "Oscars Selfie" was tweeted as the show was still in progress, it set a record with 3.4 million retweets.

Oracle DMP (formerly BlueKai) – A cloud-based DMP that helps marketing organizations personalize online, offline, and mobile marketing campaigns with information about targeted audiences.

Over-the-Top (OTT) – A streaming media service offered directly to viewers via the internet. OTT bypasses cable, broadcast, and satellite television platforms – the companies that traditionally act as a controller or distributor of such content.

P

ParseHub – A free web scraping tool.

Peek Test – A test designed to improve the use of contrast on a chart that involves the analyst taking their eyes off the chart for a period and then looking at it to see where their eyes are drawn. If their eyes are drawn to the intended location of the chart, the chart passes the peek test.

Personally Identifiable Information (PII) – Any data that could potentially be used to identify a particular person. Examples include a full name, Social Security number, driver's license number, bank account number, passport number, and email address.

Peterson, Eric – CEO at Web Analytics Demystified and the author who introduced the "Pyramid Model of Web Analytics Data."

Pets.com – A now-defunct dot-com enterprise headquartered in San Francisco that sold pet supplies to retail customers. It began operations in November 1998 and liquidated in November 2000.

PewDiePie – Felix Arvid Ulf Kjellberg, better known as PewDiePie, is a Swedish YouTuber, known primarily for his Let's Play videos and comedic formatted shows.

Photoshop – A raster graphics editor Adobe developed and published.

Photoviz – Same as dataviz but uses photos of real-world objects rather than computer-generated visuals to represent data.

Pie Chart – A circular statistical graphic which is divided into slices to illustrate numerical proportion.

Pinterest – American social media web and mobile application company. It operates a software system that enables people to discover and save information on the World Wide Web using images and, on a smaller scale, GIFs and videos.

Plan Step – The first step in the Marketing Analytics Process (MAP), during which time an analyst identifies a singular Marketing Objective that will direct their analysis. The analyst plans their approach with a planning document.

Planning Document – A document an analyst uses to record their planned approach to an analysis project. The document can take any form but must detail the Marketing Objective that will guide their analysis, the connection between the Marketing Objective and key questions the analysis will investigate, the data to be collected, and the sources of those data.

Playfair, William – Scottish engineer and political economist who introduced several innovations in the presentation of quantitative information by means of graphs and charts.

Point Solutions – Data analytics and/or visualization tools that typically center on a primary capability and feature medium data flexibility.

Postpurchase Experience – Part of McKinsey & Co.'s CDJ framework. It occurs when a consumer takes a product home and uses it.

PowerPoint – A presentation program developed as part of the Microsoft Office suite.

Preattentive Attributes – These are attributes that determine what information catches our attention.

Predictive Analysis – One of the primary categories of marketing data analysis. Closely linked to causal analysis, predictive analysis uses models to predict the future value of data attributes.

Prefrontal Cortex (PFC) – The cerebral cortex that covers the front part of the frontal lobe. This brain region has been implicated in planning complex cognitive behavior, personality expression, decision-making, and moderating social behavior.

Pre-Test Period – A period before an analyst conducts a study, during which the analyst observes behaviors of the treatment and control groups. By analyzing the pre-test period, an analyst can determine a factor that equates the behavior of the two groups to each other.

Primary Colors – The colors that cannot be formed through a combination of any other colors, specifically: red, blue, and yellow.

Probabilistic Model – A model that incorporates random variables and probability distributions to estimate an event or phenomenon. While a deterministic model gives a single possible outcome for an event, a probabilistic model gives a probability distribution as a solution.

Programmatic Media Buying – The data-intensive algorithmic purchase and sale of advertising space in real time through the use of marketing technology (i.e., "martech").

Provide Examples – The fourth step in The McCandless Method of presenting dataviz that offers substantiation for the insight revealed in the third step. Typically, these examples are highlighted through annotations or pulled from patterns in the data.

Purchase Intent – The percent of consumers who intend to purchase a product, rather than a competitor's product or a product from a set of competitive products, the next time a need arises.

Python – An open-source general-purpose programming language Guido van Rossum created and released in 1991.

Pyramid Model of Web Analytics Data – Web Analytics Demystified CEO Eric Peterson developed this concept that depicts the inverse relationship between digital data availability and digital data value.

Q

Quanteda – An R package designed to conduct quantitative analysis on text.

Questionnaire Bias – Bias in data collection that results from unanticipated communication barriers between the investigator and respondents, yielding inaccurate results. Bias may arise from the way individual questions are designed, the way the questionnaire as a whole is designed, and how the questionnaire is administered or completed.

R

R – An open-source programming language the R Foundation for Statistical Computing supports and that's used to analyze data and build dataviz.

Ranking – One of the primary categories of patterns found in data. The position in a scale of achievement or status.

Regression Analysis – An analysis technique that involves a set of statistical processes for estimating the relationships between a dependent variable and one or more independent variables.

Refined Execution – One of three critical elements of good visual form. Refined execution is the deep attention to detail and seeks to improve the legibility of a chart.

Relativity – One of the primary categories of patterns found in data. The consideration of data observations in relation or in proportion to something else.

RStudio – An integrated, visual-based development environment for R.

Randomized Controlled Trial (RCT) – A study design that randomly assigns participants into an experimental group or a control group. As the study is conducted, the only expected difference between the control and experimental groups in a randomized controlled trial (RCT) is the outcome variable being studied.

Rating Point – One percent of the potential audience.

Reach – Measurement of the size of the audience that watches an ad. Reach (%) = Gross rating points (%) / Frequency.

Refined Execution – A critical element of good visual form, refined execution expresses the attention to detail needed to ensure charts are as legible as possible.

Repeat Purchase Rate – The percent of consumers who buy a product they purchased previously.

Report Step – The fourth and final step in the Marketing Analytics Process (MAP), during which an analyst presents the story they found during their analysis in a visual form.

Repositioning the Brand – One of six primary Marketing Objectives. By repositioning the brand, an advertiser hopes to better align its product with the needs of its target consumers.

Return On Investment (ROI) – A ratio between net profit and cost of investment. A high ROI means the investment's gains compare favorably to its cost.

RGB Color Model – An additive color model in which red, green, and blue are combined to create a broad array of colors. The name comes from the initials of the three additive primary colors: red, green, and blue.

Royalty Relief – An approach to brand impact valuation that calculates the net present value of the hypothetical royalty payments an organization would receive if it were to license its brand to a third party.

RStudio – A free and open-source integrated development environment (IDE) for R, a programming language for statistical analysis.

S

Saleh, Khalid – Co-founder and CEO of Invesp, an e-commerce optimization company.

Sampling Bias – Also known as "selection bias." A bias in which a sample is collected in a way that some members of the intended population have a lower sampling probability than others.

Scheiner, Christoph – German priest, physicist, and astronomer who played an instrumental role in the early development of data collection methods.

Scripting Language – A programming language for a special run-time environment that automates the execution of tasks, such as R or Python.

Search Engine Optimization (SEO) – The process of increasing the quality and quantity of website traffic by increasing the visibility of a website or a webpage to users of a web search engine.

Search Engine Results Page (SERP) – The links to pages search engines display in response to a user's query. The SERP typically responds with ads (if relevant) and organic results.

Search Engine Management (SEM) – A form of internet marketing that involves the promotion of websites by increasing their visibility in search engine results pages, primarily through paid advertising.

Search Rank – The position that the brand's website or page is returned on the SERP.

Searchvolume.io – A free search trends analysis tool.

Second Moment of Truth (SMOT) – Part of Proctor & Gamble's three-step marketing model that describes the process of brand marketing. It begins after the consumer makes a purchase decision and brings that product home. Here, the product is evaluated against the expectations set during the consumer's evaluation process.

Second-Party (2P) Data – Data an organization owns and provides to a company.

Secondary Colors – The colors that are formed by mixing primary colors (e.g., purple is a secondary color formed by mixing red and blue).

Sensitivity Analysis – The study of how different variables or values affect a model's output.

Shape Contrast – Differences in shapes presented in a data visualization that communicate the uniqueness of each element instantly.

Share of Audience (SOA) – One way to quantify relevance. Calculate SOA by dividing the number of subscribers to a brand's OLV channel by total subscribers for brand channels in the category.

Share of Search (SOS) – One way to quantify relevance. Calculate SOS by dividing the number of searches for a brand by total searches conducted for brands in the category.

Share of Voice (SOV) – One way to quantify relevance. Calculate SOV by dividing the number of social mentions for a brand by total social mentions for brands in the category. You can also use SOV to calculate the share of advertising messages a brand produces by swapping social mentions in the calculation above with ads (or ad play time).

Shirky, Clay – American writer, consultant and teacher who focused on the social and economic effects of internet technologies and journalism.

Shuttleworth, Jamie – U.S. Chief Strategy Officer at mcgarrybowen and co-author of the "You + Big Idea" graphic, along with Ross McLean and Karl Turnbull.

Sign-Ins – The process of using usernames and passwords to manage access to digital content.

Simons, Daniel – American researcher who, along with partner Daniel Levin, introduced the Door Study to demonstrate a concept they call "change blindness." This is the psychological phenomenon that occurs when an observer doesn't notice a change in a visual stimulus.

Singer, Natasha – A journalist on the investigative team for the *New York Times*. She specializes in technology coverage and has written extensively about location tracking with partner Jennifer Valentino-DeVries.

Size Contrast – Differences in size presented in a data visualization that communicate the relative difference of elements in the chart instantly.

Smosh – American sketch comedy YouTube channel that Anthony Padilla and Ian Hecox created.

Snapchat – A multimedia messaging app used globally. It was released on July 8, 2011.

Snow, John – English physician considered one of the founders of modern epidemiology, in part, because of his work in tracing the source of a cholera outbreak in Soho, London, in 1854.

Social Media – Interactive computer-mediated technologies that facilitate the creation or sharing of information, ideas, career interests, and other forms of expression via virtual communities and networks.

SocialMention – A free, real-time social tracking tool used to collect publicly available information about a brand across social media posts, website blogs, news, videos, articles, and other pieces of content. It's particularly valuable when conducting SOV analysis.

Sophisticated Use of Contrast – One of three critical elements of good visual form. The sophisticated use of contrast seeks to draw the audience's attention to important elements of a chart while sending less important and complementary data to the background.

Spartan Test – A test that improves a chart's legibility by examining each element of the graphic to ensure it makes a positive contribution to the visual by methodically deleting unnecessary elements.

Split Complementary Color Themes – Harmonic color themes created by using colors on either side of complementary colors on the color wheel. This is among the techniques that help to create harmonious color palettes.

SPSS – A software package for interactive or batched statistical analysis. SPSS Inc. produced it until IBM acquired the company in 2009. The current versions are IBM SPSS Statistics.

Stata – A general-purpose statistical software package StataCorp created in 1985. Most users work in research, particularly in economics, sociology, political science, biomedicine, and epidemiology.

Stimulate Demand – One of six primary Marketing Objectives. By stimulating demand, an advertiser hopes to increase demand for a product using tactics, such as clarifying the need it fulfills, or introducing scarcity.

Store Visits – A measure based on tracking location data that records when a consumer enters a defined physical location.

Structured Data – Data that's neatly organized and conforms to a clear and consistent data format.

Structured Query Language (SQL) – A programming language designed for managing data held in relational databases. IBM designed it in the 1970s. Today, it's the most popular language an analyst can use to interact with a relational database.

Subtitle – A brief line of text on a chart placed below the headline that provides the insight that the audience should take away from the chart.

SurveyMonkey – An online survey development cloud-based software as a service company founded in 1999.

Sysomos – A Toronto-based social media analytics company that Meltwater owns.

T

Tableau – American interactive data visualization software company founded in January 2003 in Mountain View, California. Salesforce acquired the company on August 1, 2019.

Tags – Strings of code that initialize when someone performs an action in a browser, such as loading a webpage or clicking an object displayed on that page.

Talk-Track – The narrative of the story you're trying to tell through the visuals.

Techie – One of three roles an analyst must play. The data owner must understand how to collect and manage data in ways that ensure data quality and promote efficiency.

Term Relevance – The relative number of times a term is used in a body of text data, often visualized through a word cloud.

Tertiary Colors – Colors formed by mixing a primary color and a secondary color (e.g., blue-green, red-violet, yellow-orange, etc.).

Test-and-Learn Attitude – An attitude analysts adopt that accepts risk but mitigates its effect by allowing for programs to "fail fast." Through this attitude, analysts seek to improve a brand's marketing efforts by constantly optimizing targeting, messages, and other important elements.

Test Period – The period when an analyst performs a study.

Third-Party (3P) Cookie – A digital cookie set by a domain that's not the domain of the webpage the consumer visits. 3P cookies are typically used for targeting personalized ads to consumers and measuring conversions.

Third-Party (3P) Data – Data firms collect when they don't have direct relationships or agreements with the consumers who generate the data.

Thompson, Stuart A. – A journalist who specializes in technology coverage and is on the investigative team at the *New York Times*. He's written extensively on the subject of location tracking with partner Charlie Warzel.

Tidy Data – A standard way of mapping the meaning of a dataset to its structure. A dataset is messy or tidy, depending on how rows, columns, and tables are matched up with observations, variables, and types. In tidy data, each variable forms a column and each observation forms a row.

Time-Series Plot – A type of line graph that shows data patterns over time.

Three-Step Model of Marketing – A Proctor & Gamble framework that describes the process of brand marketing. It involves a Stimulus, the First Moment of Truth (when the consumer is at shelf, in-store making a purchasing decision), and the Second Moment of Truth (following purchase when the consumer experiences the product).

Trade Desk, The – A global technology company that markets a software platform, including a DMP. Digital ad buyers use the platform to purchase data-driven digital advertising campaigns across various ad formats and devices.

Treatment Group – The set of participants in a research study that are exposed to some manipulation or intentional change in the independent variable of interest.

Triadic Color Themes – Harmonic color themes that are created by picking three colors from the color wheel that are perfectly spaced from one another.

Trigger – Part of McKinsey & Co.'s CDJ framework. The beginning of every consumer's purchase path. Some sort of stimulus that initiates a product need.

Turnbull, Karl – Founder and Chief Strategy Officer of Cavalry and co-author of the "You + Big Idea" graphic, along with Ross McLean and Jamie Shuttleworth.

TweetReach – A free tool for analyzing Twitter hashtags, users accounts, and other activity.

Twitter – American microblogging and social networking service based in San Francisco, California. It was created in March 2006.

U

Unaided Awareness – The percent of consumers who voluntarily mention the brand or product when prompted by a generic question such as, "What brands of automobile have you heard of?" Unaided awareness clearly reveals a deeper consumer/brand connection than aided awareness.

Unicorn – A pre-IPO tech startup with a market valuation of $1 billion or more. Also, a legendary creature that's been described as a beautiful horse with a large, pointed, spiraling horn projecting from its forehead. Unicorns have delighted children since antiquity.

Unique Page Views – A website analytics metric that measures the number of unique pages a visitor views on a website.

Unstructured Data – Data that doesn't come in a predefined, standardized format. It's usually text-heavy and sometimes contains dates and numbers that don't fit a uniform description, as well as awkward (but increasingly important) data, such as images, sounds, and video.

V

Valentino-DeVries, Jennifer – A journalist who specializes in technology coverage and is a member of the investigative team for the *New York Times.* She's written extensively on the subject of location tracking with partner Natasha Singer.

Varian, Hal – An economist specializing in microeconomics and information economics. He is the chief economist at Google and holds the title of emeritus professor at the University of California, Berkeley where he was founding dean of the School of Information.

Venn Diagram – A visual chart that shows all possible logical relations between a finite collection of different sets.

Voice of the Consumer – Data collected (typically through online surveys) that measures consumer sentiment, opinions, and/or thoughts about any number of topics, including products, brands, and companies. Also known as "voice of the customer."

Visits – A website analytics metric that measures the number of times people visit a website.

Visual Cues – An element of the concept of clear meaning in good visual form, visual cues are design elements, such as arrows, boxes, and shaded areas, which can be effective additions to visuals by highlighting messages.

Visual Perception – The way our brain interprets data visually.

Visual Polish – The expert application of small but important details to a chart that improves its legibility.

Visual Website Optimizer (VWO) – A website optimization tool that allows analysts to create A/B tests and geo-behavioral targeting campaigns without having technical or HTML knowledge.

W

Warzel, Charlie – A journalist who specializes in technology coverage and is a member of the investigative team for the *New York Times*. He's written extensively about location tracking with partner Stuart A. Thompson.

Web Scraping – Also known as web harvesting or web data extraction. An analyst uses this technique to extract data from websites that's not provided through facilitated downloads or APIs. Data is copied, or "scraped," directly from the website's HTML code and typically requires the use of a web scraping tool to make the collection process efficient.

Website Analytics – The collection, reporting, and analysis of website data. The focus is on identifying measures based on organizational and user goals and using the website data to determine the success or failure of those goals.

Wickham, Hadley – Statistician from New Zealand, Chief Scientist at RStudio, and an adjunct statistics professor at the University of Auckland, Stanford University, and Rice University.

Wong, Dona – Senior Vice President, Digital Strategy, Communications, at the Federal Reserve Bank of New York and author of the *Wall Street Journal Guide to Information Graphics*.

Word Cloud – A dataviz that highlights the most frequently used words in a document or paragraph.

Wordle – An online tool to create word clouds.

X

X+ Reach (Effective Reach) – The number of people who will see an ad the most effective number of times. The most effective frequency (e.g., "1+ Reach" means everyone who saw the ad at least once).

Y

Yahoo – American web services provider headquartered in Sunnyvale, California. Verizon Media owns the company.

YouTube – American online video-sharing platform created in February 2005 and headquartered in San Bruno, California. Google purchased the platform in November 2006.

Z

Zero Moment of Truth (ZMOT) – Google introduced the concept to represent the time between the Stimulus and the First Moment of Truth in P&G's three-step marketing model. During ZMOT, consumers use online and offline information to inform their purchase decisions.

Zuckerberg, Mark – American internet entrepreneur and philanthropist who co-founded Facebook, Inc. and serves as its chairman, CEO, and controlling shareholder.

ABOUT THE AUTHOR

Kevin Hartman is an Associate Teaching Professor of Marketing at the University of Notre Dame's Mendoza College of Business.

He has decades of experience helping the world's largest organizations build deeper customer relationships, with most of that time spent leading large analytics teams at a major advertising agency and a global technology company. Kevin is a six-time winner of the Advertising Research Foundation Ogilvy Award and led the insights behind campaigns that have won Cannes Lions, Effies, Tempos, and dozens of other awards.

Kevin earned his BA in political science and economics from the University of Notre Dame and his MBA and MPP from the University of Chicago.

Made in the USA
Monee, IL
29 October 2024

68942637R00184